Reasserting the Public in Public Services

D1721112

After two decades of dominating the public sector reform agenda, privatization is on the wane as states gradually reassert themselves in many formerly privatized sectors. The change of direction is a response to the realization that privatization is not working as intended, especially in public service sectors.

This landmark volume brings together leading social scientists to systematically discuss the emerging patterns of the reassertion of the state in the delivery of essential public services. The state under these emerging arrangements assumes overall responsibility for and control over essential public service delivery, yet allows scope for market incentives and competition when they are known to work. The recent reforms thus display a more pragmatic and nuanced understanding of how markets work in public services.

The first part of the book provides the theoretical context while the second provides sectoral studies of recent reforms in healthcare, education, transportation, electricity and water supply. It includes case studies from a range of countries: Brazil, China, South Korea, Singapore, Thailand, Vietnam, USA, Hong Kong and the UK.

This book will be of interest to students and scholars in Political Science, Public Administration, Public Policy, Geography, Political Economy, Sociology and Urban Planning.

M. Ramesh is Professor of Social Policy at the University of Hong Kong. He is the author of *Welfare Capitalism in Southeast Asia; Social Policy in East and Southeast Asia* and co-author of *Studying Public Policy*. **Eduardo Araral Jr** and **Xun Wu** are faculty members at the Lee Kuan Yew School of Public Policy, National University of Singapore.

Routledge studies in governance and public policy

Reasserting the Public in Public Services

New public management reforms

**Edited by M. Ramesh,
Eduardo Araral Jr and Xun Wu**

LONDON AND NEW YORK

First published 2010
by Routledge
2 Park Square, Milton Park, Abingdon, Oxfordshire OX14 4RN

Simultaneously published in the USA and Canada
by Routledge
711 Third Avenue, New York, NY 10017

First issued in paperback 2014

Routledge is an imprint of the Taylor & Francis Group, an informa business

© 2010 Selection and editorial matter, M. Ramesh, Eduardo Araral Jr and Xun Wu; individual contributors, their contributions

Typeset in Times by Wearset Ltd, Boldon, Tyne and Wear

British Library Cataloguing in Publication Data
A catalogue record for this book is available from the British Library

Library of Congress Cataloging in Publication Data
Reasserting the public in public services: new public management reforms/edited by M. Ramesh, E. Araral and Wu Xun.
p. cm.
Includes bibliographical references and index.
1. Public administration. 2. Public-private sector cooperation–Evaluation.
3. Privatization–Evaluation. 4. Public welfare. 5. Social policy. I. Ramesh, M., 1960– II. Araral, Eduardo III. Xun, Wu.
JF1351.R385 2010
352.3'67–dc22

2009032781

ISBN13: 978-1-138-87415-2 (pbk)
ISBN13: 978-0-415-54739-0 (hbk)

Contents

Illustrations

Figures

Tables

Contributors

Eduardo Araral Jr, Lee Kuan Yew School of Public Policy, National University of Singapore

Paul A. Barter, Lee Kuan Yew School of Public Policy, National University of Singapore

George A. Boyne, Cardiff Business School, Cardiff University, UK

Gene A. Brewer, Department of Public Administration and Policy, University of Georgia, USA

Anthony B. L. Cheung, The Hong Kong Institute of Education

Scott A. Fritzen, Lee Kuan Yew School of Public Policy, National University of Singapore

Jonathan D. London, Department of Asian and International Studies, City University of Hong Kong

Ka Ho Mok, Faculty of Arts and Sciences, The Hong Kong Institute of Education, Hong Kong

Martin Painter, Department of Public and Social Administration, City University of Hong Kong

B. Guy Peters, Department of Political Science, University of Pittsburgh, USA

Jon Pierre, Department of Political Science, University of Gothenburg, Sweden

M. Ramesh, Department of Social Work and Social Administration, University of Hong Kong

Sunil Tankha, International Institute of Social Studies, Erasmus University Rotterdam, The Netherlands

Richard M. Walker, Kadoorie Institute and Department of Sociology, University of Hong Kong

Mildred E. Warner, Department of City and Regional Planning, Cornell University, USA

Wu Xun, Lew Kuan Yew School of Public Policy, National University of Singapore

1   Introduction

Reasserting the role of the state in public services

M. Ramesh and Eduardo Araral Jr

States are back, hesitatingly, even unwillingly, but it is widely accepted that they have no option but to rescue the market from itself. The financial rescue packages announced in many countries in late 2008 and early 2009 indicated some of the largest expansion in the role of the state as financier, owner and regulator in half a century. While some commentators are describing it as a sudden shift of the pendulum towards the state (Gills 2008), some scholars have observed this trend for some years now (Warner and Hefetz 2007). Regardless of when the trend started, this is certainly an opportune time for analyzing it and understanding its implications.

The debate on the extent and form of the government's role is, of course, not new, as scholars and thinkers at least as far back as Adam Smith [1759] have pondered over the issue (Sen 2009). While Smith was known for his explanation and defense of the workings of the market through his book *The Wealth of Nations* (1776) – popularized by the reference to the self-interested butcher, baker and brewer – little was known about his views on the role of the state. However, a close reading of his first book, *The Theory of Moral Sentiments* (1759) shows that Smith was also a defender of the role of the state in situations where the market fails to do so. In fact, Smith was deeply concerned with the failings of markets and the associated problems of illiteracy, poverty and relative deprivation. He expressed concern for universal education and poverty alleviation. He was concerned with institutional diversity and motivational variety and not monolithic markets and singular dominance of the profit motive. Smith argued the need for institutional solutions that fit the problems that arise rather than for institutions to serve some fixed formula or a dogma. These ideas, unfortunately, were not as attention-grabbing as reference to the butcher, baker and brewer.

Some 250 years since Smith's *Theory of Moral Sentiments*, the debate on the extent and form of the government's role is again on center stage. The current debate is new only insofar as the immediate past when it was common to deride governments as largely unnecessary and frequently incompetent. With markets collapsing and looking to governments for a lifeline, there is a danger that governments will turn to blunt interventions of the 1950s, overlooking the lessons of the last several decades suggesting more nuanced intervention in market processes.

The shift in the nature and extent of government intervention at the end of the twentieth century was built on the policy lessons of the preceding 50 years. In the years following the end of World War II, the role of the state expanded dramatically in both developed and developing countries to address adverse conditions at the time. In the developed countries, states took the lead responsibility for addressing the economic and social problems spawned by the Great Depression and the imperatives of post-war reconstruction, while in the developing countries governments expanded their role in order to expedite economic development. The result was a tremendous expansion in the size and reach of governments in all corners of the world. Described as the Keynesian Consensus, it involved government taking the lead role in macro-managing the economy, promoting industrial development, and providing social protection. The consensus began to unravel in the mid 1970s amidst spiraling inflation, unemployment and fiscal deficits accompanied by political unrest.

The economic turmoil of the 1970s created fertile conditions for the critics of the interventionist state who had never disappeared but rather receded to the sidelines in the heyday of Keynesianism. They blamed all economic ills on the state, arguing that the economic malaise was rooted in market distortions caused by governments (Brittan 1975). By muting and suppressing market signals, it was claimed that governments had fostered severe misallocations of resources which eventually emasculated the economy. Some of the critics went further and devised a formal theory of Public Choice which claimed to logically demonstrate that sub-optimal economic outcomes was an unavoidable result of state intervention (Buchanan 2003). The thrust of the Public Choice thinking – the general skepticism towards the state – became part of the mainstream thinking during the 1980s as governments began to roll back their involvement in the economy and in society generally.

The new consensus – also derisively referred to as "market fundamentalism" or "economic rationalism" – was initially confined to the English-speaking world but quickly spread to other parts of the world. The new policy thinking was actively promoted among developing countries, often backed by much-needed loans and aid from international financial institutions. Fiscal restraint; liberalization of regulations; weakening of trade and investment barriers; and privatization and marketization of goods and services produced by the government were the archstones of the new policy paradigm. Described as the Washington Consensus, the new policy framework was firmly in place by the end of the 1980s and it dominated reform debates in public policy and public management through the 1990s (Williamson 2000).

The faith in the minimalist government was, however, shaken by the economic turmoil of the late 1990s. The Mexican crisis of 1994 was followed by a much larger Asian financial crisis, with Russia and Brazil coming in the grips of a severe crisis in 1998, Turkey in 2000, and Argentina in 2002. Many countries suddenly faced with dire economic conditions had been some of the most ardent subscribers to the market-oriented reforms prescribed by the Washington Consensus. Some countries, notably China and India, that had not opened up their markets to the same extent, not only escaped downturns but actually grew rapidly (Kanbur 2005; Stiglitz 1998). The frequent crises since the mid-1990s fostered the conclusion that it was the excesses of the preceding market-oriented reforms that were to blame. Although there were many advances that benefitted society, there was also increasing recognition of the negative effects of many reforms which undermined the case that vital public services can be left entirely to the private sector.

The case of privatization of state-owned firms, the most hallowed of the 1980s reforms, illustrates the diverse, some expected and others unexpected, effects of the reforms. Empirical assessments of post-privatization experience tend to be largely positive overall. In a study of the privatization in four different countries, Galal *et al.* (1994) found net gains averaging 30 percent of pre-divestiture sales, with workers, owners and government always benefitting, and consumers benefitting in half the cases. Nellis (2003), Megginson *et al.* (1994), Boubakri and Cosset (1998) and La Porta *et al.* (1998) arrive at substantially similar results. Of all sectors, it was telecommunications in which the gains were the highest, a result of technological changes that almost eliminated natural monopoly and promoted intense competition. The case of telecommunications shows that privatization works if conditions of true market competition exist, a condition that does not exist in many sectors. Electricity transmission and water distribution (and, to a lesser extent, segments of the transportation industry such as rail tracks, airports, etc.) remain natural monopolies and their privatization led to unsatisfactory results. Although few privatized projects were cancelled outright, 74 percent of transport and 55 percent of water concessions in Latin America have had to be renegotiated (World Bank 2005).

Some of the greatest disappointments with privatization occurred in social policy sectors. In the healthcare sector, extreme market failures in the form of information asymmetries and externality effects meant that privatization expanded opportunities for providers to raise the volume and price of their services. While the quality of services improved, especially in non-clinical aspects, expenditures increased yet more. The result was an increase rather than the decrease in overall expenditures that was predicted by reformers (Wu and Ramesh 2009). The privatization of social security, most fervently pursued in Eastern Europe and Latin America, led to similarly unsatisfactory results (see Gill *et al.* 2004). The pension-related budget deficit rose instead of falling in many countries. Similarly, program coverage declined rather than increased as had been claimed, on the grounds that a closer link between contributions and benefits in a funded system would improve incentives to participate. Capital markets did not develop either, as had been predicted, because pension funds continued to hold safer government bonds. Interestingly, private pension funds proved more expensive to administer than the previous state-run systems, aggravated by the high marketing costs which reduced returns. Most significantly, the reforms did little to advance the main purpose of social security, which is to provide income security, as much of the unemployed and low-income population remained outside the privatized system.

The credibility of the market-inspired reform ideas was dealt a fatal blow by the financial crises that broke out in late 2008 which were widely blamed on inadequate government supervision of financial institutions. Governments around the world have had to launch massive financial rescue packages to shore up their economies and there is much talk of reasserting firm government control over the economy. Incidentally, the spikes in both the rhetoric and reality of government intervention are particularly large in countries most staunchly associated with rolling back the state during the 1980s: the United States and the United Kingdom.

The recent expansion is, however, only the latest phase in a longer term trend towards reassertion of the state's role. States have been reasserting themselves in a range of sectors and countries for some years now, sometimes in sectors from which they had withdrawn only a decade earlier. The revival of the state's role is being variously described as de-privatization, reverse privatization, re-balancing, re-centering, and emergence of the regulatory state. None of these descriptions are, however, entirely satisfactory as they fail to fully convey the complex, even contradictory, nature of the development. It is also not a case of the swinging back of the pendulum, because we are unlikely to be going back to the position that existed in the 1960s. What we are witnessing is not a move in one direction or the other, or even somewhere in between. It is instead a multifaceted and multi-layered phenomenon involving withdrawal in some respects and assertion in others.

The current redefinition of the role of the state is built on the belief that what is needed is effective and not minimal or maximal governments. Going beyond the tacit assumption that the choices between the state and market are mutually exclusive, the view accepts both as vital and explores ways in which the two can be combined to achieve policy goals. As Deng Xiao Ping might have said, it does not matter if it is the state or the market so long as the job gets done. The current failings of the market do not bring back rosy recollections of the state's achievements, as the abysmal failure of state planning in Eastern Europe and much of the developing world is still fresh in people's minds. But nor is the market as alluring, given the global economic turmoils it has wreaked. The last six decades have clearly shown both the potential and limitations of the state as well as the market.

It serves little practical purpose to engage in abstract debate on whether governments should or should not intervene in the market. A more fruitful question to raise is: what can governments do to ensure effective, equitable and sustainable public service? This book is an attempt to address this question by acknowledging, as a starting point, that what governments can and should do varies across sectors and nations due to conditions specific to the case in question. What is notable about the chapters in this volume, and others writing in the vein (for example, see Stiglitz 2008; Rodrik 2005), is the contingent nature of their claims. They accept that markets are a highly efficient and effective means of achieving policy goals but the extent to which their potential is realized depends on a host of conditions that must first be met. What governments should do depends on the sector in question, the interests of key actors, and the institutional context in which they operate, as the following section shows.

The new consensus: it depends

Some 250 years ago, Smith argued for the need to have institutional solutions that fit the problems that arise rather than for institutions to serve some fixed formula or a dogma. In light of the current economic crises, this argument is now worth revisiting.

The current debate on the role of the state is set in the background of the experiences of the last two decades. All in all, efforts to free up the economy through the 1980s and 1990s had mixed results at best, generating nuanced lessons. One lesson is that competition does not simply emerge by removing state ownership or regulations. And even if it does emerge on its own, the competition may not deliver results desired by the society. Governments may have to intervene to create the conditions for competition, as evident in the healthcare sector (Ramesh 2008). Sometimes, as in education and healthcare, it is necessary for the government to stifle competition in order to achieve socially desired outcomes.

There was also a shift in the thinking that promoting economic efficiency was the primary policy goal and that it was best achieved by reducing government involvement. It was realized that the resulting economic efficiency may not be accompanied by growth in not only the short but also medium and possibly long terms (World Bank 2005). The distinguishing feature of the "miracle" Asian economies of the 1980s was that they promoted economic growth rather than efficiency, and thus raised their population's standard of living. Scholars like Alice Amsden (2007) highlighted how "wrong" policies that compromised economic efficiency in the short run were crucial for laying the foundations for Korea's phenomenal economic development.

Another salient development of the 1990s was the greater acceptance in academic and policy circles that inequality and poverty are bad for economic growth (World Development Report 2008). Fairer and more equal societies enjoy more social capital which is conducive to effective decision making and implementation (Deaton 2003). The understanding led to the conclusion that governments should actively seek to reduce inequality rather than be agnostic about it in the hope that the benefits of economic growth will eventually trickle down to the entire population.

To ensure fairness and prevent corruption and abuse, the 1980s reforms had sought to establish clear and firm rules that limited discretion. But such rules also stymied growth by curbing innovation (World Bank 2005). So another significant policy lesson to be learnt was that governments need discretion, backed by clear accountability processes, in order to innovate.

The role of institutions, whose importance has been recognized for some decades, gained special salience in the 1990s. It came to be realized, for instance, that efficient markets do not simply emerge by the state's withdrawal from an area. For that, governments need to supply supporting institutions that were consistent with the country's social, economic and cultural system. There is also a need to create a demand for institutions by identifying institutional successes and failures, by experimenting with and recognizing local conditions, and opening information flows among others (World Development Report 2002).

Contributions in this volume are consistent with the emerging realization that the role of the state in the economy and society are contingent and context-specific and cannot be ordained in advance. The realization is based not only on the myriad theoretical and reflective writings on the subject (see Jomo 2008) but also solid empirical studies on privatization and deregulation over the last decade. The "it depends" line of argument is clearly evident in studies focusing on the efficiency and equity implications of privatization and regulation in sectors such as water utilities, electricity, telecommunication, transport, infrastructure, banking and social services such as health and education (Roland 2008; Parker and Saal 2003). Similar conclusions have emerged from studies on the effects of privatization on developing and transition economies (Nellis 2008; Cook and Kirkpatrick 2003, Hare and Muravyev 2003) and from studies explaining the shift towards mixed public–private delivery of urban services (Warner and Hefetz 2007).

A diagnostic framework

The new consensus "it depends" is not an entirely satisfying answer because of the question "depends on what?". Positive political theorists have proposed a diagnostic framework as a first step to answer this question. For example, building on the work of Ostrom (2005), Araral (2008) examines at least three broad sets of factors in a diagnostic framework as a starting point to the question "depends on what?". These broad factors – (1) the characteristics of the service; (2) the characteristics of the players involved; and (3) the transaction cost characteristics of institutions – are hypothesized to affect the incentive structures of players and hence the outcomes of privatization and regulation.

This approach builds on the work of scholars who suggest that institutional solutions should be designed to fit the problems that arise rather than for institutions to serve some fixed formula or a dogma. This approach is closely associated with Dewey's (1927) pragmatism which he espoused in his seminal work *The Public and its Problems*. What follows below is an examination of these three broad sets of factors and how they could affect the outcomes of privatization and regulation.

Characteristics of the good

The characteristics of the good have important implications for how it needs to be treated by the government for policy purposes. For example, primary health-care and basic education services are characterized by extensive market failures – externalities and extreme information asymmetries – that prevent markets from functioning in a way that meets social needs. And sub-optimal operation is not an option for these vital services because contemporary community standards regard healthcare and education as basic human rights that should be available to everyone who needs them. Electricity and water supply are similarly essential services, but with the difference that they are characterized by elements of natural monopoly which engender different incentive structures and hence require different responses.

Market imperfections are, of course, not static: technological and institutional innovations have made it possible, for instance, to unbundle the competitive segments of utility markets from their monopoly segments. But the potential for change cannot be assumed a priori; it must first occur before policy makers can respond to it. The innovations in wireless technology that fundamentally transformed the monopoly nature of the telecommunications industry is not found in water or electricity supply and, hence, the latter needs to be treated differently by governments. This is a consideration policy makers should have borne in mind before they privatized electricity and water supply in the wake of success with privatizing telecommunications.

Information limitations embedded in a good or service – whether the good has characteristics of search good, experience good or post-experience good – also matter in public policy. For example, monitoring the quality of the services of teachers in a classroom or doctors in a clinic is not easy since they allow much discretion by the provider that cannot be monitored easily. In contrast, a health service such as immunization is easier to monitor. Information problems embedded in urban water supply have also been identified – among others – as a reason for the widespread failure of water utilities' privatization compared to the privatization of some other utilities (Shirley 2006). Information problems, in general, limit what governments can anticipate, specify, regulate, monitor and enforce and therefore also set a limit to what can be achieved by privatization and regulation.

The choice of whether a public good or service is to be directly produced or financed by the national or local government or contracted out depends on several factors (see World Development Report 2004): (1) the ease of monitoring the qualities of the good or service (which is a function of information problems embedded in the good or service); (2) the homogeneity of client preferences; and (3) the politics of public service (i.e. whether clientilistic or public interest). If the politics of public service is oriented towards the public interest and if the service is homogenous in its traits and its quality easy to monitor, then there is a case for the service to be financed by the central government (because the service is homogenous) and contracted out to public or private service providers (since standards are easy to specify and monitor). A good example of this is immunization. However, if the service is not easy to specify and monitor – for example quality of education services – but clients are homogenous, then the central government would be a more efficient provider of the service. If preferences are non-homogenous, local governments would be more efficient and responsive to diverse demands. If standards for local public goods are easy to specify and monitor, local governments can finance and contract out the delivery of such services, for example, street cleaning. Otherwise if the standards are difficult to specify in a contract, direct local government provision would be more efficient and responsive when preferences are diverse.

Characteristics of players

The characteristics of players involved in the production and delivery of public services – the clients, service providers and policy makers, including regulators and politicians – also matter to the outcomes of the government's decision to intervene or withdraw. The interests, ideas, and power of the key actors involved facilitate the choice and execution of some decisions and hinders others. Players vary by the composition and size of their membership, financial resources, ideology, history of cooperation, social capital, and so on, and these have a decisive impact on what governments can or cannot do. As Schalager (1999: 235) puts it, "theoretical development in public policy must specify the assumptions about the actors who motivate action or change" … as well as "the context that structures, constrains, guides and influences the actions taken by the actors".

Understanding the incentives faced by government agents is important to the outcomes of government intervention. By its nature, governments have multiple, unclear and changing objectives, reflecting the delicate balance among contending societal forces they embody. The problem of striking a compromise among contending societal interests is aggravated by the need to balance concerns for efficiency with equity and sustainable development as well as concerns for citizen engagement, and so on. The discontinuities in governments resulting from change in government or replacement of key ministers or officials has a similar impact on policies.

The interests of service providers and investors also shape governments' policies. They seek to maximize returns on investment while minimizing various types of risks: commercial, regulatory and political. The extensive literature on the problem of credible commitment and political and regulatory risks are good starting points to analyze how attributes of players matter to the outcomes of the government's efforts to engage the private sector in delivering public services (for the credible commitment literature, see Williamson 1981; Qian and Weingast 1997).

Improving public service delivery requires, for instance, strengthening accountability relationships among clients/citizens, and service providers/policy makers. This would involve among other things giving clients and citizens a stronger voice in influencing policy makers and politicians in the delivery of public services. Stronger voice requires that clients have access to more information about public service delivery. Strengthening the control of policy makers over service providers requires, among other things, the use of performance-based contracts – to the extent that contracts can be clearly specified, monitored and enforced cost effectively. Again, transparency of performance-based contracts is important if they are to succeed.

Institutional context

Developments in institutional economics – particularly the theory of incomplete contracts as well as developments in information economics – have led to a better understanding of the costs and benefits of government's decision to intervene or withdraw from an activity. Roland (2008), for example, suggests that contract theory has shown that previous assumptions in favor of public ownership of natural monopolies are unwarranted and that the purported advantages of private ownership are not unambiguous either.

In industrial organization theory, the case of natural monopoly is often invoked as the main argument for public ownership because it would allow government to impose pricing and production policies on firms that increase social welfare. Critiques of this theory, however, argue that it does not necessarily follow from the argument that public ownership is the only way to improve on the limitations of the laissez-faire model. For instance, Laffont and Tirole (1993) ask why can the government not regulate private monopolies and issue appropriate incentive contracts in order to achieve socially desirable outcomes.

Contract theory suggests that if the government knows exactly what it wants the producer to make, it can specify this in a contract or regulation and enforce it. In this case, there is no difference between in-house provision and contracting out. As Williamson (2000) and Grossman and Hart (1986) emphasize, ownership structure does not matter when complete contracts can be written. From this perspective, government ownership – under certain conditions – does not matter when it can align private incentives with social objectives through contracts and regulation. However, in the world of boundedly rational individuals, it is the general case that contracts are incomplete, information is imperfect and transaction costs non-trivial. Thus, ownership and contractual arrangements do matter to the outcomes of privatization.

Asset ownership, however, is only one part of the story. Technological and institutional innovations have also led to policy prescriptions that saw the unbundling of various functions previously monopolized by governments. Functions such as policy making, regulation, asset ownership, corporate oversight and service provision are functions that can be unbundled – in theory – to improve the delivery of public services. There are certain functions – for example policy making and regulation – that must always remain a function of governments – while asset ownership, corporate oversight and service delivery could be the responsibility of either public or private agencies or jointly through partnerships. Whether or not these functions are better left to the public or private agencies or through partnership arrangements depends on the context which, as earlier argued, is shaped by the characteristics of the good/service, the characteristics of the players and the transaction cost characteristics of the institutional context.

Service provision is no longer just a choice of either public or private provider. A wide range of contractual and financing arrangements are now available that allow for customization of delivery mechanisms. For example, in the delivery of urban water services, several types of public–private arrangements are available: (1) management contracts; (2) affermage; (3) lease; (4) concession; and (5) divestiture. Each of these arrangements has different implications in terms of operational responsibilities, financial implications, asset ownership and risk profiles. Each of these arrangements can be configured in different ways between the private contractor and the public contracting authority which allows for the customization of service delivery.

In the provision of public infrastructure, governments can introduce various contractual arrangements that mimic competitive markets and encourage private sector providers to provide for efficient service. These include mechanisms such as: (1) competition for the market; (2) competition via capital markets; and (3) competition in the market. Competition for the market consists of rebidding private sector contracts at regular intervals. Because the incumbent contractor risks losing the contract at the next bidding stage, regular rebidding is an efficient way of maintaining competitive pressure to deliver high-quality services at a reasonable price. Competition via capital markets occurs when operators can purchase their competitors by buying shares on financial markets or through direct mergers.

By paying attention to the characteristics of the good, the attributes of the players and the configuration of the institutional context, policy makers now can have more nuanced approaches to solving public problems beyond the dogmatic privatization and regulation debate.

Essays in this volume

The objective of this book is to map and comprehend the recent revival of the state's role in contemporary societies. Towards this objective, contributors to this volume highlight instances of reassertion of the government's role and draw conclusions on the basis of review of the literature and case studies drawn from different sectors and from different parts of the world. Together they present a fascinating picture of governments that have expanded into different nooks and crannies of economic and social policy sectors.

In the opening chapter, Guy Peters provides a sweeping overview of the shifts in thinking and practice with regard to the role of the government in economy and society in recent decades. He focuses particularly on the attempts to overcome the conceptual and practical shortcomings of decentralization and devolution to promote efficiency in the public sector. The most recent response has been the emergence of, what he calls, metagovernance in which the bureaucracy and politics play a central steering role in setting goals and priorities and ensuring their implementation by professional managers. "Soft laws" and "steering" are the key characteristics of this form of strategic management.

In the following chapter, Mildred Warner offers a broad theoretical overview of how governments have recently stepped up intervention in economic and social affairs to correct the shortcoming of market-based solutions to public problems adopted in the 1980s and 1990s. Markets are still used widely and even increasingly, but governments play a "market structuring role". She describes this trend as not only necessary but also desirable because it balances the efficiency benefits of market-type engagement with the technical benefits of planning. But she goes beyond governments and markets and calls for the inclusion of civic groups in the design and delivery of public services. She argues that public engagement can help mitigate government and market failures and foster solutions to difficult public problems that are both efficient and socially optimal.

Pierre and Painter investigate the largely ignored subject of the legal bases of market-based reforms of the public sector. They question if markets can substitute for the state in assuming public responsibilities, as governments alone have the necessary authority and legitimacy. The population values efficiency, choice and customer-orientation in public service, but they also expect impartiality, procedural justice, and accountability from service providers. They do not believe that the recent concept of "public value" bridges the contradiction between legality and efficiency in public sector organization. Nor are they sanguine about the prospect of overcoming the shortcoming by "publicizing" the private providers through formal contractual obligations.

Richard Walker, Gene Brewer and George Boyne take a more focused approach and empirically examine one of the fundamental tenets of NPM reforms: that public organizations perform better if they behave more like their private counterparts. Just as the imperatives to meet consumer demands make private firms operate efficiently, it is assumed that client orientation will improve public organizations' performance. Using empirical data from the United Kingdom, they find only a weak relationship between market orientation and public sector performance. Their conclusions cast serious doubts on some of the key assumptions of the NPM which have guided public sector reforms in recent years.

The next chapter by Anthony Cheung provides a detailed and perceptive account of the revival of the state in recent years in Hong Kong, the supposed mecca of free market capitalism. After years of NPM reforms and faced with a recession in the late 1990s, he shows how the government under Donald Tsang in recent years has reinstated the bureaucracy's primacy and is contemplating a more active role for the government in shaping the economy.

The following three chapters are on social policy, an area in which the role of the state has always been large but expanded further in recent years. M Ramesh compares recent healthcare reforms in China, South Korea, Singapore and Thailand, and finds an expanding state role in all four instances. However, the expansions are considerably different in substance, with different implications and different chances of success. He shows that healthcare reforms in the Northeast Asian countries have (Korea) or are in the process (China) of expanding social insurance without corresponding efforts to control the providers who have been the key drivers of explosion in healthcare expenditures. In Singapore and Thailand, in contrast, the government has gradually tightened control over both financing and provision of healthcare while allowing room for private competition. He argues that the Thai and Singapore governments' more activist role has been a key reason why the two countries have been able to maintain a lid on expenditures while meeting their health policy obligations.

Jonathan London offers a similar analysis of healthcare reforms, but with reference to Vietnam. Nearly a decade after China, in the late 1980s, the Vietnamese government began to reduce funding for healthcare, forcing households to carry a greater share of the burden. Without sufficient control over providers, the result was a rapid increase in household as well as overall health expenditure financed largely out of pocket. Faced with widespread public anxiety over affordability, the government is in the process of laying out a patchwork of programs to improve affordability. Efforts include various exemptions from fees, greater funding for local health centers, and a modest national health insurance program. If the Chinese experience is anything to go by, these measures are unlikely to address the problems that are rooted in the lack of adequate supervision of the providers.

Painter and Mok's analysis of education policy reforms in China is consistent with the findings for healthcare. After allowing the private or semi-private educational institutions to mushroom through the 1980s and 1990s, the government is currently in the process of limiting their unbridled growth which had increased costs and reduced affordability. The government has not only introduced regulatory and financial reforms to rein in the excesses of private operators, it has begun to articulate a broad commitment to maintaining a certain minimum standard of social welfare for the population. There is no chance of going back to the fully nationalized education system of the past, but rather to make the market work in ways that are acceptable to the population.

Paul Barter offers a sweeping survey of public transport reforms around the globe which indicate trends towards greater state coordination of private providers. He finds that in the developing world there is a clear trend towards an expanded state role in the public transport sector that has been traditionally dominated by the private sector. He finds evidence of an emerging governance model in which the government takes responsibility for delivering transportation services but delegates the task of actual delivery to private firms under service contracts, often with competitive tendering. He calls the approach "proactive planning with service contracting". The successful reforms have involved public sector planning and control while still promoting competition.

In the next chapter, Sunil Tankha analyzes the privatization of the electricity industry in Brazil and its subsequent nationalization. Faced with widespread public disaffection with the publicly owned and operated electricity industry, and in line with the prevalent economic thinking, the Brazilian government privatized the sector in 1995. Hopes of higher efficiency were dashed as prices rose, investments declined, and the quality of supply deteriorated, prompting the government to re-nationalize the sector in 2003. But in the current nationalized phase, the government is employing a mix of centralized planning and competition in order to avoid the excesses of exclusive government or private ownership in a vital monopoly industry. Performance to date suggests the industry is performing better than was the case under private or previous public ownership.

In the final chapter, Eduardo Araral examines the *outcomes* of water utilities' privatization worldwide with a focus on the fiscal and efficiency hypotheses. The fiscal hypotheses suggest that privatization will relieve governments the burden of investment financing, particularly in the context of fiscal pressures faced by developing countries. The efficiency hypothesis on the other hand suggests that water utilities' performance will improve under private ownership because it is "obviously" more efficient than the public sector. Using meta-analyses, Araral finds little empirical support for the fiscal hypotheses that privatization would relieve governments of the burden of investment financing. Most privatization contracts often required public finance and/or guarantees from government or government-owned development banks. Private water companies also do not necessarily bring in new sources and volumes of investment finance as they rely heavily on the same sources that are available to the public sector. There has also been a stream of empirical evidence which has consistently shown that there is no systematic significant difference between public and private operators in terms of efficiency or other performance measures.

Bibliography

Amsden, Alice Hoffenberg (2007) *Escape from Empire: The Developing World's Journey Through Heaven and Hell*, Cambridge, MA: MIT Press.

Araral, E. Jr (2008) "Privatization and Regulation of Public Services: A Framework for Institutional Analysis", *Policy and Society* 27: 3, pp. 175–180.

Bonnefoy, Yves (1995) *New and Selected Poems*, edited by John Naughton and Anthony Rudolf, Chicago: University of Chicago Press.

Bortolotti, G. and Milella, V. (2008) "Privatization in Western Europe: Stylized Facts, Outcomes, and Open Issues", in Gerard Roland (ed.) *Privatization: Successes and Failures*, New York: Columbia University Press.

Boubakri, N. and Cosset, J. C. (1988) "The Financial and Operating Performance of Newly Privatized Firms: Evidence from Developing Countries", *The Journal of Finance* 53: 3, pp. 1083–1112.

Brittan, Samuel (1975) "The Economic Contradictions of Democracy", *British Journal of Political Science* 5: 2, pp. 129–159. Available at www.jstor.org/stable/193396 (accessed March 10, 2009).

Buchanan, James M. (2003) "Public Choice: The Origins and Development of a Research Program", Fairfax, VA: Center for Study of Public Choice, George Mason University. Available at www.gmu.edu/centers/publicchoice/pdf%20links/Booklet.pdf (accessed March 10, 2009).

Cook, P. and Kirkpatrick, C. (2003) "Assessing the Impact of Privatization in Developing Countries", in David Parker and David Saal (eds) *International Handbook on Privatization*, Northampton, MA: Edward Elgar Pub.

Deaton, Angus (2003) "Health, Inequality, and Economic Development", *Journal of Economic Literature* 41: 1, pp. 113–158. Available at www.jstor.org/stable/3217389 (accessed March 10, 2009).

Dewey, John (1927) *The Public and its Problems*, New York: Holt.

Galal, A., Jones, L., Tandon, P. and Vogelsang, I. (1994) *Welfare Consequences of Selling Public Enterprises: An Empirical Analysis*, New York: Oxford University Press.

Gill, Indermit S. *et al.* (2004) *Keeping the Promise of Old Age Income Security in Latin America*, Washington, DC: World Bank.

Gills, Barry K. (2008) "The Swinging of the Pendulum: The Global Crisis and Beyond", *Globalizations* 5: 4, pp. 513–522. Available at www.informaworld.com/10.1080/14747730802567389 (accessed March 17, 2009).

Graham, C. (2003) "Methods of Privatization", in David Parker and David Saal (eds) *International Handbook on Privatization*, Northampton, MA: Edward Elgar Pub.

Grossman, Sanford J. and Hart, Oliver D. (1986) "The Costs and Benefits of Ownership: A Theory of Vertical and Lateral Integration", *Journal of Political Economy* 94: 4, pp. 691–719.

Hare, P. and Muravyev, A. (2003) "Privatization in Russia", in David Parker and David Saal (eds) *International Handbook on Privatization*, Northampton, MA: Edward Elgar Pub.

Hart, Oliver, La Porta Drago, R., Lopez-de-Silanes, F. and Moore, J. (1998) "A New Bankruptcy Procedure that Uses Multiple Auctions", *European Economic Review* 41: 3–5, pp. 461–473. Available at http://dx.doi.org/10.1016/S0014–2921(97)00015–9.

Jayasuriya, Kanishka (2005) "Beyond Institutional Fetishism: From the Developmental to the Regulatory State", *New Political Economy* 10: 3, pp. 381–387.

Jomo, K. S. (2008) "A Critical Review of the Evolving Privatization Debate", in Gerard Roland (ed.) *Privatization: Successes and Failures*, New York: Columbia University Press.

Kanbur, Ravi (2005) "The Development of Development Thinking", unpublished paper, Cornell University. Available at www.people.cornell.edu/pages/sk145.

Künneke, Rolf W., Correljé, Aad F. and Groenewegen, John P. M. (eds) (2005) *Institutional Reform, Regulation and Privatization: Process and Outcomes in Infrastructure Industries*, Northampton, MA and Cheltenham, UK: Edward Elgar Pub.

Kurland, Philip B. and Lerner, Ralph (eds) (1987) *The Founders' Constitution*, Chicago: University of Chicago Press. Available at http://press-pubs.uchicago.edu/founders.

La Porta, Rafael, Lopez-de-Silanes, Florencio and Shleifer, Andrei (1998) "Law and Finance", *Journal of Political Economy* 106: 6, pp. 1113–1155.

Laffont, J-J. and Tirole, J. (1993) *A Theory of Incentives in Procurement and Regulation*, Cambridge, MA: MIT Press.

Megginson, William (2003) "The Economics of Bank Privatization", paper presented at the World Bank Conference on Bank Privatization, November 20–21, Washington, DC.

Megginson, W. L. and Netter, J. M. (2005) "History and Methods of Privatization", in David Parker and David Saal (eds) *International Handbook on Privatization*, Northampton, MA: Edward Elgar Pub.

Megginson, William L., Nash, Robert C. and van Randenborgh, Matthias (1994) "Financial and Operating Performance of Newly Privatized Firms: An International Empirical Analysis", *Journal of Finance* 49: 2, p. 403.

Nash, Robert C., Boehmer, Ekkehart and Netter, Jeffry M. (2003) "Bank Privatization in Developing and Developed Countries: Cross-Sectional Evidence on the Impact of Economic and Political Factors", paper presented at the World Bank Conference on Bank Privatization, November 20–21, Washington, DC.

Nellis, John (2003) "Privatization in Africa: What Has Happened? What Is To Be Done?", *Working Papers 25*, Center for Global Development.

Nellis, J. (2008) "Privatization in Africa: What has Happened? What is to be Done?", in Gerard Roland (ed.) *Privatization: Successes and Failures*, New York: Columbia University Press.

Ostrom, E. (2005) *Institutional Diversity*, Princeton, NJ: Princeton University Press.

Parker, D. and Saal, D. (eds) (2003) *International Handbook of Privatization*, Cheltenham: Edward Elgar Pub.

Peters, B. Guy and Pierre, J. (1998) "Governance without Government? Rethinking Public Administration", *Journal of Public Administration Research and Theory* 8: 2, pp. 223–244).

Qian, Yingyi and Weingast, Barry R. (1997) "Federalism as a Commitment to Preserving Market Incentives", *The Journal of Economic Perspectives* 11: 4 (Autumn) pp. 83–92.

Ramesh, M. (2008) "Reasserting the Role of the State in the Healthcare Sector: Lessons from Asia", *Policy and Society* 27: 2, pp. 129–136.

Rodrik, Dani (2005) "Rethinking Growth Strategies", in A. B. Atkinson *et al.* (eds) *WIDER Perspectives on Global Development*, London: Palgrave Macmillan in association with UNU-WIDER.

Roland, G. (2008) *Privatization: Successes and Failures,* New York: Columbia University Press.

Schalager, E. (1999) "Frameworks, Theories and Models", in Paul Sabatier (ed.) *Theories of the Policy Process*, Boulder, CO: Westview Press.

Sen, A. (2009) *The Idea of Justice*, London: Allen Lane.

Shirley, M. (2006) "Urban Water Reform: What We Know, What We Need to Know", paper presented at the 10th Meeting of the International Society for New Institutional Economics, Boulder, CO.

Shleifer, A. (1998) *State Versus Private Ownership*, Cambridge, MA: National Bureau of Economic Research.

Stiglitz, Joseph (1998) "Redefining the Role of the State: What Should It Do? How Should It Do It? And How Should these Decisions be Made?", unpublished paper. Available at www.worldbank.org/html/extdr/extme/redefine.pdf.

Stiglitz, Joseph (2008) "Foreword: Privatization: Successes and Failures", in Gerard Roland (ed.) *Privatization: Successes and Failures*, New York: Columbia University Press.

Tierney, J. (1988) *The U.S. Postal Service: Status and Prospects of a Public Enterprise*, Dover, MA: Auburn House.

Walker, Richard M. (1998) "Social Housing Management", in M. Laffin (ed.) *Beyond Bureaucracy? New Approaches to Public Management*, Aldershot: Ashgate, pp. 108–128.

Warner, Mildred E. and Hefetz, Amir (2007) "Managing Markets for Public Service: The Role of Mixed Public/Private Delivery of City Services", *Public Administration Review* 68: 1, pp. 155–166.

Williamson, J. (1999) "What Should the Bank Think about the Washington Consensus?", paper prepared as a background to the World Bank's World Development Report 2000. Available at www.iie.com/publications/papers/paper.cfm?ResearchID=351.

Williamson, John (2000) What Should the World Bank Think about the Washington Consensus? *The World Bank Research Observer* 15: 2 (August) pp. 251–264, Oxford University Press. Available at www.jstor.org/stable/3986418.

Williamson, O. E. (1981) "The Economics of Organization: The Transaction Cost Approach", *American Journal of Sociology* 87: 3, p. 548.

World Bank (2005) *Economic Growth in the 1990s: Learning from a Decade of Reform*, prepared by a team led by Roberto Zagha under general direction of Gobind T. Nankani, p. 364.

World Development Report (2002). *Building Institutions for Markets*. Available at http://econ.worldbank.org/WBSITE/EXTERNAL/EXTDEC/EXTRESEARCH/EXTWDRS/

EXTWDR2002/0,,menuPK:477750~pagePK:64167702~piPK:64167676~theSiteP
K:477734,00.html.

World Development Report (2004) *Making Services Work for Poor People,* Oxford University Press.

World Development Report (2008). *Reshaping Economic Geography.* Available at http://
econ.worldbank.org/WBSITE/EXTERNAL/EXTDEC/EXTRESEARCH/EXTWDRS/
EXTWDR2009/0,,contentMDK:21955654~pagePK:64167689~piPK:64167673~theSit
ePK:4231059,00.html.

Xun, Wu and Ramesh, M. (2009) "Healthcare Reforms in Developing Asia: Potentials
and Realities", *Development and Change*, forthcoming.

2 The role of the State in governing

Governance and metagovernance

B. Guy Peters

The national State has been one of the most successful social and political inventions of all time. Since the initial creation of the Westphalian State system there have been challenges to the State system in international politics, but this system of organization continues to be successful in maintaining its central position (Spruyt 1994). The creation of international political and economic organizations, as well as the structure of international politics more generally, has tended to make this format capable of weathering numerous calls for alternative organizational formats. The development of the European Union may challenge that format for its Member States, as has the creation of a number of international regimes (Rosenau and Czempiel 1992) but even in the face of these important changes the persistence of fundamental State structures and most powers is probable.

Although largely successful at the international level, the formal State model has been less successful in maintaining its dominant position at the domestic level. That is, although the State has remained the central representative of its people in the international arena the capacity of the State to maintain control over internal policy making has been weakened, and over time some degree of policy has been dispersed "up, down and out" (see Hooge and Marks 2003). Beginning at or around the time of election of leaders such as Margaret Thatcher, Ronald Reagan and Brian Mulroney (Savoie 1994), the past three decades have been a period of massive reform in the public sector, and in its relationship to the economy and society.

Although the roles of the State in social policy and in the defining activities of the state in foreign, defense and justice policies (Rose 1976) have been altered in many ways, the economic role of the State has been changed even more dramatically. Most European States had been major economic actors, owning many major industries and regulating most other aspects of economic life. Most of those assets have been sold off, albeit often through mechanisms that permitted the public sector to have some continuing influence over the firms. The transformation of the former socialist States is even more dramatic, of course, with economic privatization producing both costs and benefits for the populations of those countries. The developmental States of Asia have been perhaps the most interesting cases of transformation, going more slowly than others in privatizing yet responding to global economic pressures.

There are numerous reasons for the emphasis on economic and social policy reform during these three decades. Many scholars and policy analysts have argued that globalization has reduced the capacity of States, especially those less affluent and powerful States, to make economic and even social policy (Strange 1996). As well as the economic pressures emerging from globalization, the dominant economic ideologies of neo-liberalism have produced demands for a smaller role for the State in economic management.[1] These combined economic pressures were to lead to large-scale privatization and deregulation, and the increased reliance on the market to solve any economic problems (Megginson and Netter 2001). Likewise, managerialist ideologies of decentralization and devolution of powers within the public sector have tended to assign greater power to governmental actors outside the central government. This ideology has included building numerous autonomous and quasi-autonomous organizations typically providing one or a limited number of services.

All of the logic of decentralization and devolution, however, has not been about efficiency and the use of market criteria. Many advocates of greater movement of activities outside the State have argued that representative democracy did not work effectively to represent many interests in society, and greater democracy would be possible if policies were governed by alternative structures (Sorenson and Torfing 2007). While that logic almost certainly would not pertain to market-based reforms, it does argue for moving activities to policy networks and to sub-national government, both of which are considered to be closer to the people than formal democratic structures at the national level.

The increasing demands from social actors for involvement in making the policies that affect then, along with the perceived incapacities of State bureaucracies to govern effectively, have led to many public programs being moved outside of the formal State structures. Some of the movement has been to market actors, either through outright privatization or through contracting, partnerships, or a host of other possible market arrangements. The market has been a common exemplar for how government could perform its functions better, and even when activities have remained within the State structure itself the style of governing has been changed to reflect a market orientation (Peters 2001).

One of the major manifestations of the market orientation in governing has been the popularity of the New Public Management (NPM) in public administration (Christensen and Laegreid 2001, 2007). The consequences of NPM are not, however, confined to administering public programs but rather that approach to public administration is in effect an approach to governing more generally. In particular, not only is the capacity of markets to solve governance problems extolled, but the capacity of conventional political institutions to govern effectively is denigrated. While this political and administrative movement may retain most activities within the State, it still devalues most political involvement in making and implementing policy decisions. This is itself rather paradoxical given that the ideas of the NPM have been pushed rather vigorously by many politicians.

Some of the movement away from the State as the locus of policy making has been in the direction of involving social actors such as not-for-profit organizations, interest groups, and again a variety of other civic society actors. The most common manifestation of this movement has been in the utilization of networks (Sorenson and Torfing 2007) of social actors, perhaps also including market actors, that have been delegated the responsibility for making and implementing policy decisions. Although these structures are most common in the Scandinavian countries and the Low Countries (Klijn and Koppenjaan 2006) they are now also a component of governing in almost all industrialized democracies (Skelcher 2005; Milward and Provan 2000), as well as in many developing societies (Howell and Pearce 2001).

Although the strength of networks and some aspects of their structures may differ across country and across policy areas within countries, the basic logic is reducing hierarchial controls over policy in favor of negotiations and consensus- *Strategie?* building. These processes are assumed to mobilize the expertise of the groups involved and to produce better decisions. Further, having consensus in advance is assumed to eliminate many problems at the implementation stage. These assumptions may be excessively optimistic, and there are numerous problems associated with decision making in networks. Further, there are numerous problems of accountability and control that may reduce the desirability of these structures, but it is clear that this solution provides one means of reducing public sector failures and of enhancing internal democracy (of a sort) in the processes of governing.

Even if activities have remained in the public sector per se, they often have been delegated either to sub-national governments, to autonomous organizations such as "agencies" (Pollitt and Talbot 2004), or to quasi-governmental organizations that themselves reside on the boundary between the State and society.[2] As with the other forms of delegation (Huber 2004) and devolution, the logic is to improve the performance of public programs. Further, the use of various internal governance instruments such a lay boards might also facilitate the involvement of members of the community and enhance the democratic performance, as well as the policy performance, of the programs.

The above statements have been expressed in very general terms, and there are some common patterns of change across most countries of the world. That having been said, however, there are also some important comparative differences across those political systems. For example, among the industrialized democracies the smaller countries of Northern Europe have been stressing the network model of engaging civil society actors, while the Anglo-American countries have tended to emphasize market-based solutions, along with decentralization to lower levels of government[3] rather than the use of market solutions. The market model has been more popular in the Antipodes and the United Kingdom, but even in those cases some of the gloss has worn off the model.

The logic for the movement away from an Étatiste model of the past has been very clear, but once these changes were implemented the problems associated with the new styles of governing have also become apparent. To some extent the assessment of the strengths and weaknesses of the various approaches to changing the State, and its relationship to economy and society, have been based on ideologies, but there is also some clear evidence about the consequences of reforms. The next section of this chapter will discuss some of the issues arising from the reforms, and will be followed by a discussion of the reactions to those reforms. In particular, I will be arguing that the decentralizing and delegation of the "governance" models have necessarily been followed by the return of the State to a more authoritative position, using strategies of "metagovernance" to reimpose some controls. That having been said, however, the fundamental changes in governing that have occurred do not permit a return to the *status quo ante* but rather require a rethinking of strategies for public sector intervention.

These changes in patterns of governing have tended to produce much weaker States, at least when considered from a hierarchical perspective. The capacity of the State to govern through command and control has been weakened substantially, so that the hierarchical style associated with that conventional governance has been delegitimated. As we will point out below the State is still in business and performing many of its traditional functions, but may be doing so in very different means, and also may be willing to accept a wider range of variation in outcomes than had been true of the more dirigiste conceptions of government.

The move away from the State: consequences for governance

These various movements away from conventional patterns of governing have been referred to as "governance". That term has been used in a variety of different ways (see Tiihonen 2004), but they all refer to basic, and often quite fundamental, changes from State domination over policy toward models in which there is a more mixed involvement of State and societal actors in making and implementing public policy. As noted, even the State itself has altered its involvement in policy, tending to utilize more autonomous organizations than in the past, and also utilizing sub-national governments more extensively, even in States that nominally are centralized. The State may still intervene but in a less direct manner.

While these movements away from conventional government mechanisms for delivering public services may have generated some gains in efficiency and perhaps some gains (of a type) in democratization they have also created a number of important governance problems, so that the costs of the reforms may outweigh the benefits that were created. The problems created by the transformation of the styles of governing – the decentering of the State already mentioned – are for the most part familiar governance issues that have been plaguing governments since their inception. These problems have, however, been exacerbated and to some extent transformed by movements away from the conventional means of governing.

One of the most important issues for governance by decentering is coordination and coherence. Since the inception of specialized government organizations there have been difficulties in getting those organizations to work together effectively, because of conflicts over scarce resources within government as well as sincere disagreements on the appropriate priorities for the public sector. The decentering of the State has created more organizations that need to be coordinated, and also has tended to empower managers to make their own decisions.[4] The creation of agencies has been central both to improving the delivery of some public services and in creating the need to bring the decentered public sector back together.

The empowerment ideas alluded to above have also played a major role in reducing the internal coordination of the public sector. The ideology of New Public Management emphasized empowering senior managers in the public sector so that they would have greater latitude to manage their programs for greater economy and efficiency. The participatory approach to reforming the public sector emphasized empowering the lower levels of public organizations and also empowering the clients of public programs to have greater influence over the way in which their programs were managed. These various directions of empowerment may engender political conflicts (Peters and Pierre 2000) among the various actors involved in delivering public programs, and they also tend to increase the sense among public organizations that they are immune from external controls.

Reactions to "governance" initiatives

Although they are sometimes discussed together, there have been several different movements attempting to alter the role of the State in governing society. As noted, some, such as New Public Management and the dismantling of many aspects of the Welfare State, focus on market solutions. These approaches to reform are distinct and to some extent are contradictory, given that some rely on rather impersonal and political market forces, while others are highly political and involve fostering the involvement of civil society actors and creating alternative avenues for political participation. Despite those differences, their net effect is to minimize the conventional role of the State, especially in the management of the economy but to some extent in all aspects of governance.

Just as the movements away from State involvement have been complex and to some extent contradictory, so too have the reactions of State actors and their allies to those movements. The State is not the inert, inept actor that it appears in some depictions of its being downsized and removed from the center of governing. Rather, the State has proven more adaptable and creative than predicted by its critics, and political and administrative actors have made effective responses to the pressures being imposed from within and outside its own structures.

The Neo-Weberian State

From one perspective the State may not be withdrawing from its policy-making role in any significant manner, and in some areas may actually be increasing its involvement. One academic reaction to the hyperbolic statements by both scholars and practitioners about the triumph of New Public Management and other market mechanisms has been the concept of the Neo-Weberian State (Pollitt and

Bouckaert 2004). This concept means that there the State will maintain a strong position in governance and employ many of its traditional instruments for governance, but that this legalistic form of governance will be supplemented by some of the techniques of the market in order to enhance efficiency, or perhaps to create the appearance of enhanced efficiency.[5] This response has been largely administrative, rebuilding the public bureaucracy and its capacity to both make policy and implement policy decisions made elsewhere.

The reassertion of the State role in governing, or perhaps the mere recognition that this role never really disappeared, to some extent emphasizes the extent to which New Public Management was not just a set of ideas about administration. In reality NPM was, and is, a theory about governing taken more broadly. However, while the theory embedded within NPM has tended to denigrate many aspects of conventional government, and has tended to laud the governance abilities of managers as opposed to political leaders, many of the goals of NPM can not be attained through the market or through a highly disaggregated political system. Perhaps as discussed by the advocates of the concept of the Neo-Weberian State, to be effective the actors in governance, including those using the techniques of New Public Management, may require a strong State.

Thus, the movement toward creating the Neo-Weberian State (NWS) should not be seen as just returning public governance to the *status quo ante* but rather conceptualized as a new form of public sector intervention (see Jayasuriya 2005). The NWS is to some extent a composite of many aspects of the older, legalistic State with some components coming from the leaner, market-oriented State. The question posed for leaders in this response to decentering the State becomes not so much the ideological one of what should the State do, or not do, but rather how can it best undertake the tasks that it (or more precisely its leaders and citizens) choose to undertake.[6] That having been said, however, focusing on the means for providing governance may also help identify those areas of public policy in which the State may be ill-suited to attempt to exercise its control.

The primacy of politics

A second reaction to challenges posed by decentering of the State has been to reassert the primacy of politics. That is, many political leaders facing the task of governing found that they did not have the "levers" at their disposal for controlling public action that they might have expected when they assumed office. Although political leaders have encountered some of those problems for some time (Rose 1974), the decentering of the State had eliminated many of those levers and had to some extent delegitimated many of the basic ideas about public sector control over the economy and society.

The reassertion of the primacy of politics has taken several forms, all representing attempts to impose greater central control over policy choices and the implementation of those policies. One of the most important of the political reactions to the loss of control over policy has been to search for greater coordination and coherence in governing. For example, after several decades of privatization, decentralization, and agencification one of the first priorities of the Blair govern-ment in Britain was to create a "joined-up" government that would bring together many complementary programs. This was but one example from among a number of countries that sought to make the public sector work as a "whole of government" rather than as a set of more or less autonomous organizations.

In addition to simply coordinating existing programs and improving public sector efficiency, other political leaders attempted to create more strategic approaches to governing (see below). The strategic approach required identify-ing not only how various programs can work together but also what the major priorities of the public sector should be. Those priorities tend to cut across estab-lished program and organizational lines, and attempt to integrate those pre-existing policy approaches into more generalized and comprehensive systems.

Metagovernance

Although the first two reactions to the decentering of the State capture much of the transformation of the public sector, the idea of "metagovernance" can extend the argument further and point to a range of options that involve more direction but which do not represent as many returns to conventional patterns of govern-ing as the first two options.

Metagovernance – the governance of governance – accepts many of the changes in governing discussed above but seeks to impose some form of steering over those more or less transformed policy systems. Although metagovernance does not necessarily involve the direct application of public authority (as in the Neo-Weberian State) it may, however, still involve attempts of the center to steer the society by less direct methods.[7]

Although I am discussing metagovernance as a separate reaction to the prob-lems generated by decentering the public sector, to some extent it is related to the two previous approaches, most notably the "primacy of politics". That is, political actors may well attempt to reassert their control through relatively indi-rect mechanisms but they still are attempting to exert that control. Although gov-ernance approaches have generated their problems, they also have demonstrated the utility of some softer forms of governance, and approaches to metagovern-ance may also be effective if they utilize somewhat "softer" approaches to steer-ing and attempts to create control over many aspects of governing while at the same time attempting to allow some of the benefits of more decentralized and autonomous public organizations.

One of the most important mechanisms for metagovernance is priority setting, and the creation of a strategic sense of governing within public sectors that often are highly fragmented and concerned with producing immediate results, whether for political or for managerial reasons. Much of the emphasis on reform in the public sector over the last several decades has emphasized the operational elements of governing and has tended to assume that efficient administration will solve the problems being confronted by citizens. Further, as noted above the emphasis on administration has tended to denigrate the role of the central, political actors in governing in favor of managers. Priority setting, on the other hand, tends to drive control back toward the center, but does so in a relatively less hierarchical manner than was true for conventional hierarchical forms of control.

The development of strategic formats for performance management has been one of the most important mechanisms for priority setting and recentering management. Most performance management systems tend to focus attention on individual programs and organizations, and therefore may lessen the strategic and integrative capacity of the center of government (Peters 1998). If, however, systemic goals as well as programmatic goals are included in the performance system then the organizations can be used to steer the policy-making system and its priorities.[8] It should be noted, however, that performance management in general also can be used as a form of soft steering from the center and metagovernance. By establishing goals for organizations and then permitting those organizations to devise their own means of reaching those goals, performance management does provide some direction without direct hierarchical controls over those organizations. While the imposition of the goals may be considered to be exercising hierarchical control over organizations, in many performance systems these goals can be negotiated.[9] Further, even if the performance goals are not negotiated performance management systems still permit greater latitude for the individual programs than would be available in hierarchical forms of management.

Although performance management provides a rather technical mechanism for priority setting and strategic management there are other, more political approaches. Most of these political approaches tend to emphasize the role of political leaders and their central agencies in deciding on a limited set of priorities. For example, the Program Management system in Finland involves the coalition government negotiating a limited set of priorities for their term of office and then linking the on-going organizations in government with those priorities. While this may again appear to be imposing hierarchical control over actors within the public sector, the availability of incentives for the organizations tends to minimize the direct command and control elements in favor of negotiation.[10]

The general theme of shifting away from command and control patterns of governance mentioned above to the concepts of "soft law" and "soft steering" are also central to the development of metagovernance in contemporary States. Traditional forms of control over society and elements of the State itself relied on command and control and the use of public authority. Further, these traditional forms of control tended to emphasize "point compliance", demanding the subjects of the regulation to attain rather exact levels of compliance. Some legal requirements have been more exacting than others, but the general pattern has been to force close compliance with pre-set standards.

The logic of soft law that has been developing over the past decade is to establish more general guidelines for the targets of the controls. Words such as "frameworks", "guidelines", "benchmarks" and "standard-setting" have been used to characterize the mechanisms that are used to control those targets. The basic idea therefore is that there are goals for policy and the targets of the policy but that the actual compliance may be variable and progressive. Further, the standards and the compliance may be negotiated between the State agency and the actor. The idea here is to permit some latitude and to have the State exercise a much lighter hand in governing.

The notion of "soft steering" is not dissimilar to that of soft law. The basic idea here is that the State steers, but does so "at a distance" (Kickert 1995). The instruments for soft steering, or for the "New Governance" discussed by Salamon (2002), are expressed mainly in terms of incentives and perhaps moral suasion[11] as much as they are in terms of formal demands on the participants in the process. As argued for the basic idea of soft law, this approach to governing provides direction over participants without the stringent controls associated with the conventional forms of control. As noted below, however, the mailed fist may always be hidden in the velvet glove and the State may choose to revert to harder forms of governance if the softer forms are not successful.

One of the best contemporary examples of the use of soft law or soft steering is the Open Method of Coordination in the European Union (Borras and Jacobsson 2004). The major product of the Lisbon Summit of the European Union in 2000 was the commitment to an economic program designed to make Europe the most productive economy in the world by 2010. The use of the word "designed" is, however, perhaps inappropriate given that there was no set of mandates or programs but rather primarily a set of goals along with some suggested benchmarks for achieving those goals. The individual countries could therefore decide how best to achieve those goals, often involving coordinating a range of different programs in innovative ways.[12]

The Open Method of Coordination also points out that the use of softer methods may permit governments to intervene in areas in which they might not ordinarily expect to be successful, or even welcome. Although the European Union does have clear competencies in many aspects of economic policy, the productivity initiative involved areas such as education and social policy that were not directly in its area. However, by creating rather sweeping goals and permitting the Member States to decide how to reach those goals, the EU was able to intervene effectively (see Begg and Ardy 2002). Thus, somewhat paradoxically, soft mechanisms for governance may actually provide extra strength to the public sector.

The metagovernance of networks and other informal modes of governance is central to the reassertion of the State and its governance capacity. A good deal of the network literature assumes that networks are self-organizing and capable of managing their own affairs after their creation (see Rhodes 1996). That assumption seems extremely optimistic in practice, and the evidence is that the public sector is often involved in creating and framing networks. If nothing else, the willingness of the State to become involved with networks, and to delegate at least some aspects of policy making to those networks, establishes the opportunity structures for these social actors to organize structures outside the State.

The State may attempt to metagovern networks in ways that go beyond their formation or offering the opportunities for involvement. For example, governments may become heavily involved in the management of networks as in their formation. The management may involve framing the issues to be considered, and by shaping the agenda to some extent also shaping the outcomes. Further, there is always the "shadow of hierarchy" under which the networks may function, meaning that if they do not produce effective decisions, or they make the "wrong" decisions, the State can always reassert its inherent capacity to control.

Finally, the center of government may be able to exercise some metagovernance through maintaining controls over a limited number of components of the actions of its targets. The traditional mode of governing from the center was to impose controls over almost all aspects of action, especially within the public sector. One set of reforms often associated with New Public Management has been internal deregulation within the public sector (DiIulio 1994; Peters 2001). This deregulation meant removing *ex ante* controls over central features of governing such as personnel, procurement and the budget, and therefore giving managers substantially greater latitude to make their own decisions.

One strategy for metagovernance is to reassert some controls over at least some of these inputs into the delivery of public services. The usual candidate for control is the budget, with Ministries of Finance or their equivalents using financial controls to metagovern organizations in the public sector and/or perhaps the social actors involved in governance arrangements (see Wanna *et al.* 2004). This aspect of metagovernance does come very close to traditional hierarchical governance within the public sector. However, the important difference is the limited spans of the controls being implemented.

To these points, I have, implicitly or explicitly been singing hymns of praise to the idea of metagovernance. The argument is that this style of governing permits substantial control over the actions of the public but does so through the softening of internal controls within the public sector. Although this relative informality and the possibilities for enhanced involvement of social actors does appear very positive, there may be other normative questions about the metagovernance. Like the informality associated with governance itself the loose controls and the absence of clear standards may raise questions about accountability in these steering arrangements.

The desirability of informality and metagoverance strategies may also vary markedly according to the policy area being considered. For example, the defining functions of government (Rose 1976) might still be best managed more directly, while the social and economic functions of the public sector are more amenable to the involvement of social actors and steering at a distance. The defining functions of government such as justice often deal with the rights of citizens that may not be as suitable a locus of benchmarks and guidelines as are social benefits or the developmental activities of government.

Summary and conclusions

Ideas about how best to govern and to organize the public sector tend to change frequently, and tend to swing much as a pendulum. Whenever the governing apparatus goes too far in one direction, e.g. specialization, the virtues of the alternative extreme, e.g. coordination, become apparent. The reforms of the State during the past several decades have been undergoing something of a pendulum movement such as that. The "decentering" reforms associated with New Public Management and with what has come to be known as the "governance" style were successful, or perhaps too successful, in creating autonomy and independence within the public sector, but they have now provoked some reaction.

The attempts of political and administrative leaders to regain some control over the processes of governing represents the movement of the pendulum back in the direction of State management of major policy issues and processes. Although the creation of greater autonomy for both public sector organizations and private actors has had real benefits for societies and for government itself, it has also exacerbated underlying coordination problems in the public sector and increased problems of accountability in the public sector. Therefore, political leaders in particular have sought to establish some capacity to control the public sector more effectively.

This chapter has argued that although there have been some attempts simply to reassert old-fashioned forms of command and control regulation over other actors, the more interesting responses, however, have focused on providing "softer" means of exercising control. These methods may be able to retain some of the gains achieved through decentering the State, while at the same time to provide some general direction to the policy making and governing institutions. Knitting together these two strands of governing poses a significant challenge to political and administrative leaders in developing metagovernance.

Notes

1 Choices of this type were made endogenously by most of the industrialized democracies, but were imposed on most less-developed countries as part of the "Washington consensus" coming from the donor community.

2 That boundary is vague and increasingly permeable, and a clear distinction between these two sectors is often not possible. Some of the more important activities of the public sector may be delegated to these organizations in the "twilight zone", simply because they will be less subject to immediate political pressures and may be able to make "credible commitments" that more directly public organizations could not. These policy advantages may be purchased, however, at the cost of some level of democracy.

3 That having been said, many of the administrative reform processes of the United States and Canada have emphasized participation of both clients and of lower echelon workers.

4 The reforms of New Public Management have, in fact, empowered managers, lower level officials, as well as clients (Peters and Pierre 2000) thereby creating the appearance that coordination is not a crucial value for governing.

5 Some of the techniques derived from the market model of governing, e.g. pay for

performance, have proved to be spectacularly unsuccessful in producing the intended results but persist because they appear to work.

6 In some ways this is a reassertion of the old politics–administration dichotomy. The choice of what to do is bracketed and left to the political institutions of the State, while the administrative institutions may choose to employ, or be encouraged to employ, a range of different instruments in order to achieve those purposes. In reality, of course, the dividing line between the two functions is not distinct but the rhetoric associated with some aspects of contemporary governance makes it appear so. Further, as Woodrow Wilson pointed out the choice of goals through politics is largely an art.

7 The goals of metagovernance may also extend to controlling other aspects of the public sector itself, albeit through relatively indirect means. Thus, understanding metagovernance may involve unpacking several levels of softer controls over governmental and social actors.

8 For example, the Performance Management System implemented in New Zealand contains Strategic Results Areas that are linked to Key Results Areas managed by the individual organizations. Some of the same approach is now being implemented by both the United States and Canada.

9 For example, the Government Performance and Results Act in the United States involved extensive negotiations between the Office of Management and Budget and the individual organizations, with the General Accounting Office being the referee between the two principals.

10 One cannot deny, however, the importance of cultural elements emphasizing cooperation and compromise in making this type of steering system perform as effectively as it appears to.

11 The development of soft law and soft steering represent to some extent an expansion of the toolkits used by government, or at least a recognition of the wide variety of instruments that have been available but which governments often eschewed in favor of the familiar command and control instruments.

12 After the success of this mode of intervention for the Lisbon goals the European Union has adopted similar modes of governance for a number of other policy areas, again often those for which it has the least direct authority.

Bibliography

Begg, I. and Ardy, B. (2002) "The European Employment Strategy: Policy Integration by the Back-door?", *Current Politics and Economics in Europe* 11(3): 187–203.

Borras, S. and Jacobsson, K. (2004) "The Open Method of Co-ordination and New Governance Patterns in the EU", *Journal of European Public Policy* 11(2): 185–208.

Christensen, T. and Laegreid, P. (2001) *New Public Management: Transformation of Ideas and Practice*, Aldershot: Ashgate.

Christensen, T. and Laegreid, P. (2007) *Transcending New Public Management: The Transformation of Public Sector Reforms*, Aldershot: Ashgate.

DiIulio, J. J. (1994) *Deregulation*, Washington, DC: The Brookings Institution.

Hooge, L. and Marks, G. (2003) "Unraveling the Central State, but How? Types of Multi-Level Governance", *American Political Science Review* 97(2): 233–43.

Howell, J. and Pearce, J. (2001) *Civil Society and Development: A Critical Appraisal*, Boulder, CO: Lynne Reinner.

Huber, J. D. (2004) *Delegation*, Cambridge: Cambridge University Press.

Jayasuriya, K. (2005) "Beyond Institutional Fetishism: From the Developmental to the Regulatory State", *New Political Economy* 10(3): 381–7.

Kickert, W. J. M. (1995) "Steering at a Distance: A New Paradigm of Public Governance in Dutch Higher Education", *Governance* 8(1): 135–57.

Klijn, E-H. and Koppenjaan, J. (2006) *Managing Uncertainties in Policy Networks*, London: Routledge.

Megginson, W. L. and Netter, J. M. (2001) "From State to Market: A Survey of Empirical Studies of Privatization", *Journal of Economic Issues* 39(2): 321–89.

Milward. H. B. and Provan, K. G. (2000) "Governing the Hollow State", *Journal of Public Administration Research and Theory* 10(2): 359–79.

Peters, B. G. (1998) "Managing Horizontal Government: The Politics of Policy Coordination", *Public Administration* 76(2): 295–311.

Peters, B. G. (2001) *The Future of Governing*, second edition, Lawrence, KS: University Press of Kansas.

Peters, B. G. and Pierre, J. (2000) "Citizens Versus The New Public Manager: The Problem of Mutual Empowerment", *Administration & Society* 32(1): 9–28.

Pierre, J. and Peters, B. G. (2001) *Governance, Politics and the State*, Basingstoke: Palgrave.

Pollitt, C. and Bouckaert, G. (2004) *Public Management Reform: A Comparative Analysis*, second edition, Oxford: Oxford University Press.

Pollitt, C. and Talbot, C. (2004) *Unbundled Government: A Critical Analysis of the Global Trend to Agencies, Quangos and Contractualisation*, London: Routledge.

Radin, B. A. (1996) *Challenging the Performance Movement: Accountability, Complexity and Democratic Values*, Washington, DC: Georgetown University Press.

Rhodes, R. A. W. (1996) "The New Governance: Governance Without Government", *Political Studies* 44(4): 652–67.

Rose, R. (1974) *The Problem of Party Government*, London: Macmillan.

Rose, R. (1976) "On the Priorities of Government", *European Journal of Political Research* 4(3): 247–89.

Rosenau, J. N. and Czempiel, E. O. (1992) *Governance Without Government*, Cambridge: Cambridge University Press.

Salamon, L. M. (2002) "Introduction", in L. M. Salamon (ed.) *The Handbook of Policy Instruments*, New York: Oxford University Press.

Savoie, D. J. (1994) *Reagan, Thatcher, Mulroney: In Search of a New Bureaucracy*, Pittsburgh, PA: University of Pittsburgh Press.

Skelcher, C. (2005) "Jurisdictional Integrity, Polycentrism, and the Design of Democratic Governance", *Governance* 18(1): 89–110.

Sorenson, E. and Torfing, J. (2007) *Theories of Democratic Network Governance*, Basingstoke: Palgrave.

Spruyt, H. (1994) *Sovereign State and Its Competitors: An Analysis of System Change*, Princeton, NJ: Princeton University Press.

Strange, S. (1996) *The Retreat of the State: The Diffusion of Power in the World Economy*, Cambridge: Cambridge University Press.

Tiihonen, S. (2004) *From Government to Governance*, Tampere: University of Tampere Press.

Wanna, J., Jensen, L. and De Vries, J. (2004) *Controlling Public Expenditure: The Changing Role of Central Budget Agencies – Better Guardians?*, Cheltenham: Edward Elgar.

3 Reversing privatization, rebalancing government reform

Markets, deliberation and planning

Mildred E. Warner

Introduction

Experimentation with contracting out (privatization) of local government services grew over the 1980s and 1990s, but we have begun to see reversals in that trend. Compulsory competitive tendering has been abolished in the UK and Australia; New Zealand elected a new prime minister focused on rebuilding internal government service delivery capacity; and US local government managers began to bring previously contracted services back in house in a process of reverse privatization. This reassertion of the public role is not the direct government monopoly of the past. Instead we see local governments using markets, but playing a market structuring role in building competition, managing monopoly and reducing transactions costs of contracting. But market management is not the only role of government. Managers also see the importance of engaging citizens in the public service delivery process. This chapter describes both theoretically and empirically how this new approach to governmental reform balances the efficiency benefits of market-type engagement with the technical benefits of planning and the civic benefits of public engagement.

There has been a shift in understanding of the role of the state in public service delivery over the last few decades. The old public administration emphasized direct government delivery, hierarchical control, and a separation of politics and management to ensure due process for citizens and limit outside influence among public employees. This system was criticized as too slow and inflexible by proponents of the New Public Management who argued market-type management approaches could be effectively applied to the public sector (Hood 1991; Osborne and Gaebler 1992). New Public Management emphasized speed and flexibility and touted the advantages of markets for both greater private sector engagement and consumer voice for citizens (Savas 1987). Market solutions suffer from high transactions costs and this has led to a new emphasis on network governance based on relational contracting and trust (Goldsmith and Eggers 2004; Brown *et al.* 2007). However, the close relationships between contractors and government in network governance undermine democratic accountability. The lack of control and accountability in contracting networks has led others to emphasize citizens are more than consumers and government more than a contract manager (DeLeon and Denhardt 2000; Denhardt and Denhardt 2003; Sclar 2000; Starr 1987).

One of the intellectual foundations for market approaches to public goods is public choice theory (Tiebout 1956). However, the public choice reliance on aggregated individual preferences in a market-type system can lead to public value failures because it allows no space for a deliberative social process of public participation (Bozeman 2002). Problems with preference misalignment cause the aggregation of individual preferences to diverge from the collective social preference (Lowery 1998). However, democratic approaches to aggregate individual preferences through voting may not be socially optimal or stable either according to social choice theory (Sager 2002a). What is missing in both these approaches is a space for deliberation to identify collective needs and common solutions. Recent work in communicative planning and deliberative democracy shows that through deliberation individuals shift preferences toward more collective goals and thus arrive at a more socially optimal choice (Sager 2002b; Lowery 2000; Frug 1999). When combined with markets and voting, deliberation may be both democratic and efficient.

In this chapter, I argue there is a rebalancing of government reform that capitalizes on the efficiency of markets, the technical expertise of planning, and the social choice of democracy without the problems of accountability and decision cycling that occur under any of these strands alone. This chapter explores the theoretical basis for the emergence of such a balanced position, and provides evidence this is occurring in local government practice. Public managers have moved beyond the dichotomy of markets *or* planning, and instead embrace a mixed position which complements the advantages of markets with the benefits of public engagement. This balance between deliberation and markets recognizes citizens are more than consumers, and government is more than a market manager. Government creates the space for collective deliberation to occur and through this process a sense of the social is built. See Figure 3.1.

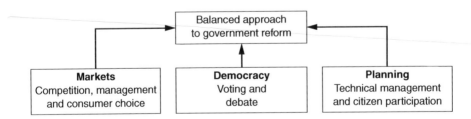

Figure 3.1 Rebalancing government reform.

Shifts in theory

Understanding the difference between market and government

The New Public Management revolution in local government promotes market-based management techniques to increase efficiency and citizen choice, but it fails to consider the subtle and important ways in which markets and government differ. Markets are based on the principle of utility maximization. Adam Smith articulated the notion of an invisible hand whereby producers and consumers in a market (motivated by individual utility maximization) would create competitive price pressure, promote innovation and ensure service quality thus securing socially optimal production. The key to this happy result was competition. But many services are natural monopolies, and thus do not benefit from the invisible hand of Adam Smith's competitive market. Competition erodes, and with it the guarantee of this market-based socially optimal result.

Key to the challenge of using markets for public goods is recognition of what creates a public good in the first place. Public goods, by definition, arise from market failure as self-interested individuals undersupply critical social goods or free ride on common resources. Congestion, pollution, and public health are all examples of market-failed public goods which require some collective intervention to address. Typically this intervention is in the form of government regulation or production. With increased urbanization, externalities become more pronounced (congestion, public health impacts, etc.), more services experience market failures, and citizen demand for public provision increases. This has led to the expansion of local government service delivery over time into new arenas of service delivery – e.g. garbage collection, water distribution, environmental management, infrastructure provision and human services.

However, market delivery mechanisms still may be possible for some of these goods. The potential of voluntary bargaining to address externalities, first articulated by Ronald Coase in his article on the Problem of Social Cost (1960), rests on the notion of a bargaining framework where individuals with full information and clear property rights pay producers of positive (negative) externalities to increase (reduce) them in a voluntary scheme. When the link between the supplier and the consumer is close, such payment schemes are easier to arrange. When larger numbers of actors are involved, these voluntary solutions tend to break down and government organization of production is preferred (Coase 1960; Webster 1998).

Recent scholarship suggests that in dense urban settings, the possibilities of voluntary solutions may be larger than once thought. For example in squatter settlements where government is unwilling or unable to extend basic services, individuals come together to provide services – urban transportation, water delivery – that might traditionally be provided by government (Gilbert 1998). That people have voluntarily organized to meet collective needs attests to the power and potential behind voluntary market solutions. In arguing for the "spontaneous order" created by markets, Webster and Lai (2003) suggest government delivery may hamper such private solutions through regulation and intervention that raises costs and restricts access, especially for the poor. This has been one of the rationales behind the promotion of market-delivered services for the poor (Graham 1998).

While these market approaches show promise, they still require a significant government role. Where these market solutions are most pronounced (e.g. squatter settlements), property rights of consumers are least secure. This tilts the bargaining power toward the private producers of public goods and can lead to problems in price and quality due to inadequate government oversight. It also promotes an economic conception of citizenship where rights to basic services – even those critical to life such as water – are based on ability to pay. Especially in developing countries, where market-based schemes for water delivery have been promoted by foreign donors, we have seen large increases in consumer prices which have led to civic protest, most notably the water riots in Cochabamba, Bolivia (Kohl 2004). These market solutions promote a version of citizen choice and empowerment based on market-based bargaining, that has been challenged as a veil to reduce citizenship rights to basic services (Miraftab 2004). Even in developed countries, such as Canada, privatization has been challenged as an assault on both citizenship and democracy (CUPE 2001).

There is something more fundamental than cost and service quality in the public goods equation. Citizens expect involvement, voice and control over government decisions. Deliberation is key to democracy. But anonymous and spontaneous markets do not create a space for deliberation. The individual can choose to buy or not, but deliberation on the nature of the choice is not typically part of a market. Markets, as aggregations of individuals, do not become social spaces for deliberation unless market governance is designed that way. Recall that the efficiency benefit of Adam Smith's invisible hand was that it did not require deliberation. But as market solutions have been applied to public service delivery, problems with preference alignment have been found (Lowery 1998). When individual preferences are substituted for public preferences (e.g. a private provider's preference for profit versus the public interest in access and service quality), we have failure of public goods again. Consumers may substitute individual preferences for public objectives when they shop as individuals in a privatized market for public goods. This has been found in voucher schemes for education, child care and job training where socially suboptimal choices are made by individual consumers who, due to lack of information or time, choose convenience over quality and thus undermine the intended societal educational benefits (Hipp and Warner 2007; Meyers and Jordan 2006; Lowery 1998).

Recent research has shown that through deliberation, citizens shift their individual preferences more toward collective well-being (Lowery 2000; Sager 2002b). Creating the space for such democratic deliberation is a key function of government. Frug (1999) has argued that such community building is the ultimate public good. Citizens in a democratic society must develop the capacity to engage difference, see common problems and craft socially optimal solutions. In planning, this has led to a new subfield of communicative planning which emphasizes how power imbalances can be altered through a deliberative process which allows more citizen voice and participation (Forester 1999; Healey 1996). In public administration attention is shifting back to a focus on citizenship, participation and public value. The role of government is not simply to steer a market process; it also must serve citizens (Denhardt and Denhardt 2003, 2000). Governments must have the capacity to help citizens come together to identify problems and to debate choices (Nalbandian 1999, 2005). Citizen engagement is more than the consumer orientation and competition advocated by New Public Management (Osborne and Gaebler 1992). Citizens need more than the exit option of markets; they need the opportunity to stay, exercise voice, and invest in their community (Frug 1999). Participation in local decision making is seen as the foundation for a democratic society. Learning to solve collective problems, to engage the heterogeneous diversity found in the urban landscape, and to practice deliberation – these are the foundations for a democratic society.

Recognizing the civic within the market

In order to use markets for public goods, more attention must be given to the civic foundations of markets and the potential for deliberation within them. The social construction of markets challenges the anonymity of the invisible hand, and shows the importance of trust and embeddedness in creating the social norms that permit markets to function (Granovetter 1985; North 1990). This line of research has been especially important in the transition literature on Eastern Europe and China. Market emergence requires a state role in creating the legal framework necessary to support market functioning (bonding, insurance, property rights). It also requires attention to social networks and changing social norms (Nee 2000). Market entrepreneurship requires contestation and competition. Neither was encouraged under state socialism, and so building the norms for contestation and competition is part of the sociological foundation both for civic engagement and market emergence (Warner and Daugherty 2004).

Some have argued that democracy and market economies are mutually reinforcing (Przeworski 1991), and indeed this was the philosophy behind most international donor investment in Eastern Europe after the transition. However, inadequate social foundations for market functioning led to corruption and concentration of privatized assets into the hands of a few, understood as gangster capitalism or "the great stealing" in much of the region, especially Russia (Holstrom and Smith 2000).

Markets naturally concentrate power. A laissez-faire market does not naturally emerge. Absent state regulations to ensure more competitive market functioning, and social norms and networks to ensure broader bargaining power, concentration is an expected result. Even mathematical models of market systems show that wealth concentrates, and competition disappears as the models play out over time (Hayes 2002). This is especially common in many publicly provided services which are natural monopolies, or tend toward monopoly – water, waste collection, electricity, etc.

Lowery (1998) has warned that public service contracting markets are, at best, quasi markets of one buyer (government) and a few sellers. Thus these markets fail to create competition. This may be why local governments show more stability in their use of contracting for public goods if they focus on managing monopoly. Warner and Bel (2008), in their comparative study of water distribution and solid waste disposal contracting in the US and Spain, found Spanish local governments had both higher levels of contracting and more stable contracts than in the US. They attributed these differences to the Spanish focus on managing monopoly through mixed public/private firms which enjoy the benefits of natural monopoly (economies of scale) and private sector management, but retain public values and accountability. In the US, by contrast, local governments focus on promoting competition between government and private firms. This resulted in less contracting overall and much higher rates of reversals.

Lack of competition is not the only failure. Market-based solutions also create preference alignment problems as individuals substitute private preferences (convenience) for public preference (quality) (Hipp and Warner 2007). Markets also can lead to preference errors on the part of purchasers due to information asymmetries and transactions costs (Lowery 1998). Some of these market failures can be addressed through investments in the social foundation – public education, regulatory standards or anti-trust laws. The important challenge is to understand the social foundations of markets. The late twentieth century was an experiment to see how far we could push the boundaries of market into state provision of market-failed public goods. However, if we want to use markets for public goods, then we must understand what is needed for those markets to work.

Market solutions for public goods promoted in both developing countries and Eastern Europe failed to give sufficient attention to the failures of quasi markets outlined above or the important social foundations of markets which help ensure their smooth functioning. Polanyi (1944) argued that human interaction is based on more than market exchange. Reciprocity and redistribution are key. When markets subordinate other aspects of human life, there will be a counter movement to moderate them. This may help explain the strong anti-privatization movement in water in Bolivia and South Africa. It also may explain the growth in reverse privatization we are seeing in the US and the shifts away from competitive tendering among the early privatizers: the UK, Australia and New Zealand.

Privatization requires government capacity to manage markets and citizen/consumer capacity to effectively engage them. Privatization is not a reduction in the role of the state as some pro-privatization theorists argue (Savas 1987), but rather a shift in state role (Schamis 2002) toward managing new tools (Salamon 2002) including a more direct market management role. The structuring of contracts, regulation of price and quality, as well as direct action as a supplier or purchaser in the market are all tools governments have used to engage markets more effectively in public service delivery. Privatization does not allow government to contract out and walk away; instead government must remain actively engaged as a market player directly providing services and contracting out in a dynamic process to ensure competition, efficiency, service quality and broader public objectives (Warner and Hebdon 2001; Hefetz and Warner 2004, 2007; Warner and Hefetz 2008).

The promise and failure of market approaches

One of the purported advantages of market approaches to government was that they would give the consumer citizen more choice and voice in government service delivery. Tiebout (1956) showed that, especially at the local government level, a public market of competing local governments gave mobile residents choice in the tax/service mix of their communities, and provided competitive pressure for local governments to remain efficient. At a time of rapid suburbanization and geographic mobility in the post World War II US, a public choice model based on mobility seemed reasonable. Later studies of such Tiebout sorting have challenged the assumption that decisions are based primarily on efficiency considerations. Sorting by race and class has had a major impact on the landscape of fiscal and service inequality in metropolitan areas (Warner and Pratt 2005; Troutt 2000; Frug 1999; Lowery 2000).

A strong sense of localism has led to the notion that public services are private, club goods, available only to residents within a particular jurisdiction (Frug 1999). This narrowing of the public view has undermined efforts to cooperate at the regional scale. While such localism may promote democracy and choice, the need for planning at the metropolitan regional scale suggests the region may be the appropriate scale for a local focus today (Briffault 2000). The challenge is how to create the appropriate forum for a regional democratic conversation (Frug 2002). Both technocratic planning "things regionalism" and private market approaches "privatization" have been shown to exacerbate inequality and narrow voice to growth coalition elites (Warner and Hefetz 2002, 2003, 2008; Warner 2006b; Bollens 1997; Logan and Molotch 1987). We need a "people regionalism" that incorporates both the technical and the market but subjects it to social debate.

One of the promises of privatization is that it would give consumer citizens even more voice than voting (which is infrequent), or changing communities (which requires the means to move). By privatizing government services, citizen consumers would enjoy market choice and could shop for services on a more regular basis than they can vote or move between communities. However, empirical analysis of US contracting behavior shows that attention to citizen voice is lower among municipalities that privatize more (Warner and Hefetz 2002). Because privatization is typically a contract between government as purchaser and one or a small group of suppliers, the citizen consumer does not see a choice of providers.

Similarly, market approaches could allow governments to obtain economies of scale at the regional level. Privatization and inter-municipal cooperation are popular local government reforms. However, neither promotes intra-regional equity. Privatization is favored by richer suburbs over rural or core urban communities (Warner and Hefetz 2003, 2008; Warner 2006a; Kodrzycki 1994), and inter-municipal cooperation, because it is voluntary, does not lead governments to choose to cooperate with their less well-off neighbors (Warner 2006b).

Efficiency gains, another promise of the market model, have been fleeting. US research shows that only with monitoring did local governments experience efficiency gains under privatization (Warner and Hefetz 2002). Meta analyses of privatization and cost studies show inconsistent results, but the majority of studies do not show cost savings under privatization (Bel and Warner 2008; Boyne 1998; Hodge 2000; Hirsch 1995). Some have attributed this lack of efficiency gains to the high transactions costs of contracting (Sclar 2000; Hefetz and Warner 2004). Contract specification and monitoring have turned out to be more challenging and costly than first thought (Prager 1994; Pack 1989). While some of these costs can be controlled through a more careful market management role, transactions costs do not form a sufficient framework for understanding the challenges of contracting (Hefetz and Warner 2007; Bel and Warner 2008).

Combining deliberation and markets

We have seen above that markets do not ensure equity, voice or efficiency. Markets are a tool that can be used in public service delivery but they must be managed carefully to achieve the desired goals. Local government must have the capacity to structure markets and engage citizens in a deliberative process.

While the experiment with market reforms has been proceeding in public administration, in the field of planning renewed interest has been focused on deliberation and communication. Building from Habermasian dialogue, a field of communicative planning has arisen which focuses on the process of public participation and communication in planning decisions (Forester 1999; Healey 1996). Communicative planning sees a special role for the planner in clarifying options and challenging misinformation (Forester 1989; Healey 1997; Innes 1995). While some critique communicative planning theory for being too focused on consensus and failing to adequately address power differences – especially the naïve assumption that the planner can be abstracted from his/her structural position in a nexus of power and professional expertise (McGuirk 2001), others argue that planners can facilitate an advocacy planning process that challenges existing power structures and gives more voice to the poor (Krumholz and Clavel 1994; Reardon 1999).

Although market-based reform efforts have fueled negative views of government among citizens and the media; local government managers show increasing interest in serving public values (Allmendinger *et al.* 2003; Moore 1995). Public opinion research in the US has found that citizens typically equate government with self-serving politicians or unresponsive bureaucracy, leading to a negative view (Bresette and Kinsey 2006). But when the dialogue is reframed in terms of government creating the public structures that promote economic efficiency and security, then citizen views become more positive. The challenge is to rebuild the capacity of government to lead, and of citizens to participate in a collective deliberative process. Local government has a progressive potential exhibited by leadership at the municipal scale to promote innovation (Clavel 1986). John Nalbandian (1999, 2005) has articulated government capacity as the capacity to bring a community together to solve problems in a way that does not rend the social fabric, so they can come together again to solve the next problem. Based on the exciting innovations in Puerto Alegre, Brazil, city leaders around the world are experimenting with new models of citizen engagement – citizen budgets, citizen visioning, and encouraging neighborhood control over service delivery (Osborne and Plastrick 1997; Abers 1998; Potapchuck *et al.* 1998).

In this regard, the planner's role is similar to the local government manager's role, though the planner is primarily focused on process and the government manager on direct service delivery. How to incorporate this need for deliberation in the context of a more market-based system of government service delivery is the challenge.

Public choice theory incorrectly assumed that consumer choice in a competitive market could address public goods problems. Likewise, democratic alternatives, such as majority voting, have been shown to lead to unstable decision cycles and manipulation. Social choice theory has documented the impossibility of solutions which are both efficient, democratic and serve the public interest. Cycle-free decisions involve some form of expert sovereignty (Sager 2001, 2002b).[1] So neither voting nor consumer choice alone can yield a stable, democratic and socially optimal solution. Sager (2002b) suggests that deliberation can be used as a supplement in an iterative process that circumvents these problems.

> Deliberation brackets preferences and voting brackets the giving of reasons, but shifting between these decision-making modes can bring both types of information into play ... which helps to explain why decision cycles do not occur as frequently in practice as predicted by social choice theory.
>
> (Sager 2002b p.376)

Through deliberation individuals can see the need to shift toward more socially beneficial decisions (Lowery 2000; Frug 1999). This is the promise of a deliberative and democratic planning process. However, deliberation alone can lead to the same kind of impossibility problems as voting (Sager 2002b). So the challenge is to use a process that combines planning, markets, voting and deliberation.

Shifts in practice

The first section of this chapter documented a shift in theory from an emphasis on market approaches, to a more balanced concern with democracy and planning. I argue that local government, in its practice, is moving beyond the either/ or dichotomy of planning or markets, and embracing a more balanced mixed position. Three brief examples will suffice.

New Zealand and the United Kingdom were early and radical innovators promoting extensive privatization through compulsory competitive tendering. In New Zealand, we are seeing a shift back with the new 2002 local government law which recognizes the need to rebuild government capacity to both manage markets and build the local foundation for democracy. Local government is seen as the forum where a balance between economic development, environmental and civic interests can be crafted. In the United Kingdom we have seen a shift away from compulsory competitive tendering toward a "best value" regime which includes a broader range of objectives than just efficiency. While terms such as "contestability" and "scrutiny" emphasize competition and accountability, there is also emphasis on citizen engagement. In the US, privatization was never compulsory, but support for market-based government is strong. However contracting out peaked in 1997 and reverse contracting is now larger than new contracting out. Concerns with reductions in service quality and lack of cost savings drove this shift. In each of these cases market approaches are not jettisoned; rather use of market is balanced by recognition of the need for a government management role – both to structure the market and to ensure a deliberative space for citizens.

New Zealand

New Zealand was an early leader in implementing market-based approaches to government. They tested the notion of enterprise units – focused on meeting goals and using a private sector management approach which promoted competition, outsourcing, privatization and a customer service orientation. Many services were sold off or privatized. New Zealand's approach to reform served as an exemplar for other countries, especially the United States (Osborne and Plastrick 1997). At the local level private companies emerged to manage roads, which are one of the largest budget areas for local government. New Zealand local government managers became experts in contract management. Contracting networks were viewed as more flexible than direct government and considered the wave of the future. As they moved from market management to partnerships, they recognized that partnerships need management and accountability.

However, the results of privatization were only partly satisfactory. Regulation alone was not enough; an accountability framework was needed, along with professional local government management. In the late 1990s New Zealand made a course correction and reasserted a government role. The election of Prime Minister, Helen Clark, in 1999, reflected in part a desire to rebuild government capacity.

> Certainly a not inconsiderable part of my government's time has been spent in rebuilding public sector capacity to deliver the results the public demands.... The public sector reform which went on in the 1980s and 1990s was aimed at making government agencies more efficient, but it was undoubtedly also aimed at ensuring that there was less government. Our

reforms have banked the efficiency gains, but have looked to build effectiveness as well ... a high performance and highly skilled public sector is required.

(Clark 2004)

In 2002 a new local government law was passed (Local Government New Zealand 2003). This law recognized that local government must balance competing objectives: economic development, social well-being, environmental management and civic engagement. This process is too complex for a simple market mechanism. The law recognized that citizens are more than market-based service customers. Local government must give more attention to the importance of a democratic base and citizen consultation.

New Zealand is ahead of the US in many respects. It has undertaken more privatization and outsourcing at the local level. Its performance management systems are more sophisticated, and it has an explicit audit and accountability framework. It undertook a significant amalgamation of local government in 1989 which created a structural framework for regionalism based on more sensible urban and ecological boundaries (e.g. regionalism that encompasses a watershed, or links city and suburb). Although a clearer framework for local government has been laid out, there are still problems creating effective regional collaboration and crafting the balance between environmental, social, economic and cultural objectives, especially in areas with development pressures. Consultation is not without its problems. A deliberative process can lead to more social choices, but too much consultation can lead to "governance exhaustion." However the notion of a more balanced position involving markets, democracy and planning has been articulated. Local government leaders are attempting to balance deliberative process with the efficiency of markets.

United Kingdom

The United Kingdom was another early innovator in privatization. With Margaret Thatcher, emphasis on competition and breaking the monopoly of government power was paramount. Competitive tendering was made compulsory from 1988 to 1998. But results suggest the program was not that successful in breaking the monopoly of local government control, as a large percentage of contracts were won by local government teams (Szymanski and Wilkins 1993). Nor was the program successful in saving money, as most cost savings eroded over time (Szymanski 1996). With the election of Tony Blair in 1997, a shift back toward a more balanced position began. The "best value" framework was implemented in 1999 in recognition that local government needed to balance more objectives than simple cost efficiency. Greater attention was given to accountability and citizen engagement (Martin 2002). Best value gave attention to speed, service quality and citizen voice in the service delivery process. Although the national government was keenly interested in promoting local government innovation and viewed contestability as a core reform, it also recognized the need to engage local government managers as partners, not rivals, in the reform process (Entwistle and Martin 2005). Local government managers' reluctance to externalize services reflected a public service ethos, the need for control and market management, and the need to retain core competencies within the public sector (Entwistle 2005). More detail on the UK reforms can be found in the chapter by Walker *et al.* in this volume.

United States

In the United States public discourse at the national level regarding local service delivery was not as pronounced as in New Zealand or the United Kingdom. Local government reform is controlled at the state level and this leads to great diversity and more local government independence.

However, support for privatization was strong in the US. In 1982 the professional association of city managers, the International City/County Management Association, commenced a Survey of Alternative Service Delivery to measure the level of privatization. That survey has been repeated every five years since. This permits tracking trends over time, something not possible in other countries. Although trends were relatively flat, there was increasing experimentation with privatization after 1992. But contracting out peaked in 1997, and in 2002 (the latest data available) we see a return to public delivery and a dramatic increase in mixed public and private delivery (Warner and Hefetz 2008). See Figure 3.2. As contracting out has fallen, mixed public/private delivery has

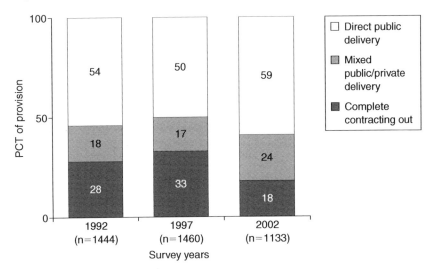

Figure 3.2 Trends in local government service delivery, 1992–2002 (source: reprinted from Warner and Hefetz (2008: 151)).

Notes
Percent of provision averaged across all responding governments. Provision is percent of total number of services provided on average. Provision Rates: 66%, 61%, 53% for 1992, 1997, 2002 respectively. Author analysis based on data from the International City/County Management Association, Profile of Alternative Service Delivery Approaches, US Municipalities, 1992, 1997, 2002, Washington, DC.

grown. This mixed delivery occurs when governments both provide a service directly and contract out a portion. This creates competition between public and private providers, maintains government capacity and internal knowledge about the process of service delivery, and ensures continued citizen involvement in the service delivery process (Warner and Hefetz 2008). Regression models for 1992, 1997 and 2002 show priority for market management concerns, but emergence of a balanced concern with market management *and* citizen voice in 2002. The challenges of local government service delivery are about more than efficiency. Local government leaders and citizens alike recognize the need to balance multiple objectives: service quality, citizen participation and economic efficiency. This explains the emergence of a mixed market position.

Reverse privatization also grew dramatically over the decade from 12 percent of all service delivery in the 1992–1997 period, to 18 percent of all service delivery from 1997–2002 (Hefetz and Warner 2007). See Figure 3.3. ICMA added a question to its 2002 survey asking why managers brought previously contracted work back in house and the primary reasons were problems with service quality, lack of cost savings, internal process improvement, and citizen support for bringing the work back in house (Warner and Hefetz 2004). A similar survey fielded in Canada the following year found exactly the same rank order of reasons for reverse privatization (Hebdon and Jalette 2008).

Statistical analyses of this shift over the decade 1992–2002 (Hefetz and Warner 2007) show the increase in reverse contracting is only partially explained by transactions costs (asset specificity, monitoring). What is more important are place characteristics and citizen voice. Reverse contracting is part of a market management approach, but also is a response to increased attention to citizen

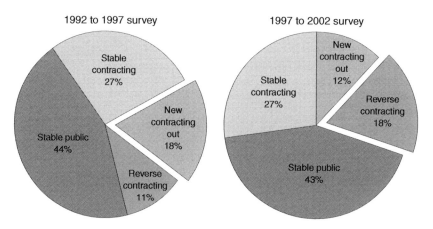

Figure 3.3 Dynamics of local government service delivery, 1992–2002 source: reprinted from: Hefetz and Warner (2007: 557)).

Notes
Author analysis based on data from the International City/County Management Association, Profile of Alternative Service Delivery Approaches, Survey Data 1992, 1997, 2002, Washington, DC.

voice. These results confirm the existence of a new balanced model of local government reform which gives attention to both markets and citizen voice.

Conclusion

The last decades of the twentieth century witnessed a profound experiment to increase the role of markets in local government service delivery. However, that experiment has failed to deliver adequately on efficiency, equity or voice criteria. This has led to reversals. But this reverse privatization process is not a return to the direct public monopoly delivery model of old. Instead it heralds the emergence of a new balanced position which combines use of markets, democracy and planning to reach decisions which may be both efficient and more socially optimal.

Local governments play a key role in community problem solving and this is the fundamental public good. To do so, they must move beyond market models of government and promote deliberation and public participation. The New Public Management reforms focused on competition and entrepreneurialism. But competition is ephemeral in public service markets and provides a poor foundation for equity. Entrepreneurship encourages secrecy and risk taking that may be inappropriate for critical public services (Kelly 1998; DeLeon and Denhardt 2000). Government is meant to be a stabilizing force, designed to reduce risk and ensure security. It is structured around principles of openness and stewardship where participation and representation are the foundation, not competition.

The privatization experience of the late twentieth century has taught us that markets require governance. Managing markets for public services is both challenging and costly. These market networks limit traditional government mechanisms to ensure public control, accountability, representation and balance of interests. Using markets alone can lead to economic conceptions of citizenship (e.g. citizen rights defined by ability to pay, limited sense of public space, little collective sharing of externalities). Recognizing the democratic deficit in these arrangements has led to greater emphasis on public planning and democratic engagement. We see this in the reverse privatization trends and the emergence of a more balanced position that combines market approaches with participation and planning. At the beginning of the twenty-first century, this balanced approach is the new reform.

Note

1 Research on social choice argues the impossibility of decision processes that are both manipulation-free and democratic (the Gibbard–Satterthwaite theorem), the impossibility of combining individual liberty and respect for unanimous preference rankings (Sen theorem), and the impossibility of amalgamating individual preference rankings in a way that is both consistent and democratic (Arrow theorem). For more detail on these theorems see: Arrow, K. J. (1963) *Social Choice and Individual Values,* New York: John Wiley; Gibbard, A. (1973) "Manipulation of Voting Schemes: A General Result," *Econometrica* 41: 587–601; Satterthwaite, M. A. (1975) "Strategy-proofness and

Arrow's Conditions: Existence and Correspondence Theorems for Voting Procedures and Social Welfare Functions," *Journal of Economic Theory* 10: 187–217; Sen, A. (1970) "The Impossibility of a Paretian Liberal," *Journal of Political Economy* 78: 152–157.

References

Abers, Rebecca (1998) "From Clientelism to Cooperation: Local Government, Participatory Policy, and Civic Organizing in Porto Alegre, Brazil," *Politics and Society* 26.4: 511–537.

Allmendinger, P., Tewdwr-Jones, M. and Morphet, J. (2003) "Public Scrutiny, Standards and the Planning System: Assessing Professional Values within a Modernized Local Government," *Public Administration* 81.4: 761–780.

Bel, G. and Warner, M. E. (2008) "Challenging Issues in Local Privatization," *Environment and Planning C: Government and Policy* 26.1: 104–109.

Bollens, Scott (1997) "Concentrated Poverty and Metropolitan Equity Strategies," *Stanford Law and Policy Review* 8.2: 11–23.

Boyne, G. A. (1998) "The Determinants of Variations in Local Service Contracting – Garbage In, Garbage Out?" *Urban Affairs Review* 34.1: 150–163.

Bozeman, B. (2002) "Public-Value Failure: When Efficient Markets May Not Do," *Public Administration Review* 62.2: 145–161.

Bresette, Patrick and Kinsey, Marcia (2006) "Public Structures: A Constructive Model for Government," *Public Briefing No. 6*, New York, NY: Dēmos: A Network for Ideas and Action. Available at http://demos.org/talkaboutgov/toolkit/docs/publicStructures_es.pdf.

Briffault, R. (2000) "Localism and Regionalism," *Buffalo Law Review* 48.1: 1–30.

Brown, T., Potoski, M. and van Slyke, D. (2007) "Trust and Contract Completeness in the Public Sector," *Local Government Studies* 33.4: 607–623.

Canadian Union of Public Employees (CUPE) (2001) *Dollars and Democracy: Canadians Pay the Price of Privatization, Annual Report on Privatization*, Ottawa, Canada: CUPE. Available at www.cupe.ca/issues/privatization/arp/default.asp.

Clark, Helen (2005) "Patterson Oration: Helen Clark – Full transcript," Australian and New Zealand School of Government, May 6, 2004, in ANZSOG, Carlton, Victoria, Australia. Available at www.anzsog.edu.au/images/docs/news/Patterson_Oration.pdf.

Clavel, P. (1986) *The Progressive City: Planning and Participation, 1969–1984*, New Brunswick, NJ: Rutgers University Press.

Coase, R. H. (1960) "The Problem of Social Cost," *Journal of Law and Economics* 3: 1–44.

DeLeon, L. and Denhardt, R. B. (2000) "The Political Theory of Reinvention," *Public Administration Review* 60.2: 89–97.

Denhardt, J. V. and Denhardt, R. B. (2003) *The New Public Service: Serving, Not Steering*, Armonk, NY: M.E. Sharpe.

Denhardt, R. B. and Denhardt, J. V. (2000) "The New Public Management: Serving Rather Than Steering," *Public Administration Review* 60.6: 549–559.

Entwistle, T. (2005) "Why Are Local Authorities Reluctant to Externalise and Do They Have Good Reason?" *Environment and Planning C: Government and Policy* 23.2: 191–206.

Entwistle, T. and Martin, S. (2005) "From Competition to Collaboration in Public Service Delivery: A New Agenda Research," *Public Administration* 83.1: 233–242.

Forester, J. (1989) *Planning in the Public Domain*, Berkeley, CA: University of California Press.

Forester, J. (1999) *The Deliberative Practitioner: Encouraging Participatory Planning Processes*, Cambridge, MA: MIT Press.

Frug, G. E. (1999) *City Making: Building Communities without Building Walls*, Princeton, NJ: Princeton University Press.

Frug, G. R. (2002) "Beyond Regional Government," *Harvard Law Review* 117.7: 1766–1836.

Gilbert, Alan (1998) *The Latin American City*, New York, NY: Latin America Bureau.

Goldsmith, S. and Eggers, W. (2004) *Governing by Network: The New Shape of the Public Sector*, Washington, DC: Brookings Institution Press.

Graham, Carol (1998) *Private Markets for Public Goods*, Washington, DC: Brookings Institution Press.

Granovetter, M. (1985) "Economic Action and Social Structure: The Problem of Embeddedness," *American Journal of Sociology* 34.2: 481–510.

Hayes, B. (2002) "Follow the Money," *American Scientist* 90.5: 400–405.

Healey, Patsy (1996) "The Communicative Turn in Planning Theory and its Implications for Spatial Strategy Formations," *Environment and Planning B: Planning and Design* 23.2: 217–234.

Healey, P. (1997) *Collaborative Planning: Shaping Places in Fragmented Societies*, Vancouver: UBC Press.

Hebdon, R. and Jalette, P. (2008) "The Restructuring of Municipal Services: A Canada–United States Comparison," *Environment and Planning C: Government and Policy* 26.1: 144–158.

Hefetz, A. and Warner, M. E. (2004) "Privatization and Its Reverse: Explaining the Dynamics of the Government Contracting Process," *Journal of Public Administration Research and Theory* 14.2: 171–190.

Hefetz, A. and Warner, M. E. (2007) "Beyond the Market vs. Planning Dichotomy: Understanding Privatisation and its Reverse in US Cities," *Local Government Studies* 33.4: 555–572.

Hipp, Magdalena and Warner, Mildred (2007) "Market Forces for the Unemployed? Training Vouchers in Germany and the U.S.," *Social Policy and Administration* 42.1: 77–101.

Hirsch, W. Z. (1995) "Contracting out by Urban Governments – a Review," *Urban Affairs Review* 30.3: 458–472.

Hodge, G. A. (2000) *Privatization: An International Review of Performance*, Boulder, CO: Westview Press.

Holstrom, N. and Smith, R. (2000) "The Necessity of Gangster Capitalism: Primitive Accumulation in Russia and China," *Monthly Review,* February, 1–15.

Hood, C. (1991) "A Public Management for All Seasons?" *Public Administration*, Spring, 69: 3–19.

Innes, J. (1995) "Planning Theory's Emerging Paradigm: Communicative Action and Interactive Practice," *Journal of Planning Education and Research* 14.4: 183–191.

Kelly, R. M. (1998) "An Inclusive Democratic Polity, Representative Bureaucracies, and the New Public Management," *Public Administration Review* 58.8: 201–208.

Kodrzycki, Y. K. (1994) "Privatization of Local Public Services: Lessons for New England," *New England Economic Review*, May/June, 31–46.

Kohl, Benjamin (2004) "Privatization Bolivian Style: A Cautionary Tale," *International Journal of Urban and Regional Research* 28.4: 893–908.

Krumholz, N. and Clavel, P. (1994) *Reinventing Cities: Equity Planners Tell Their Stories*, Philadelphia: Temple University Press.

Local Government New Zealand (2003) *The Local Government Act of 2002: An Overview*, Wellington, NZ: LGNZ.

Logan, J. R. and Molotch, H. L. (1987) *Urban Fortunes: The Political Economy of Place*, Berkeley, CA: University of California Press.

Lowery, D. (1998) "Consumer Sovereignty and Quasi-Market Failure," *Journal of Public Administration Research and Theory* 8.2: 137–172.

Lowery, D. (2000) "A Transactions Costs Model of Metropolitan Governance: Allocation Versus Redistribution in Urban America," *Journal of Public Administration Research and Theory* 10.1: 49–78.

McGuirk, P. M. (2001) "Situating Communicative Planning Theory: Context, Power, and Knowledge," *Environment and Planning A* 33.2: 195–217.

Martin, Steve (2002) "The Modernization of UK Local Government: Markets, Managers, Monitors and Mixed Fortunes," *Public Management Review* 4.3: 291–307.

Meyers, Marcia and Jordan, Lucy (2006) "Choice and Accommodation in Parental Child Care Decisions," *Community Development: The Journal of the Community Development Society* 37.2: 53–70,

Miraftab, Faranak (2004) "Neoliberalism and Casualization of Public Sector Services: The Case of Waste Collection Services in Cape Town, South Africa," *International Journal of Urban and Regional Research* 28.4: 874–892.

Moore, M. H. (1995) *Creating Public Value: Strategic Management in Government*, Cambridge, MA: Harvard University Press.

Nalbandian, J. (1999) "Facilitating Community, Enabling Democracy: New Roles for Local Government Managers," *Public Administration Review* 59.3: 187–197.

Nalbandian, J. (2005) "Professionals and the Conflicting Forces of Administrative Modernization and Civic Engagement," *American Review of Public Administration* 35.4: 311–326.

Nee, Victor (2000) "The Role of the State in Making a Market Economy," *Journal of Institutional and Theoretical Economics* 156: 64–68.

North, D. (1990) *Institutions, Institutional Change and Economic Performance*, New York: Cambridge University Press.

Osborne, D. E. and Gaebler, T. (1992) *Reinventing Government: How the Entrepreneurial Spirit Is Transforming the Public Sector*, Reading, MA: Addison-Wesley.

Osborne, D. E. and Plastrick, P. (1997) *Banishing Bureaucracy*, Reading, MA: Addison-Wesley.

Pack, J. R. (1989) "Privatization and Cost Reduction," *Policy Sciences* 11.2: 1–25.

Polanyi, K. (1944) *The Great Transformation*, Boston, MA: Beacon Press.

Potapchuck, W., Crocker, J. and Schechter, W. (1998) *The Transformative Power of Governance*, Washington, DC: Program for Community Problem Solving.

Prager, J. (1994) "Contracting out Government Services: Lessons from the Private Sector," *Public Administration Review* 54.2: 176–184.

Przeworski, Adam (1991) *Democracy and the Market: Political and Economic Reforms in Eastern Europe and Latin America*, Cambridge: Cambridge University Press.

Reardon, Kenneth M. (1999) "Promoting Community Development through Empowerment Planning in East St. Louis, Illinois," in W. Dennis Keating and Norm Krumholz (eds) *America's Poorest Urban Neighborhoods: Urban Policy and Planning*, Thousand Oaks, CA: Sage Publications, pp. 124–139.

Sager, T. (2001) "Positive Theory of Planning: The Social Choice Approach," *Environment and Planning A* 33.4: 629–647.

Sager, T. (2002a) *Democratic Planning and Social Choice Dilemmas: Prelude to Institutional Planning Theory*, Aldershot, Hampshire, England; Burlington, VT: Ashgate.

Sager, Tore (2002b) "Deliberative Planning and Decision Making: An Impossibility Result," *Journal of Planning Education and Research* 21.4: 367–378.

Salamon, Lester (2002) "The New Governance and the Tools of Public Action: An Introduction," *The Tools of Government: A Guide to the New Governance*, Oxford, New York: Oxford University Press, pp. 1–47.

Savas, E. S. (1987) *Privatization: The Key to Better Government*, Chatham, NJ: Chatham House Publishers.

Schamis, Hector E. (2002) *Re-forming the State: The Politics of Privatization in Latin America and Europe*, Ann Arbor, MI: University of Michigan Press.

Sclar, E. (2000) *You Don't Always Get What You Pay For: The Economics of Privatization*, Ithaca, NY: Cornell University Press.

Starr, P. (1987) *The Limits of Privatization*, Washington, DC: Economic Policy Institute.

Szymanski, S. (1996) "The Impact of Compulsory Competitive Tendering and Contracting Out in Refuse Collection," *Fiscal Studies* 17.3: 1–19.

Szymanski, S. and Wilkins, S. (1993) "Cheap Rubbish? Competitive Tendering and Contracting Out in Refuse Collection," *Fiscal Studies* 14.3: 109–130.

Tiebout, C. M. (1956) "A Pure Theory of Local Expenditures," *Journal of Political Economy* 64.5: 416–424.

Troutt, D. D. (2000) "Ghettoes Made Easy: The Metamarket/Antimarket Dichotomy and the Legal Challenges of Inner-City Economic Development," *Harvard Civil Rights–Civil Liberties Law Review* 35.2: 427–507.

Warner, M. E. (2006a) "Market-Based Governance and the Challenge for Rural Governments: U.S. Trends," *Social Policy and Administration: An International Journal of Policy and Research* 40.6: 612–631.

Warner, M. E. (2006b) "Inter-municipal Cooperation in the U.S: A Regional Governance Solution?" *Urban Public Economics Review/Revista de Economia Pública Urbana* 7: 132–151. Available at http://government.cce.cornell.edu/doc/pdf/UPER6artWARNER.pdf.

Warner, M. E. and Bel, G. (2008) "Competition or Monopoly? Comparing US and Spanish Privatization," *Public Administration: An International Quarterly* 86.3: 723–735.

Warner, M. E. and Daugherty, C. W. (2004) "Promoting the 'Civic' in Entrepreneurship: The Case of Rural Slovakia," *Journal of the Community Development Society* 35.1: 117–134.

Warner, M. E. and Hebdon, R. (2001) "Local Government Restructuring: Privatization and its Alternatives," *Journal of Policy Analysis and Management* 20.2: 315–336.

Warner, M. E. and Hefetz, A. (2002) "Applying Market Solutions to Public Services: An Assessment of Efficiency, Equity and Voice," *Urban Affairs Review* 38.1: 70–89.

Warner, M. E. and Hefetz, A. (2003) "Rural–Urban Differences in Privatization: Limits to the Competitive State," *Environment and Planning C: Government and Policy* 21.5: 703–718.

Warner, M. E. and Hefetz, A. (2004) "Pragmatism over Politics: Alternative Service Delivery in Local Government 1992–2002," *The Municipal Yearbook 2004*, Washington, DC: International City County Management Association, pp. 8–16.

Warner, M. E. and Hefetz, A. (2008) "Managing Markets for Public Service: The Role of Mixed Public/Private Delivery of City Services," *Public Administration Review* 68.1: 150–161.

Warner, M. E. and Pratt, J. E. (2005) "Spatial Diversity in Local Government Revenue Effort Under Decentralization: A Neural Network Approach," *Environment and Planning C: Government and Policy* 23.5: 657–677.

Webster, C. J. (1998) "Public Choice, Pigouvian and Coasian Planning Theory," *Urban Studies* 35.1: 53–75.

Webster, C. J. and Lai, L. W. C. (2003) *Property Rights, Planning and Markets: Managing Spontaneous Cities*, Cheltenham, UK; Northhampton, MA: Edward Elgar.

4   Why legality cannot be contracted out

Exploring the limits of New Public Management

Jon Pierre and Martin Painter

New Public Management (NPM) emerged in the 1980s and 1990s as a new model of public administration, albeit with antecedents in earlier debates in several countries on how to modernize the public administration and increase its efficiency. Various market-type mechanisms as well as other forms of decentralization or autonomization were adopted in the name of efficiency and customerization. Since then, it has become increasingly clear that there are values inherent in traditional systems of public administration, which still matter a great deal. Citizens still appreciate impartiality, procedural justice, legal security and equal treatment at the same time as they favor customer choice and market-based service delivery. This problematic is far from a theoretical artifact; public service institutions around the world daily face the issue of balancing objectives of efficiency and cost-cutting against the mission to uphold due process, equality, equity, and legality. This raises the question of the consistency of NPM with traditional legalistic values which are embedded in public administration systems. These values are more pronounced in some systems than others; while Europeans define most of these values in terms of a *Rechtsstaat* model of public administration, many Anglo-Americans would probably prefer the notion of the public interest.[1] That having been said, observers on both sides of the Atlantic agree that the public administration is a keystone of democratic governance, and tampering with the exchange patterns between society and the administration is essentially tampering with the democratic process.[2]

We need to know more about this problematic relationship between legality on the one hand and market-based reform on the other. This chapter will look critically at how NPM relates to the legal and procedural dimensions of public administration. We will rehearse the recent debate on the extent to which NPM as a system of production is compatible with a public administration system as a system of procedure. We will review the debate on the capacity of market actors to assume some degree of public authority, or at least to act as if they had that authority, and the mechanisms of accountability that go with that legal status. The overall argument in the chapter, as the title indicates, is that legality cannot – and, as several observers seem to agree, should not – be transferred from the public to the private sector.[3] Since legality and its associated procedural mechanisms are a keystone of legitimacy for the public administration, this has posed, and continues to pose, a major challenge to NPM.[4] As governments and theorists seek to find ways to redress the balance with measures to 'publicize' what has been privatized (without fully going into reverse) they miss the point. While the NPM advocates maintain that legitimacy in their management philosophy is tied to performance and not to procedure, we believe that values such as legality and accountability remain important sources of public sector legitimacy and trust, requiring direct assertion of state responsibilities.

The remainder of the chapter is organized as follows. The chapter first looks at the roots of the legality-based public administration and describes the logics of that system as well as the market-based model of public administration The next section traces the impact of NPM-style administrative reform on the legal dimension of the public administration. Following that, we discuss the recent notion of 'public value' as a potential, but also dangerous, strategy of bridging the gap between legality and efficiency. From that discussion, the chapter focuses on attempts at bringing legal norms and a public sector ethos into the market sector in the process of contracting out service delivery before a concluding section wraps up the chapter.

NPM, legality and public sector management

Traditional public administration was associated with the emergence of civil service systems in countries undergoing industrialization in the second half of the nineteenth century. A constellation of norms and practices became attached to these systems in forms that embodied the 'legal–rational' mode of organization. These embodied a set of rules about merit-based recruitment and promotion, security of tenure and the payment of a fixed and decent salary and were often entrenched in the form of laws and regulations which were overseen and implemented by more or less independent personnel authorities. The important principle was also established that the civil service was a neutral but obedient instrument of the state or of the sovereign (increasingly, the latter took the form of an elected political executive). Their relation to the public was also that of a detached and neutral interpreter and implementer of the laws and of the policies of the day. Thus, the civil service came to enjoy a status as a symbol of stability and continuity and as an impartial guardian of the public interest. It was concerned not only with economy and efficiency but with procedural regularity in pursuit of democratic values such as equity of treatment in the delivery of public goods.

From the late nineteenth century, when the US progressive movement called for administrative reforms such as the separation of politics from administration and the employment of professional managers, the example of business management has had a strong hold on the minds of public sector reformers.[5] Practices that developed in the private sector were the principal source of the 'public management' model, or 'managerialism' as it has sometimes been labelled.[6] The public management paradigm dislikes rigid rules, formal procedures and uniform systems, such as prevail in the traditional civil service. It emphasizes the 'hands-

on' skills of the manager and the need for managers at all levels to exercise initiative. At the same time, the 'science of management' should be brought to bear
to help managers solve generic management problems. These ideas were
espoused by many businessmen and management experts brought in to review
government efficiency throughout the twentieth century in both the US and in
Europe. Diverse sets of management techniques drawn from management
science and doctrine were adopted, depending on the 'business needs' or the
'business model' of the particular organization. Such techniques as performance
budgeting, management by objectives and strategic planning would enable each
organization to adapt its practices to its particular objectives and circumstances.

The seeds of NPM were clearly evident in this managerialist paradigm, but
the distinctive feature of NPM is its association with a belief that the market
works better than government in the production of public services. The characteristic tools of NPM are competition, marketization, autonomization, disaggregation and deregulation. Techniques such as performance management and
benchmarking are borrowed from the corporate sector while micro-economic
theories of consumer sovereignty are drawn upon in order to align management
or policy goals with consumer needs and demands. The 'customerization' of
public service delivery is a key feature of NPM and is to be seen in a variety of
forms, ranging from service delivery disaggregation via contracting out to the
use of technologies that allow for immediate client interface and response, in
particular 'e-government'. Consumer sovereignty most crucially means that all
service provision should be 'demand-driven' rather than 'supply-driven'. For
example, user-charges are viewed as a key regulator to bring supply and demand
into balance and help promote efficiency. Competition between providers in
some form is viewed as an ideal way to 'get the price right' while improving
service quality and responsiveness. Ultimately, regulated markets in which customers are provided the means to enter the marketplace for a public service – for
example through 'vouchers' or other entitlements – and where all suppliers are
in a strictly competitive relationship with each other are viewed as an ideal
arrangement.

For our purposes, the primary point of contrast between NPM and traditional
public administration is between a model based on business production values
(including a consumer focus) and a model based on legal and procedural values.
The contrast is evident in a number of ways. In NPM's predominantly
production-oriented approach to management, the policy making and administrative processes are decoupled through insisting that political control and
accountability should be confined by and large to two functions: first, setting
objectives; and second, evaluating and adjusting policy based on assessments of
results, or outcomes. In the business production model, each production unit has
a core, unequivocal purpose or set of production goals related to its often narrowly defined purpose and a specific set of consumers. Disaggregation and
'agencification' seek to achieve this single-mindedness of purpose. Values that
are, in traditional public administration, embedded in legislation or in public
service procedures and receive careful attention by a whole range of guardians

and overseers, are separated out into, on the one hand, a limited set of 'core business' values and, on the other hand, a broader set of 'risks' to be 'managed' during the course of meeting narrow production targets and consumer satisfaction.

The core business values invariably emphasize customer service requirements, sometimes embodied in 'citizen charters' or 'performance pledges'. As a consequence, 'customer rights' and 'service quality' get primary attention, while wider democratic principles such as citizen entitlements or third-party participation rights may be sidelined. Integration of goals and values across related service functions and activities in larger, more 'general-purpose' public service organizations, which are monitored by more diffuse and diverse sets of policies and values, is sacrificed for the sake of being clearly focused on a single set of service objectives and clearly defined clients or customers. The clarity and simplicity of marketplace expectations such as 'good service' and efficient production are preferred to the ambiguity and complexity of conflicting political and social values.

By contrast, in the traditional public administration model, politics and administration are kept distinct in theory but in practice are closely coupled through mechanisms of control and accountability that are in principle unified and consistent across the public sector (albeit in pursuit of multiple and sometimes conflicting policy goals and procedural values). At the core of this system is a generalized hierarchy of political control focused on the political executive, embodying not only the immediacy of policy control over operational matters but also a clear principle that public administration is regulated through universal attention to procedure for the sake of core democratic values of equity and access. Customers are no more prioritized than the general citizenry or specific constituencies of stakeholders, represented in many guises through multiple accountability mechanisms. Diverse procedural standards are given pervasive but often shifting attention: economy, attentiveness, integrity and probity, accuracy and dispatch, promptness, fairness and equity, anti-discrimination, preserving the environment or local amenity and so on (Dunsire 1986: 337). Underpinning all of them is legality.

In this traditional model, the organization of government is often less concerned with allocating separate service delivery tasks to production units than with collecting together related functions and activities within more common-purpose, inclusive politico-administrative structures. Thus, in traditional public administration, large-scale bureaucratic organizations tend to predominate over more disaggregated units focused on particular clients. They facilitate procedural consistency and, where there is ambiguity, its resolution through hierarchical authority. Where this aggregation becomes too cumbersome (and particularly when it is based on an incoherent division of labor) multiple accountabilities are often handled by 'hiving off' or 'tacking on' para-state organizations or local self-governing bodies that reflect particular communities of interest. If these concerns can be handled through a dispersal of authority and power without doing damage to overall consistency or the coverage of more universal procedural values, the 'representative' principle is often preferred to more technical, efficiency-based production values. Decentralization is not inconsistent with traditional public administration, but (unlike NPM's single-minded production-unit principle of disaggregation) it can be organized democratically as a set of devolved general-purpose local self-governing bodies or as a form of disaggregated government such as Sweden's system of devolved 'agencies', which embodies traditional public administration's procedural universalism through both top-down controls and also extensive external monitoring by citizens and the law (for example, in freedom of information provisions).

Clearly, many of these features of traditional public administration can lead to a range of consequences that seem to beg for the remedies of managerialism and NPM. Multiple accountabilities create procedural delay and obfuscation; clients and customers lose their way in the labyrinths of multiple jurisdictions; those in authority lose control of the increasingly complex machinery; managers are deflected from their service delivery and production roles by the tasks of coordination and accountability; and so on. Thus, it is readily understandable why, for service delivery activities in particular, the precepts and practices of NPM have been widely adopted. The advantages of being able to focus clearly on productive efficiency and consumer responsiveness are not lost on politicians eager to win support from citizens weary with high tax bills and declining service quality. Service reform is thus focused on squeezing higher productivity from the system and on customer service or client responsiveness measures, leading to various forms of autonomization and disaggregation, including the use of market-type mechanisms and the increasing use of private sector partnerships.

But such a model clearly carries dangers of sacrificing some of the values associated with a system focused on maximizing procedural ends as well as production outputs. The common response to this concern among defenders of NPM is that private organizations, while focused on their 'bottom line' and on their customers, are just as much accustomed to regulation by multiple overseers, monitors and auditors as are government bureaucrats: legality is an imperative for business as much as it is for government. On this count, NPM advocates argue that it is not immediately obvious why regulation within government to ensure legality should be any easier than regulation outside of government: both face the same problems in principle, namely information asymmetry between principal and agent and hence high enforcement costs. From their perspective of the self-interested bureaucrat, they might claim that achieving legality within government is possibly more difficult, as it is more prone to collusion and lack of transparency than is regulation in the marketplace, where competitors monitor each other for their compliance and the courts are more likely to be called upon. That is, legality is more likely, not less, under NPM regimes.

Yet the whole logic of NPM (at least in its initial phase) is to deregulate, or at least to strip away some of the regulatory overburden of bureaucratic proceduralism in order to focus on the core values of consumer sovereignty. Multiple accountabilities and monitoring are deliberately sidelined for the sake of simply enforcing production-related contracts. Thus, for example, public service contractors and partners are generally excused the normal freedom of information requirements and the more complex and often tougher employment regulations prevailing in the 'public sector proper'. This, in turn produces some backlash: it turns out that customers and citizens want some channels of redress other than the customer hot-line and sometimes expect 'whole person' treatment of the kind they might get at their MP's local clinic, rather than just the contractor's refund under the performance pledge or citizen's charter. Politicians want to know how they can intervene to redress breakdowns in integration and coordination or – increasingly commonly – contractor default and failure. They want to see things joined up again.

Another way of looking at the potential conflicts between NPM and legality is to address the question of the extent to which a production model of public management can be followed in some areas of government, if not in others. That is, how much of government is actually 'just like running a business'? In the next section, we address this issue and conclude that in practice, most areas of government are concerned inextricably with both production and also procedure. That being the case, we look more closely at the strategies NPM and traditional public administration have suggested for coping with this situation. This leads into a discussion in a later section of some of the 'second wave' of management reform where some of these issues have been addressed through trying to 'retrofit' legality and procedural fidelity into newly privatized and deregulated milieux, and we explore the limits of this as against more wholesale root-and-branch reversal.

NPM and legality: necessary evil or collateral damage?

At a very basic level, all public administration systems can be said to play two basic roles in society. One is to deliver public service, as part of the implementation of public policy. In terms of budgetary allocation and staff intensity, this is by far the most demanding role of the public administration. This aspect of the public administration includes hospitals, day care, maintenance of public utilities and so on. This is a work-intensive sector where economies of scale can be difficult to obtain. Professional skills vary from highly specialized, such as in the health-care sector, to relatively low. Many, but far from all, positions have requirements that are typical to the public sector. The other basic role of a public administration is to enforce the law and to exercise public authority. The organizational emphasis in this sector is on professional training and a public sector ethos. In theory, at least, budgetary considerations are subordinated to getting the job done correctly. Public sector-specific requirements are frequent and are critical to evaluation.

These two roles – production of service and enforcing legal authority – overlap to a greater or smaller extent. Even in such typical service production areas as health care or day-care centers for children, there are professional and legal codes specifying the relationship between the institution and the individual. Similarly, even in typical cases of public authority like issuing permits, passports and driver's licenses or even enforcing the law, there is an obvious element of service provision. As a general rule, however, we could say that the weaker the element of service production and the stronger the element of public authority, the more difficult the implementation of NPM becomes. Going back to the early writings on market-based public sector reform, it is striking to see that this is a philosophy which is clearly aimed at that part of the public sector which has the lowest degree of public sector specificity, that is to say, service production.[7] It is here that the NPM model can produce best results by opening up for competition, developing economies of scale, creating organizational flexibility, increasing customer satisfaction by offering a choice of service providers and tailored services, and – for the most part – cutting costs.

The Anglo-American democracies were quick to adopt NPM as a general philosophy of administrative reform. But, even in many countries that were explicitly tentative towards market-based reform in the public sector, these achievements (potential or real) of NPM were too attractive to disregard.[8] In much of Europe, and with substantive variation among individual countries, NPM-style reform was introduced, often in a piecemeal fashion and without reassessing the basic normative foundation of the public administration. Objectives such as improved performance management and measurement, quality, flexibility, efficiency and customer satisfaction were gradually introduced into the public sector vernacular while traditional values such as due process, legality, equal treatment and legal security remained core elements of the public sector ethos.[9] Public bureaucrats were expected to be service-minded, flexible and, not least, efficient, at the same time as they upheld due process and equal treatment.

As the philosophy of NPM spread across the public sector, it soon became clear that many of the obstacles to implementing such reform were, in fact, related to the legal framework of the public administration and the public authority dimension of service production. Also, while NPM seemed to perform well in the service production sector of the public administration, it had yet to be implemented on a wider scale in the public authority domain of the public sector. Eventually, this raised two fundamental questions about the extent to which the two models of public sector modus operandi can be integrated: to what extent is NPM a viable and efficient model of administrative reform in the public authority domain of the public service; and, equally challenging and complex, to what extent can legality as an organizational norm be conveyed into private sector organizations operating under contract with public organizations? We will address the first question here and return to the second question in a later section of the chapter.

In order to address the question of whether NPM can serve as an organizational philosophy in that domain of the public sector which is concerned with the exercise of public authority, we need to look briefly at what appears to be the normative underpinning of NPM. As discussed earlier, market-based public sector reform rests on the assumption that the key factors explaining the low efficiency in the public sector are related to the organizational structure, management, and normative framework of the public sector. While this list of features could be seen as being common to any organization, the point we wish to make is that the public sector has a different organizational philosophy to the corporate sector with regard to the objectives guiding decisions on organizational structure, management and normative framework. Unlike corporate organizations, the public sector has a multitude of objectives guiding these three dimensions, of which efficiency is but one. Thus, Weberian notions about the structure, the role of the individual in the organization and the hierarchical pattern of command and control still loom large in many public sector organizations. Together with other Weberian objectives such as legality, due process and equal treatment, these norms and values define the specificity of public sector organizations compared to all other organizations in society.[10] And, since NPM's departure point is a conviction that this specificity contains the main obstacles to efficiency, market-based reform at some stage will clash with the traditional normative foundation of the public service. Management, in the NPM philosophy, is a 'generic' concept which is not (and, normatively speaking, should not be) typical to either the private or the public sector; it is essentially the same kind of challenge, with similar obstacles and similar solutions.[11]

Given this situation, the architects of market-based reform seem to be confronting a choice between two strategies of reform. One strategy is to look at legality – as shorthand for the traditional legal and normative framework of public administration – as a 'necessary evil', that is, to acknowledge that these are values that to a large extent express the environment's expectations on the public administration and thus provide its legitimacy. Such process-based legitimacy is thus purchased at the expense of efficiency; NPM advocates are convinced that the public service would have been far more efficient, had some of the legality restrictions been lifted. However, the idea of altering societal views on the public administration by changing its internal modus operandi is not very credible – NPM would have to be part of a larger, neo-liberal project to influence those values – thus the 'necessary evil' strategy may have some merit.

The alternative strategy is to impose NPM on the public administration and to look at its impact on legality as some form of collateral damage. This would be a more aggressive and challenging strategy of reform, where the basic philosophy is that if legality is reduced, so be it. If the legitimacy of the public administration is jeopardized, it is a form of legitimacy which is based on procedure. NPM is essentially a philosophy of performance, and the clients (or customers) of public services will soon find that the market-reformed public administration delivers. Thus, the 'collateral damage' strategy of market-based reform is more far-reaching and encompassing than the other reform strategy in that it presupposes a shift over time in the environment's perception of the public service.

It appears as if one of the key explanations to the current situation in many countries, with emerging 'hybrid organizations' in the public sector, is that neither elected politicians nor the senior levels of the public administration have fully addressed the question of how to resolve the inconsistencies between NPM and legality. As a result, public sector organizations in many countries today are squeezed between NPM objectives of efficiency and flexibility on the one hand, and objectives of legality, due process and continuity on the other. The two reform strategies, while easy to grasp in theory, display a more complex image in the real world. The strategy of perceiving legality as a 'necessary evil', which has been more common outside the Anglo-American democracies, introduces NPM selectively in the public administration and causes problems of competing models of leadership, control, accountability and relationship with the surrounding society.

But perhaps there is a 'middle way' based on a new perspective on the mix of production and procedural values that characterize the public sector. The next section addresses one such possible solution.

Towards a functionalist perspective: creating 'public value'

While the public management model originates in an admiration for business-like efficiency, more recently a version has evolved that focuses on 'creating public value'.[12] Such a view counters the 'bottom line' mentality derived from many business models and encourages a more complex orientation, focusing on management of multiple stakeholders and conflicting values. The significance of this view of public management is best understood as a reaction to what are seen by some as the excesses of NPM, which is a particular version of the public management approach. Here, NPM is defined as both a particular doctrine and a distinctive tool-kit of administrative techniques. As a doctrine, it combines insights from economic theories of institutions with practical lessons from business management, the latter being selectively chosen because they conform to these theories. The theories begin with the assumption that everyone is motivated by the desire to maximize their personal preferences. From this assumption, such models as 'principal–agent' and the 'budget-maximizing bureaucrat' are derived.[13] Thus, in order to align the agent's self-interest with the principal's objectives, they are monitored by rules, constraints and performance agreements that incorporate incentives, rather than according to principles of obedience, trust and the building of joint commitment. Once these contractual arrangements are in place (in an agency budget or in a contract of employment, for example), the agent can be left to 'self-manage', rather than being instructed or closely supervised. To take another example, if a government wants to provide just the right amount of a service at the desired quality and at the lowest feasible cost, then 'market disciplines' will provide the right constraints and incentives to bring this outcome about. Hence, such instruments as internal markets, user charges and contestability or contracting out are advocated.

Moore's argument about the need for 'creating public value' also echoes the public-choice debate of the 1970s where neo-liberal economists advocated a closer and more visible linkage between taxes and fees going into the public service and the resultant performance. Several observers are skeptical towards the notion of public value. Rhodes and Wanna argue that Moore's model is based on a depoliticization of the public service which is alien to Westminster systems.[14] Perhaps more importantly, the 'public value' model seems to assume that clients, or 'customers', only appreciate discrete, material returns from their tax money. It is probably true that citizens will be more inclined to pay taxes if they receive visible returns from their money but that is a perspective which completely overlooks, and denies, other key societal roles played by the public administration. Moore conveniently draws an introductory example from sanitation, but how is national defense, the Foreign Service, foreign aid and the judicial system supposed to deliver 'public value'? Furthermore, 'public value' in this perspective appears to be something that has to be continuously reproduced in service delivery. But are there not a number of core 'public values' endogenous to the administrative process, manifested in norms and values like transparency, legality, equality, accountability?[15]

There are also several complex issues surrounding the relationship between 'public value' and regulation. The targets of regulation and the recipients of 'public value' frequently tend to be different actors. Regulating the amount of pollution from an industry incurs a significant cost on that industry but offers potential 'public value' to those who live downwind from the plant.

Thus, the functionalist perspective that underlies Moore's 'public value' model assumes that public and private services only differ with regard to the nature of the commodity delivered, not with regard to the legality surrounding the service. It is not so much a philosophy of transferring legality to the market, as it is an implicit strategy of denying the legality of public services and the presence of politics in designing public service altogether.[16]

The softer touch: legality as an emerging private-sector organizational norm

In the 'second wave' of management reform, following privatization and contracting out, the increasing exchange between public and private organizations has created patterns of institutional isomorphism. Concerns about weakening legitimacy appear to have induced purchasing agents in the public administration to require that the private provider operates in accordance with public, legal norms. Thus, if public sector organizations sometimes are said to emulate private sector organizations as a result of NPM, this pattern of institutional isomorphism, which Rosenbloom and others refer to as 'retro-fitting' thus brings legality in through the back door of corporate organizations involved in public service delivery.[17] While retrofitting helps make private organizations better equipped to enter the sphere of public service delivery, this diffusion of legality as an organizational norm could be believed to be too instrumental and incomplete to solve the problem of NPM's lack of attention to legality as a steering system in the public sector.

That having been said, several scholars maintain that private sector organizations are fully capable of both assuming a quasi-public role and also of observing constitutional and administrative values and norms. Jody Freeman, UCLA Professor of Law refers to this process as 'publicization', in which 'private actors increasingly commit themselves to traditional public goals. /.../ So rather than compromising democratic norms of accountability, due process, equality and rationality ... privatization might extend these norms to private actors through vehicles such as budgeting, regulation, and contract.'[18] Freeman thus takes a positive and optimistic view on the role of private organizations and providers of public services and as carriers of public values. The chief reason for their willingness to do so is financial, i.e. if contracts are contingent on conformity with public values. This could however, as Freeman concedes, be more complicated than it might appear at first glance. Providing proper training and education in public norms would be a costly matter to potential contractors. Publicization, she therefore concludes, 'will turn private firms into public agencies and undermine gains from privatization'.[19]

'Publicization', thus, would essentially resolve the tension between NPM's philosophy of focusing on costs and efficiency on the one hand, and the traditional philosophy of legality as the foundation for public administration on the other. It would be a model of public administration which is consistent with a globalized society and 'the new governance'.[20] It is a distinctly functional perspective on public administration in which it is strictly the delivery of services which matters. It begs the question of whether private firms are able and willing to deliver public services at a lower price than public agencies while subscribing to public values. And it does not escape the tricky questions about control, contract management, and accountability.

The functional perspective on public administration in the context of 'publicization' could be accompanied by the market perspective on private businesses. To become agents of 'publicization' private contractors would have to make significant investments in staff training and be willing to, as Freeman suggests, become quasi-agents of the state. While some contractors probably would be happy with that arrangement provided the contract was sufficiently lucrative, it would mean that the contractor would gradually adapt his business to public sector service and put all his eggs in one basket. The company would become tailored for those specific purposes and services and thus find it difficult to compete for contracts in the private market where there is no demand for the special, 'public' skills of the staff. This is a scenario which would serve as a disincentive to most private contractors.

At the end of the day, Freeman's analysis of 'publicization' begs the question of the rationale of contracting out in the first place. The costs for the public sector associated with 'publicization' – designing and managing by contracts, careful evaluation of potential contractors, evaluation of the performance of the final contractor, and so on – raises the issues of how much money is actually saved by contracting out services where adhering to public norms is paramount. The market logic is not in favor of 'publicization'; a related question is whether the public sector logic would support such an arrangement.

Concluding discussion

We have argued throughout this chapter that legality is a key requisite of public administration as we know it. This is because the public administration is more than a service-producing system; it enforces the law, exercises public authority and, as such, makes decisions which may have significant repercussions on the citizens. It is precisely because the public administration harbors such extensive powers and capabilities that legality is a necessary framework to prevent abuse of that power. And, it is precisely because the public administration is keystone of democratic governance, in its role in implementing policy and as one of the most important points of contact between the state and the citizen, that the public administration must be transparent and accountable. The advocates of NPM reform suggest that market-like mechanisms can be introduced into the public service without challenging these core values. With regard to public service production – which has been NPM's shop-window case of success – the record so far has been quite good. However, that analysis tends to forget that public administration is also about exercising public authority and it is here that public values clash with performance-based values. Public service, in the original meaning of that concept, will not be of better quality just because it produced quicker or cheaper results.

An intriguing aspect of NPM is to what extent such reform can be contained within only some designated NPM sectors of the public administration and not to be allowed to enter other areas of the public sector. We believe that such 'hybrid organizations' will suffer from a number of complicated problems. One such problem relates to leadership. NPM draws on a philosophy of de-politicization and managerial autonomy. Although the constitutional idea of the legalistic public administration, too, separates politics from administration, that system is to some extent predicated on informal contacts between politicians and bureaucrats. However, such exchanges are faux pas in NPM. Another problem relates to the degree of autonomy which should be given to the lower levels of the organization. NPM takes a more positive view on empowering lower-level public servants than does the traditional model of public administration, as we argued earlier. Finally, traditional public administration emphasizes process while NPM emphasizes performance. We do not believe that performance, however excellent, can compensate for a flawed process. It is true that NPM has helped administrative reform target inefficiency and rigidities in the public sector, but there is the downside risk that, in the process of reform, it challenges the democratic and normative foundation of public administration.

In sum, the various remedies suggested in the literature – 'retro-fitting', asserting 'public values' and 'publicization' – somehow miss the point. To some extent, we believe that the present debate on market solutions in the public sector has become too focused on pursuing a fixed solution while forgetting the complexity of the problems which initiated the debate. Market reform was introduced where a case could be made that contracting out or privatization could save public sector resources while maintaining a high level of public service.

Subsequently, market reform as such became the objective and the problem became how to redesign public services, including the exercise of public authority, so that they could be marketized. Thus, means became ends. The need to retreat from dogma and face up to the complexities of a more pragmatic approach to the complexities of achieving service quality while maintaining due process has become clear as the state reasserts itself in pursuit of public ends.

Notes

1 B. Guy Peters (2001) *The Future of Governing.*
2 Ezra Suleiman (2003) *Dismantling Democratic States.*
3 H. George Frederickson (1991) 'Toward a Theory of the Public for Public Administration'; Suleiman, op. cit.; and, interestingly, David Osborne and Ted Gaebler (1992) *Reinventing Government.*
4 Bo Rothstein (2007) 'Creating State Legitimacy: The Five Basic Models'.
5 Donald F. Kettl (2002) *The Transformation of Governance: Public Administration for Twenty-first Century America.*
6 Christopher Pollitt (!990) *Managerialism and the Public Services.*
7 See, for instance, Osborne and Gaebler, op. cit.
8 Tentative and skeptical responses were often due to differences in political culture. See, for example P. Munk Christiansen (1998) 'A Prescription Rejected: Market Solutions to Problems of Public Sector Governance'.
9 Christopher Pollitt and Geert Bouckaert (2004) *Public Management Reform: A Comparative Analysis.*
10 Jon Pierre (2000) 'Externalities and Relationships: Rethinking the Boundaries of the Public Service'.
11 B. Guy Peters, op. cit.
12 See Mark H. Moore (1995) *Creating Public Value: Strategic Management in Government*; R. A. W. Rhodes and J. Wanna (2007) 'The Limits to Public Values, or Rescuing Responsible Government from the Platonic Guardians'; Janine O'Flynn (2007) 'From New Public Management to Public Value: Paradigmatic Change and Managerial Implications'.
13 Jonathon Boston *et al.* (1996) *Public Management: the New Zealand Model.*
14 Rhodes and Wanna, op. cit.
15 See Jon Pierre (2008) 'Not Just Service Production, Not Just Paper Pushing: Exploring the Limits of Markets and Legality in the Public Sector', paper presented at Scancor's 25th Anniversary Conference, November 21–22, 2008.
16 See Stoker.
17 David H. Rosenbloom (2000) *Building a Legislative-Centered Public Administration: Congress and the Administrative State, 1946–1999*; David H. Rosenbloom (2000) 'Retrofitting the Administrative State to the Constitution: Congress and the Judiciary's Twentieth-Century Progress'.
18 Jody Freeman (2003) 'Extending Public Law Norms through Privatization', quotation from p. 1285.
19 Jody Freeman, op. cit., p. 1339.
20 Alfred C. Aman, Jr (2002) 'Globalization, Democracy, and the Need for a New Administrative Law'.

Bibliography

Aman, Alfred C. Jr (2002) 'Globalization, Democracy, and the Need for a New Administrative Law', *UCLA Law Review* 49(6): 1687–716.

Boston, Jonathan, Martin, John, Pallott, June and Walsh, Pat (1996) *Public Management: the New Zealand Model*, Auckland: Oxford University Press, pp. 16–41.

Christiansen, P. Munk (1998) 'A Prescription Rejected: Market Solutions to Problems of Public Sector Governance', *Governance* 11(3): 273–95.

Dunsire, Andrew (1986) 'A Cybernetic View of Guidance, Control and Evaluation in the Public Sector', in Franz-Xavier Kaufmann, Giandomenico Majone and Vincent Ostrom (eds) *Guidance, Control and Evaluation in the Public Sector*, Berlin and New York: Walter de Gruyter, pp. 327–46.

Frederickson, H. George (1991) 'Toward a Theory of the Public for Public Administration', *Administration and Society* 22(4): 395–417.

Freeman, Jody (2003) 'Extending Public Law Norms through Privatization', *Harvard Law Review* 116: 1285–352.

Jorgensen, Torben Beck and Bozeman, Barry (2007) 'Public Values: An Inventory', *Administration and Society* 39(3): 354–81.

Kettl, Donald F. (2002) *The Transformation of Governance: Public Administration for Twenty-first Century America*, Baltimore, MD: John Hopkins University Press.

Moore, Mark H. (1995) *Creating Public Value: Strategic Management in Government*, Cambridge, MA: Harvard University Press.

O'Flynn, Janine (2007) 'From New Public Management to Public Value: Paradigmatic Change and Managerial Implications', *Australian Journal of Public Administration* 66(3): 353–66.

Osborne, David and Gaebler, Ted (1993) *Reinventing Government*, MA: Addison-Wesley.

Peters, B. Guy (2001) *The Future of Governing*, Lawrence, KS: University Press of Kansas.

Peters, B. Guy and Savoie, Donald J. (2000) *Governance in the 21st Century: Revitalizing the Public Service*, Montreal and Kingston: McGill/Queens University Press.

Pierre, Jon (2000) *Externalities and Relationships: Rethinking the Boundaries of the Public Service*, B. Guy Peters and Donald J. Savoie (eds) pp. 332–57.

Pierre, Jon (2008) 'Not Just Service Production, Not Just Paper Pushing: Exploring the Limits of Markets and Legality in the Public Sector', paper presented at Scancor's 25th Anniversary Conference, November 21–22, in Stanford University, California.

Pollitt, Christopher (1990) *Managerialism and the Public Services*, Oxford: Blackwell.

Pollitt, Christopher and Bouckaert, Geert (2004) *Public Management Reform: A Comparative Analysis* (second edition), Oxford: Oxford University Press.

Rhodes, R. A. W. and Wanna, J. (2007) 'The Limits to Public Values, or Rescuing Responsible Government from the Platonic Guardians', *Australian Journal of Public Administration* 66(4): 406–21.

Rosenbloom, David H. (2000) *Building a Legislative-Centered Public Administration: Congress and the Administrative State, 1946–1999*, Tuscaloosa: The University of Alabama Press.

Rosenbloom, David H. (2000) 'Retrofitting the Administrative State to the Constitution: Congress and the Judiciary's Twentieth-Century Progress', *Public Administration Review* 60(8): 39–46.

Rothstein, Bo (2007) 'Creating State Legitimacy: The Five Basic Models', paper presented at the APSA conference, August 29–September 2, Monash University, Australia.

Suleiman, Ezra (2003) *Dismantling Democratic States*, Princeton, NJ: Princeton University Press.

5 How far has market orientation penetrated public organizations?

An empirical test on customer satisfaction

Richard M. Walker, Gene A. Brewer and George A. Boyne

Introduction

The past 30 years have seen many governments around the world aggressively alter their bureaucratic structures and managerial processes in an attempt to improve the productivity and performance of the administrative state. This worldwide trend has been based on a model of "economic individualism" based upon market processes, downsizing public institutions and making public employees more productive (Bozeman 2007). In short, the public sector has been moving toward a business-like model of governance that emphasizes managerialism; champions efficiency; favours competition, outsourcing, and privatization; and recasts government organizations as suppliers, public managers as entrepreneurs, and citizens as customers. This new public sector is conforming more and more to the normal disciplines of the private sector.

Public choice theory has provided the theoretical backdrop for New Public Management (NPM), and market orientation has formed its backbone. One common denominator is a bold effort to separate politics from administration; thus there is an emphasis on agencification and autonomization in some countries. The movement also emphasizes managerialism and touts efficiency. Its driving themes are "let managers manage" and find the "one-best-way" to "make government work better and cost less". Competition is introduced by contracting out and privatization, thus forcing public administration to become more market-oriented and business-like.

During 2008 and 2009 events on the international stock markets began to raise questions about the effectiveness of private market-based models to deliver. The financial crisis that led to the nationalization of banks in a number countries has led to the state reasserting its role in a number of domains. Many of the problems associated with the global financial collapse are those very values and characteristics that scholars have generally been critical of in the NPM movement and have pointed out many of its flaws; e.g. poor accountability mechanisms, devaluation of public sector values, tendency to reduce political questions to administrative trivia, and lowered emphasis on the core administrative values of equity and fairness (see for example Bozeman 2007). Many have noted the fundamental trade-off between efficiency and accountability, and the related dysfunctions of managerialism. Others have argued that short-run increases in efficiency are being purchased at a long-range cost in governmental and administrative capacity.

While it is possible that developments in the very early part of the twenty-first century will come to represent a paradigm change in our understanding of the ways in which public service delivery is managed and organized, public management researchers have been slow to place NPM's theoretical infrastructure under the empirical microscope. This study attempts such a test. We operationalize the theory of market orientation and examine its effects on public service performance in the context of English local government. Market orientation is at the extreme end of the NPM reform movement, because it implies that governmental organizations will perform better if they behave like private organizations that operate in a competitive market environment and compete with rival firms to meet consumer demands. We believe that this is an opportune time to undertake this examination and that the evidence gleaned can be used to assist thinking about the role of the state.

In the next section, the literature is reviewed and the theory of market orientation is introduced. Then, we develop a model of public service performance and describe how the key variables – including market orientation and performance – are measured. Our data and methods are described next. We then estimate two models and report the results, which are lacklustre for the theory of market orientation in general and the market orientation–performance hypothesis specifically. Finally, we conclude by discussing some limitations of this study, some suggestions for future research, and some broader implications for public administration theory and practice.

Market orientation

A variety of government publications over many years have argued for "choice and voice" for citizens in service delivery (in the UK context, see Blair 2002; OPSR 2002, 2003 for recent examples). This policy discussion typically emphasizes providing what customers want: this implies listening to them and offering alterative forms of service delivery, as necessary. This view is consistent with the business norm that "customers know best" and the economic principle of consumer sovereignty, which states that in free markets consumers know what they want and should be able to get it. The normative hypothesis that follows from this discussion is that public organizations should have a market orientation with a strong consumer or customer culture, and that the adoption of such a culture will lead to public service improvement.

While the policy documents referenced above clearly draw on the popular and academic management literature, there has been no academic examination of this topic in the public management community. No theoretical framework has been advanced, and certainly no empirical analysis has been undertaken. In this chapter we will draw upon the management literature to suggest a model and empirically test it in the context of English local government.

The model adopted in this chapter is known as market orientation. In short, market orientation is an attempt to strategically align an organization with its external environment and includes making the organization more customer-oriented and market-driven (Shapiro 1988; Harris 2001). As such, market orientation is an aspect of organizational culture that is predicated on the marketing concept, which includes "a fundamental shared set of beliefs and values that puts the customer in the center of the firm's thinking about strategy and operations" (Deshpande and Webster 1989: 3).

The market orientation concept is further defined by Kohli and Jaworski (1990, cited in Narver and Slater 1990: 21) as: "the organization-wide information generation and dissemination and appropriate response related to current and future customer needs and preferences". Thus, market orientation is categorized as an organizational culture that most effectively and efficiently creates the necessary behaviours that result in "continuous superior performance" (Narver and Slater 1990: 21). These necessary behaviours include:

- customer orientation: the sufficient understanding of one's customers to be able to create superior value for them continuously;
- competitor orientation: an organization understands the short-term strengths and weaknesses and long-term capabilities and strategies of both its key current and key potential competitors: and
- interfunctional coordination: the coordinated utilization of company resources in creating superior value for target customers. The achievement of interfunctional requires an alignment of functional areas, incentives, and the creation of dependency so that internal cooperation is achieved.

Narver and Slater (1990: 22) argue that the approach has relevance to non-profit organizations: for non-profit organizations, the objective analogous to profitability is survival, which means earning revenues sufficient to cover long-run expenses and/or otherwise satisfying all key constituencies in the long run. Operationally, this means that English local authorities need to satisfy key stakeholders: government (CPA, BVPIs), staff (internal perceptions of performance) and customers (BVPIs).

Next, empirical research on the relationship between market orientation and performance is reviewed. Market orientation has long been discussed in the business literature, but several developments in the early 1990s stimulated a flurry of empirical research on the market orientation–performance hypothesis. In particular, conceptual refinement of the market orientation concept by Kohli and Jaworski (1990) and Narver and Slater (1990) set the stage for subsequent empirical work testing the relationship between market orientation and performance, notably in studies by Narver and Slater (1990), Jaworski and Kohli (1993) and Slater and Narver (1994). These studies triggered an explosion of research that has since tested the hypothesis in many different contexts. Results from these studies suggest that the relationship between market orientation and performance is robust cross-nationally (Deshpande and Farley 1998: 221).

Yet Harris (2001) reviewed this literature and found that the alleged relationship between market orientation and performance was largely based on the analysis of subjective measures of performance. On such measures, market orientation was associated with performance only in certain environmental conditions. When objective measures of performance were examined, the range of conditions narrowed. In Harris' study, these conditions included high levels of competition and low market turbulence. When the conditions were reversed, developing a market orientation had a detrimental effect on performance.

Several recent meta-analyses have further examined the empirical record and concluded that the market orientation–performance hypothesis is viable, but that the strength of association between market orientation and performance varies in different contexts and under certain conditions (Kirca *et al.* 2005; Ellis 2006; Shoham *et al.* 2006). The general trend is toward more complex specifications of the relationship.

In summary, empirical studies have shown that the relationship between market orientation and performance is more complex and variable than the theory suggests. Results seem sensitive to context, type of performance measure, and other conditions. Perhaps the greatest limitation of these studies has been their almost exclusive focus on private sector organizations and their neglect of public and non-profit sector applications, which are considerable as a result of NPM-related reforms. This study attempts to fill this gap in the literature: specifically, we will use the dominant theory of market orientation from the business literature to operationalize and test the market orientation–performance hypothesis that underlies NPM. In the sections that follow, we describe the setting for this study, identify the data sources, and provide information on the measurement of key constructs.

Unit of analysis

This study is situated in the English local government sector. English local governments are politically elected bodies with a Westminster-style cabinet system of political management. They are multi-purpose authorities delivering education, social services, regulatory services (such as land-use planning and environmental health), housing, libraries, leisure services, and welfare benefits in specific geographical areas. In urban areas, authorities deliver all of these services; in rural areas, a two-tier system prevails with county councils administering education and social services, and district councils providing environmental, welfare and regulatory functions. Authorities are not all-purpose; for example, health care is provided by health authorities. Yet they employ professional career staff, and receive around two-thirds of their income, and guidance on the implementation of legislation, from the central government.

Data sources

Two measures of consumer satisfaction are used as dependent variables in this study. The first is taken from the Best Value Performance Indicators (BVPI) dataset. We refer to this dependent variable as *objective consumer satisfaction* because it consists of independent measures of market orientation from the consumers' point of view. The second comes from a large-scale survey of English local government. This dependent variable is labelled *subjective consumer satisfaction* because it represents the viewpoints of the producers of local services – local government officers. These dependent variables and the datasets they come from are described in more detail below.

The objective measure of consumer satisfaction is found in the BVPI dataset. This dataset is collected by central government, the major external stakeholder for local authorities in England. (Central government creates and abolishes individual local government units, provides around 75 per cent of their funding, and bestows or removes service responsibilities.) The BVPIs are based on common definitions and data are obtained from councils for the same time periods with uniform collection procedures. Local authorities are expected to collect and collate these data in accordance with the Chartered Institute of Public Finance and Accountancy "Best Value Accounting Code of Practice". The figures are then independently verified, and the Audit Commission assesses whether the management systems in place are adequate for producing accurate information. Consumer satisfaction data for local authorities as a whole are available in the BVPI datasets for 2000/01 and 2003/04.

The next data source is a survey of local authorities. The survey collected data from multiple informants at the corporate and service levels.[1] This strategy was adopted to address the weakness of prior studies that have utilized elite surveys, which typically collect evidence on organizational leaders' aspirations rather than actual organizational innovations, and overlook the range of different perceptions within organizations (Bowman and Ambrosini 1997; Walker and Enticott 2004). Two echelons were used to overcome the sample bias problem faced in surveying large numbers of informants from one organizational level. For this sample, a simple organizational mean would drown out the voices of the smaller numbers of corporate officers surveyed. Corporate officers and service managers were selected because past research has shown that attitudes differ between these positions (Aiken and Hage 1968; Walker and Enticott 2004). By calculating an organizational mean from a mean of corporate officers and a mean of service officers, variations across organizations are maintained and categorical data are converted to continuous data.

The survey was electronic.[2] It explored informants' perceptions of organization and management, notably culture, structure, strategy making and strategy content, together with drivers of service improvement, background variables and the management reform regime called "Best Value" (Boyne *et al.* 2004).[3] In each authority, questionnaires were sent to up to three corporate informants, chief officers in each of seven service areas, and three managers in each of these service areas.[4] All survey questions were in the form of a seven-point Likert scale and informants were asked to rate their authority (for corporate respondents) or service (for chief officers or service managers) on different dimensions of organizational culture and management.

At the core of the survey is a representative sample of 100 English local authorities. Representativeness is based upon background variables including deprivation, population, and performance (see Martin *et al.* 2003). The survey was conducted annually from 2001 until 2004. This analysis draws upon data from 2001 and 2002. The maximum number of authorities included in our analysis is 116 – for some of the models this falls to 73. The number of authorities falls because of variations in response rates from year to year. For example, in 2001, 314 authorities replied to the survey and in 2002, 100. Second, we remove all district councils from our analysis: there were 25 such authorities in our sample in 2002. These were removed because of the relatively small number of respondents in some councils, thereby undermining our rationale for conducting a multiple informant survey. Furthermore the CSP variable is only available for upper tier authorities. Finally, non-response to some questions results in the omission of a small number of authorities.

Measures

Dependent variables

The BVPI on consumer satisfaction is collected tri-annually, based upon a random sample of local addresses drawn from the Post Office Small Users Address File (PAF). These surveys gauge the extent to which local authorities are having a positive effect on the quality of life experienced by local residents. The survey includes an item assessing residents' satisfaction with "the way the authority run things" as a whole (Department of the Environment, Transport and Regions 1999: 110). The surveys are conducted in accordance with guidance provided by central government (Office of the Deputy Prime Minister 2003), with the ensuing returns submitted to the government department responsible for local government before the Audit Commission independently verifies them.

The measure of subjective consumer satisfaction is one of eight dimensions of performance in the survey. Respondents (local government officers) were asked to rate their service in comparison to others on a four-point scale ranging from one (bottom quartile) to four (top quartile). The item gauging internal perceptions of consumer satisfaction thus provided us with a measure that was directly comparable with the measure of external perceptions of consumer satisfaction taken from the BVPI dataset.

Independent variables

Market orientation variables were obtained from 21 measures in our local government survey. All items were measured on a seven-point Likert scale anchored by one (disagree) and seven (agree). Informants were asked to respond to questions in relation to their immediate area of work. Items were matched to the market orientation categories of customer orientation, competitor orientation and interfunctional coordination. Multiple items were identified for each category of market orientation. Within each category, groups of variables represented distinct conceptual areas and were isolated to test reliability. Reliability was tested via confirmatory factor analysis and by calculating scale reliability values. All survey items loaded onto one factor and all factors except integration had Cronbach alpha coefficients above 0.7. The alpha of 0.6389 for integration is acceptable for new scales, those with a small number of items and in exploratory research (Nunnally 1978). Table 5.1 presents the items, factor analytic results and Cronbach alphas.

In the private sector model of market orientation, customer orientation and competitor orientation "...include all of the activities involved in acquiring information about the buyers and competitors" (Narver and Slater 1990: 21). For public agencies the most appropriate customer market is not that of buyers per se but of a number of stakeholders. In this study, we measure customers to include users, the public, other local agencies and local businesses. The measures identified fell into two distinct groups: those concerned with *customer focus*, i.e. attitudes toward customers or a customer culture; and those associated with gathering information about the customer environment, labelled *consultation*. Measures of competitor orientation similarly fell into two groups of variables, both concerned with searching or scanning the external environment for data and information. The measures focused on two specific groups in the environment, other local authorities and the private sector. The first set of measures are labelled *compare public* and are concerned with making comparisons with other local authorities in the areas of costs, outcomes, management and performance. The second variable is titled *competitiveness*. Measures focus on market testing, externalization and attitudes toward working with private agencies.[5]

Interfunctional coordination is concerned with "...the coordinated utilization of company resources in creating superior value for target customers" (Narver and Slater 1990: 22). Local government has been encouraged to develop corporate strategies by its key external stakeholders, central government and in particular the Audit Commission. Corporate strategies are seen as a method to coordinate information and activities within local authorities. Notable has been the promotion of performance management regimes to manage information and integration to bring together different services and parts of the organization in meeting a common goal or mission. In order to achieve both sets of outputs, information technology, information systems and communication are required. Such behaviour is argued to result in higher levels of organizational performance. These three aspects of interfunctional coordination are measured by variables labelled *performance management, integration* and *IT & communication*. Performance management captures performance management systems, linkages between the objectives and priorities of services and the whole authority, and information that allows managers to meet goals and targets. Integration measures flexible structures, coordination, joint and cross-cutting work – all integrative

Table 5.1 Reliability analysis

Customer orientation	Customer focus	Most managers place the needs of users first and foremost when planning and delivering services	0.651
		Strategy is made in consultation with our external stakeholders	0.789
		Working more closely with users	0.717
		Users' demands	0.815
		Eigenvalue/% variance/Cronbach alpha	2.225/55.622/0.7202
	Consultation	Consult – the public as a whole	0.764
		Consult – service users	0.688
		Consult – other local agencies	0.766
		Consult – local businesses	0.731
		Eigenvalue/% variance/Cronbach alpha	2.177/54.429/0.7081
Competitor orientation	Comparison public	Compare – other local authorities	0.743
		Comparisons – generic management	0.637
		Comparisons – costs	0.762
		Comparisons – outcomes	0.826
		Comparisons – performance	0.891
		Eigenvalue/% variance/Cronbach alpha	3.013/60.269/0.8230
	Competitiveness	Competitiveness – market test all or part of the service through open competition	0.770
		Competitiveness – test opportunities for strategic alliances and partnerships	0.695
		Competitiveness – test for externalization of the service	0.831
		Competitiveness – develop the market in order to encourage alternative providers	0.777
		The authority/service welcomes partnership with the private sector	0.473
		Eigenvalue/% variance/Cronbach alpha	2.594/51.883/0.7657

Interfunctional coordination		
Performance management	There is a well-developed framework of clear performance measurement and targets to drive what we do	0.818
	There are clear links between the objectives and priorities of the service and those of the authority as a whole	0.748
	Our management information systems enable service managers to judge their progress towards meeting goals and targets	0.887
	Our management information systems enable the authority's senior management team to judge their progress towards meeting goals and targets	0.903
	Eigenvalue/% variance/Cronbach alpha	2.830/70.739/0.8605
Integration	We frequently transfer or second staff to different departments/ services	0.681
	Enhancing coordination and joint working	0.829
	Cross-departmental/cross-cutting working	0.795
	Eigenvalue/% variance/Cronbach alpha	1.783/59.420/0.6389
IT and communication	New information technology	0.796
	New management information systems	0.886
	Internal communications	0.865
	Eigenvalue/% variance/Cronbach alpha	2.166/72.190/0.8017

methods promoted to break down internal barriers between typically professional service areas. IT and communication examines information technology hardware and software together with communication.

Control variables

Three external constraint variables are used in this study. These archival measures of the environment include service need, diversity, and the extent to which need has changed over time. Measures of level of affluence, such as income data, are not readily available at the local authority level. The level of *service need* is consequently operationalized through a measure of deprivation. The average ward score on the Index of Multiple Deprivation (Office of the Deputy Prime Minister 2000a) was used as a measure of the level or quantity of service need. This deprivation score is the standard population-weighted measure of deprivation in England used by central government. It provides an overview of the different domains of deprivation (e.g. income, employment and health). As the range of service providers becomes more varied, it becomes harder for local authorities to determine the relative needs of different groups and to provide standardized services that meet their requirements. We use ethnic diversity to measure variations in the level of service need (*diversity of need*) (Andrews *et al.* 2006). A Hehrfindahl index was created by squaring the proportion of each ethnic group (taken from the 2001 census, Office for National Statistics, 2003) within a local authority and then subtracting the sum of the squares of these proportions from 10,000. The resulting measure is a proxy for "fractionalization" within the local authority area, with a high level of ethnic diversity reflected in a high score on the index. High and diverse levels of need result in lower levels of performance (Andrews *et al.* 2005, 2006). The final archival measure looks at change in population to measure *change in need*. This measure captures features of a dynamic area because evidence suggests that in areas of population growth new residents are likely to be economically skilled and socially enterprising (Armstrong and Taylor 2000). Thus, local authorities with higher levels of population change are likely to achieve higher levels of public service performance.[6]

Findings

Next, we test the market orientation–performance hypothesis with two autoregressive models reported in Table 5.2.[7] These models estimate the effects of the market orientation and control variables on the two variables measuring consumer satisfaction.

Both models produce strong, statistically significant explanations of public service performance.[8] Their explained variance is 64 per cent for M1 and 63 per cent for M2, and a quick glance across the models reveals that prior performance does most of the heavy lifting and is the most consistent and effective predictor variable with effect sizes of 0.6922 and 0.5918 respectively. The family of market orientation variables produce some marginal effects, and these are some-

Table 5.2 Market orientation matters most to objective consumer satisfaction

		M1		M2	
		Subjective consumer satisfaction		Objective consumer satisfaction	
		B	se	B	se
Customer orientation	Customer focus	0.1149	0.0063+	−0.2591	0.8954
	Consultation	−0.0003	0.0047	−2.1580	0.7209**
Competitor orientation	Compare public	−0.0002	0.0056	3.1959	0.8561***
	Competitiveness	−0.0059	0.0042	1.3361	0.6355*
Interfunctional coordination	Performance management	−0.0006	0.0014	0.4140	0.2054*
	Integration	−0.0039	0.0049	−1.9956	0.7645**
	IT and communication	−0.0025	0.0062	0.4054	1.0384
External constraints	Service need	0.0005	0.0003†	0.0069	0.0046
	Diversity of need	−0.0000	0.0000*	0.0000	0.0000
	Change in need	0.0040	0.0041	1.3610	0.7209+
Prior performance		0.6922	0.0087***	0.5918	0.0700***
	F	12.60***		13.12***	
	Adjusted R^2	0.64		0.63	

Notes
† $p<0.1$; * $p<0.05$; ** $p<0.01$; *** $p<0.001$.

times weak across the two models and others tend in the wrong direction. None of the market orientation variables reach significance in both models. Each model is discussed in turn.

None of the market orientation variables are significant predictors in M1, our subjectively measured consumer satisfaction model, save the customer focus measure which is significant at the lower 0.1 level. However, five market orientation variables are significant predictors in M2, our objectively measured consumer satisfaction model. Two of these variables (competitiveness and performance management) achieve significance at the 0.05 level, while two others produce negative coefficients indicating that they are actually undercutting rather than improving public service performance (consultation and integration). The fifth variable is highly significant at the 0.001 level and it appears to be contributing to the model's explanatory power. This variable – a competitor orientation measure labelled "compare public" – represents authorities making comparisons with other local authorities in the areas of costs, outcomes, management and performance. Such benchmarking appears to be helpful in producing higher levels of objective consumer satisfaction.

Overall, M2 produces a fair number of statistically significant findings, most notably on the competition variables which run in the hypothesized direction. Since similar results are not present in M1, it appears that the public may hold different views from other stakeholders, who in this model are inside public organizations. Moreover, since the public sector version of market orientation theory seems to focus attention on the public as its customers, one can argue that M2 provides limited support for the theory.

To recap, there are no consistent predictors of performance among the market orientation variables. Levels of significance and directions of impact are highly variable across the models. Several variables only achieve significance at the lower 0.1 or 0.05 levels, and several others turn in the wrong direction –actually doing violence to public service performance.

Finally, Table 5.2 shows that the control variables have little effect. The only one that achieves statistical significance at the 0.05 level is diversity of need, which shows up in M1. However, its unstandardized coefficient of –0.0000 reveals that this variable is not having much effect on public service performance. Two other control variables achieve statistical significance at the lower level of 0.1 in M1 and M2, respectively. These variables are service need in M1, and change in service need in M2. These findings are not unexpected as effects of these controls are largely captured in the measure of prior performance.

Conclusion

This study has tested the backbone theory of New Public Management – that market orientation improves public service performance. We thus report the first known empirical evidence on the market orientation–performance hypothesis in the public sector. Overall, our findings show that market orientation does not explain public service performance very well. This weak relationship further suggests that the theory of market orientation is an inadequate and possibly inappropriate model for public service improvement. More important, this finding raises fundamental questions about public choice theory and NPM which rely heavily on market-based processes and solutions for public service improvement. Perhaps these applications are inappropriate.

Among our models, the objectively measured consumer satisfaction model seems to respond better to the theory of market orientation, with five of the seven variables reaching statistical significance (although two are in the wrong direction). This is in contrast to most private and non-profit sector tests of the market orientation–performance hypothesis that have marshalled stronger support for the theory using subjective measures of performance.

Overall, though, we are struck by the fact that the theory of market orientation does such a poor job of explaining performance in public organizations. The interior relationships in the models are not necessarily as hypothesised – possibly because the models are inappropriately specified. Here we have replicated Narver and Slater's (1990) study which tests independent effects of the three aspects of market orientation. However, we believe that the effects of consumer orientation, competitor orientation and functional integration may in fact be interactive. For example, information on consumer requirements may be unrelated to organizational results unless a sophisticated system of performance management is in place. Future research should examine this possibility. Moreover, other definitions and measures of market orientation need to be tested, both in the UK local government context and elsewhere.

Yesterday's NPM is today's public sector, meaning that many market orientation reforms have already been adopted and institutionalized in the public sector. During the first few years of the twenty-first century, the NPM-based theory of market orientation, and its offspring, the market orientation–performance hypothesis, continues to be very influential. In the USA President George W. Bush said: "Government should be market-based – we should not be afraid of competition, innovation and choice. I will open government to the discipline of competition" (Executive Office of the President, Office of Management and Budget 2002: 17). Mr. Bush subsequently made competitive sourcing a high priority item on the President's Management Agenda, proposed outsourcing 850,000 Federal government jobs to the private sector, and began subjecting Federal agencies to strict market-based competition. Similar reforms are underway (and often more advanced) in the UK and other highly developed countries. Thus while the global financial crisis that took hold in 2008 has signalled a new resurgent role for the state in the management of national economies, and the election of President Obama in late 2008 signals a new set of public values, many NPM-based reforms are still being implemented across the globe. It will take time for the practice of public management to change to the nearly emerging agenda; nonetheless it is not too late for public management researchers to shine the light of empirical investigation on NPM-type reforms to develop a more comprehensive appreciation of their impact on organizational performance. The next generation of public sector reformers will, in addition, hopefully pursue a more evidence-based reform agenda.

Notes

1 Corporate officers include the chief executive officer and corporate policy officers with cross-organizational responsibilities for service delivery and improvement. Service officers include chief officers who are the most senior officer with specific service delivery responsibility and service managers or front-line supervisory officers. In each authority, survey questionnaires were sent to up to three corporate informants and four managers across seven service areas.
2 The survey was conducted by email following a pilot in 17 local authorities that tested the survey administration technique and item quality (Enticott 2003). Email addresses were collected from authorities and questionnaires delivered as an Excel file attached to an email. The electronic questionnaires were self-coding and converted to SPSS for analysis. Informants had eight weeks to answer the questions and return the file by email. During the survey period, three reminders were sent to informants who had not yet responded. There were no statistically significant differences between late and early respondents (Martin *et al.* 2003).
3 A copy of the full questionnaire is available at www.clrgr.cf.ac.uk or on request from the authors.
4 The seven key services were surveyed: education, social care, land-use planning, waste management, housing, library and leisure, and benefits.
5 At the time of the surveys, English local authorities were required to undertake environmental scanning activities associated with consultation, comparison and competitiveness as part of the Best Value regime, referred to above in relation to the purpose of the study (Boyne *et al.* 2004).
6 Descriptive data for external constraints include: Service need, mean 27.69, sd 11.03; Diversity of need, mean 2491.35, sd 2214.07; Population change, mean 0.7342, sd 0.7767.
7 These models are autoregressive and use the most recently available data. Thus, the subjective consumer satisfaction model has a one-year lag between the collection of the independent (2001) and the dependent variables (2002), with a 2001 autoregressive term. The objective consumer satisfaction model has a longer gap with the dependent variable recorded in 2003 and prior performance in 2000.
8 The average variance inflation factor is 1.9 and the highest individual score recorded was 3.7 meaning that multicollinearity is not a problem.

References

Aiken, Michael and Hage, Jerald (1968) "Organizational Interdependence and Intra-organizational Structure", *American Sociological Review* 33.6: 912–930.

Andrews, Rhys, Boyne, George A. and Walker, Richard M. (2006) "Strategy Content and Organizational Performance: An Empirical Evaluation", *Public Administration Review* 66.1: 52–64.

Andrews, Rhys, Boyne, George A., Law, Jennifer and Walker, Richard M. (2005) "External Constraints and Public Sector Performance: The Case of Comprehensive Performance Assessment in English Local Government", *Public Administration* 83.3: 639–656.

Armstrong, Harvey W. and Taylor, James (2000) *Regional Economics and Policy*, Oxford: Blackwell.

Audit Commission (2002) *Comprehensive Performance Assessment*, London: Audit Commission.

Blair, T. (2002) "The Courage of our Convictions: Why Reform of the Public Services is the Route to Social Justice", *Fabian Ideas 603*, London: Fabian Society.

Bowman, Cliff and Ambrosini, Veronica (1997) "Using Single Respondents in Strategy Research", *British Journal of Management* 8.2: 119–132.

Boyne, George A., Martin, Steve and Walker, Richard M. (2004) "Explicit Reforms, Implicit Theories and Public Service Improvement", *Public Management Review* 6.2: 89–210.

Bozeman, Barry (2007) *Public Values and Public Interest. Counterbalancing Economic Individualism*, Washington, DC: Georgetown University Press.

Department for Environment, Transport and Regions (1999) *Best Value and Audit Commission Performance Indicators for 2000/2001*, London: DETR.

Deshpande, Rohit and Farley, John U. (1998) "Measuring Market Orientation: Generalization and Synthesis", *Journal of Market Focused Management* 2.3: 213–232.

Deshpande, Rohit and Webster, Frederick E. (1989) "Organizational Culture and Marketing: Defining the Research Agenda", *Journal of Marketing* 53.1: 3–15.

Ellis, Paul D. (2006) "Market Orientation and Performance: A Meta-Analysis and Cross-National Comparisons", *Journal of Management Studies* 43.5: 1089–1107.

Enticott, Gareth (2003) "Researching Local Government Using Electronic Surveys", *Local Government Studies* 29.2: 52–67.

Executive Office of the President. Office of Management and Budget (2002) *The President's Management Agenda: Fiscal Year 2002*, Washington, DC: Government Printing Office.

Harris, Lloyd C. (2001) "Market Orientation and Performance: Objective and Subjective Empirical Evidence from UK Companies", *Journal of Management Studies* 38.1: 17–43.

Jaworski, B. J. and Kohli, A. K. (1993) "Market Orientation: Antecedents and Consequences", *Journal of Marketing* 57(July): 53–70.

Kirka, Ahmet H., Jayachandran, Satish and Bearden, William O. (2005) "Market Orientation: A Meta-Analytic Review and Assessment of its Antecedents and Impact on Performance", *Journal of Marketing* 69.2: 24–41.

Kohli, Ajay K. and Jaworski, Bernard J. (1990) "Market Orientation: The Construct, Research Propositions, and Managerial Implications", *Journal of Marketing* 54.2: 1–18.

Martin, Steve, Walker, Richard M., Ashworth, Rachel, Boyne, George A., Enticott, Gareth, Entwistle, Tom and Dawson, Lynn (2003) *The Long Term Evaluation of Best Value and its Impact: Baseline Report*, London: Office of the Deputy Prime Minister.

Narver, John C. and Slater, Stanley F. (1990) "The Effect of a Market Orientation on Business Profitability", *Journal of Marketing* 54.4: 20–35.

Nunnally, Jum C. (1978) *Psychometric Theory*, New York: McGraw-Hill.

Office for National Statistics (2003) *Census 2001. National Report for England and Wales*, London: HMSO.

Office of the Deputy Prime Minister (2000a) *Best Value Performance Indicators for 2000/2001*, London: HMSO.

Office of the Deputy Prime Minister (2000b) *Index of Multiple Deprivation*, London: HMSO.

Office of the Deputy Prime Minister (2003) *Best Value Performance Indicators for 2003/2004*, London: HMSO.

Office of Public Service Reform (2002) *Reforming our Public Services. Principles into Practice*, London: HMSO.

Office of Public Service Reform (2003) *Leading from the Front Line*, London: HMSO.

Shapiro, Benson P. (1988) "What the Hell is 'Market Oriented'?", *Harvard Business Review* 66.6: 119–125.

Shoham, Aviv, Ruvio, Ayalla, Vigoda-Gadot, Eran and Schwabsky, Hitza (2006) "Market

Orientations in the Nonprofit and Voluntary Sector: A Meta-Analysis of Their Relationships with Organizational Performance", *Nonprofit and Voluntary Sector Quarterly* 35.3: 453–476.

Slater, Stanley F. and Narver, John (1994) "Does Competitive Environment Moderate the Market Orientation-Performance Relationship?", *Journal of Marketing* 58.1: 46–55.

Walker, Richard M. and Enticott, Gareth (2004) "Using Multiple-Informants in Public Administration: Revisiting the Managerial Values and Actions Debate", *Journal of Public Administration Research and Theory* 14.3: 417–434.

6 Repositioning the state and the public sector reform agenda

The case of Hong Kong

*Anthony B. L. Cheung**

Introduction

Together with Singapore, Hong Kong ranks as the forerunner of public sector reform in Asia along the lines of the New Public Management (NPM) paradigm (Cheung 2004). As a former colony of Britain until 30 June 1997, Hong Kong had been subject to the influence of British-style NPM reforms since the 1980s. However, public sector reform was driven more by domestic political and bureaucratic factors, particular those that shaped Hong Kong's political trans-ition to become a special administrative region (SAR) of China in July 1997 (Cheung 2006). Whereas public sector reform in the West was often driven by economic and fiscal decline, as well as the rising public backlash to 'big govern-ment', Hong Kong's public sector reform first took place in the absence of these factors but embraced a pro-civil service agenda (Cheung 1996a). It was only after the 1997 handover, when a prolonged economic recession resulted in fiscal stress and the need for retrenchment, that the government began to embark on more ambitious plans in civil service reform, public sector downsizing and pri-vatization. Most lately, as the economy rebounds and fiscal surplus re-accumulates, both the pace and emphasis of reform have begun to readjust; the privatization programme has slowed down and government starts to recruit civil servants again.

Public sector reform is part of the process of repositioning public governance, and should be understood within the wider context of the change in the role and scope of functions of the state. In the West, NPM came hand in hand with the movement to reposition governance as regards how the society and economy should be run – resulting in the concurrent taming of the administrative bureauc-racy and the transformation of the public sector. Among OECD countries, this meant 'the rolling back of the welfare state, the modification if not abandonment of the socialist ambitions, and an embrace of liberal capitalism, private enter-prise, and Big Business (as opposed to Big Government)' (Caiden 2007: 12). In the case of Hong Kong there has been, on the reverse, a steady shift towards a pro-state regime, in contrast to the *laissez-faire* state in the heyday of colonial rule. Because of its defective constitutional design, the SAR government has to deliver more policy and service outputs in order to earn legitimacy. Post-colonial sentiments have also fuelled rising expectations and the expansion of government responsibility in social and economic development, amid a more restless and demanding population eager to find a new sense of identity and future for the SAR. The need for economic restructuring in light of globalization further requires more strategically directed government actions. All these have added up to an enhanced state role and a more regulatory regime, somewhat contradictory to the official rhetoric of minimum government. Caught at a crossroads of transition, between legacies of small government and non-interventionism on the one hand, and new exogenous and endogenous needs for expansion and interventions on the other, the government faces the paradox of having both to reassert the 'public' and the role of the state in economic and social management, and to emphasize the use of more market-oriented means to achieve its public goals. Reviewing Hong Kong's trajectory of public sector reform and state role, this chapter seeks to explain and conceptualize the rise of a nascent developmental regime.

Public sector reforms: from administrative to political–economic agenda

Hong Kong's public sector reform is not just a passive response to, or convergence with, the new global trend to improve the efficiency of the public service through adopting NPM methods (OECD 1995). It has had its own longstanding trajectory of administrative reform since the 1970s to modernize its public service and to shore up the capacity of its administrative state (Cheung 1999). Such trajectory can be divided into four main phases: the colonial modernization phase; the 1990s reform phase; and the post-1997 reform phase, and current reversion phase. Table 6.1 highlights those significant reform measures.

Modernization and expansion of the colonial state: administrative self-improvement

In the aftermath of the pro-communist 1967 riots which exposed serious government–people gaps, the British colonial administration in Hong Kong began to embark on a series of administrative reforms as substitutes for political and constitutional reforms, in order to cope with a perennial legitimacy crisis of an unelected state (Scott 1989). The government machinery, in particular Government Secretariat (the policymaking centre), was reorganized following the recommendations of a commissioned management consultancy review (McKinsey & Co. 1973). New policy branches with ministerial roles (re-titled 'bureaus' in 1997 under the SAR government) were established, resource management processes streamlined, and a new corporate management approach adopted. The civil service had grown and localized rapidly, along with the expansion in government functions, public services and infrastructural development. An Independent Commission Against Corruption (ICAC) was created in 1974 to promote clean government and integrity, with an anticorruption brief extending to the private

Table 6.1 Significant public sector reforms in Hong Kong since the 1970s

Period	Reform measures
1970s-1980s (Administrative modernization)	Setting up of the Independent Commission Against Corruption (ICAC) (1974) McKinsey reform of government machinery (1974) Better forecasting techniques and longer term planning cycles introduced Financial management reforms – e.g. Introduction of 'controlling officer' in departments to be held accountable for expenditure (1979); devolution of authority to heads of departments to create non-directorate posts (1980); amalgamation of line items in budget; and introduction of inter-departmental charging
1990s (Public sector reform during political transition)	Launch of 'Public Sector Reform' (1989) Corporatization of public hospital services under new Hospital Authority (1990) Monitoring customer satisfaction – Introduction of performance pledges Private Sector Participation (including contracting out and divestiture) Improving productivity and reinventing front-line services Setting up trading funds 'Serving the Community' initiative (1995) Code of Access to Information Resource Assessment Exercise, Baseline Budgeting, and Fundamental Expenditure Reviews New management frameworks – Devolution of financial and human resource management responsibilities to policy branches and departments Managing for Results and Performance Review system
1997 onwards (Public sector reform during SAR period)	Target-based Management Process (TMP) (1997) Enhanced Productivity Programme (EPP) (1998) Civil Service Reform – Review of civil service pay adjustment mechanism; voluntary retirement schemes for civil servants; target for reducing civil service establishment; use of non-civil service contracts New executive accountability system for principal officials (or ministers) (2002) Private Sector Involvement (PSI) – including outsourcing and public private partnerships (PPP) Financial management reforms – Envelope Budgeting; '3Rs + 1M' (reprioritizing, reorganizing, reengineering, market-friendly) Privatizations – Partial privatization of the Mass Transit Railway Corporation (MTRC) (2000); privatization of public housing estates retail and car parking facilities (2005); public consultation on partial privatization of the Airport Authority (2005) Merger of MTRC and KCRC (Kowloon–Canton Railway Corporation) (2007)

sector. The 1970s and 1980s also saw the growth and proliferation of government departments, specialist grades in the civil service and para-governmental organizations.[1]

Public sector reform during 1990s: politics behind an efficiency agenda

Echoing the worldwide NPM trends, Hong Kong launched its own Public Sector Reform programme in 1989 (Finance Branch 1989). Although reform in the 1990s had displayed the usual NPM-like managerial initiatives such as budgetary devolution, contracting out, trading funds, customer-orientation and performance pledges, it was more than an efficiency agenda. At a time when the bureaucracy was subject to the rising challenges from newly emerging electoral politics and a more demanding and vocal population as the city entered the final stage of the pre-1997 political transition, public sector reform articulated a programme of institutional reconfiguration to redefine the relationship between the government centre and departments, and to provide a new buffer of managerialism to shield the bureaucracy from undue societal politicization (Cheung 1996a, 1996b). Opting for a consumerist orientation of public service also had the advantage of re-empowering service managers through the back door (Cheung 1996c). Behind the official *efficiency discourse* was a subtle *legitimation discourse* geared towards preserving and reinventing public bureaucratic power. Until then Hong Kong lacked any ideological bashing of 'Big Government' or the public bureaucracy.[2] Market supremacy had always been recognized but this had not prevented the extension in social functions of the colonial bureaucracy during the latter part of British rule. Public sector reform was implemented top down in the 1990s even though a strong macro-economic or macro-political premise for change seemed absent. However, the new '*management-speak*' did provide a handy reform rhetoric that helped to rationalize and legitimize changes motivated and shaped mainly by endogenous factors.

Post-1997 public sector reform: economic and political factors

After the change of sovereignty a shift in the public sector reform agenda was induced by a combination of economic, political and institutional factors. Economically, whereas the pre-1997 period was marked by a high growth which helped to sustain the public sector's fiscal capacity to expand and to satisfy public demands, a period of prolonged economic downturn and fiscal deficits had set in as a result of the Asian financial crisis. The costs of government did matter now; economic difficulties drove the public towards growing dismay with government performance. There were rising calls for revamping the bureaucracy to improve productivity and accountability. Politically, the civil service had suffered a dual efficiency and political crisis. The efficiency crisis was partly a sequence of administrative and policy failures. Shortfalls in efficiency, effectiveness and probity were attributed to the lack of political accountability of a civil service institution that had long operated within the so-called 'executive-led' polity. Initially, the bureaucracy engaged the same strategy as before to meet the criticism, by launching an 'efficiency enhancement programme' (EPP) of cost savings, and a broad-range civil service reform (Civil Service Bureau 1999; Cheung 2001). Once again, managerial solutions were used to deal with political challenges as during the colonial era (Cheung 1999); but this time, merely an administrative response had proved to be far from sufficient.

Former Chief Executive Tung Chee-hwa (1997–2005) blamed the failure of his first five-year term on the rigidity and inefficiency of the civil service, as well as their lack of enthusiasm and support for his policy agenda. His answer to the efficiency problem was to push for more extensive civil service reform; his solution to the political problem was to implement a new system of executive accountability for principal officials, substituting top mandarins by political appointees as 'ministers' (Tung 2002; Burns 2004: Ch. 5).[3] Government by bureaucrats was gradually giving way to a SAR regime embracing political goals beyond administrative contingency and self-preservation. The rise of electoral and legislative politics, as well as rising public expectations on service quality and accountability, also helped pave the path for bigger change. In stark contrast to the pro-civil service agenda of the 1990s, a new public sector reform agenda driven by economics and politics with bureaucrat-sceptic sentiments began to take shape. Reform now served to legitimize both government restructuring and an overhaul of the civil service (e.g. to downsize it through freezing new recruitment, extensive contracting out, outsourcing, non-civil service contract appointment, and voluntary retirement).

Current phase: reversion to pro-bureaucracy agenda to support state role

If reform implemented in economic adversity and amidst a downsizing environment had harmed the welfare and morale of the bulk of the civil service (mainly middle-level and rank-and-file staff), the new 'ministerial' system of political appointments had hit at the very heart of the bureaucracy – namely the interest and morale of the elite 'administrative class' (the Administrative Officers or AOs). This suspected 'disempowerment' of AOs was, however, short-lived. It came to a halt when Tung resigned in March 2005 and was replaced by former Chief Secretary for Administration (and head of the civil service) Donald Tsang, an ex-AO with over three decades of service. Tsang saw the civil service as the backbone of his new administration. Without derailing the new ministerial system, he encouraged those bureaucrats who wanted to participate in politics to leave the civil service to take up political appointment (Tsang 2005). As opposed to Tung's 2002 reform which aimed to recruit outsiders into government and retained some former civil servants as ministers only as a transitional arrangement, Tsang now opted for a reverse direction – retaining a few 'outsiders' but otherwise tapping on the civil service (mainly the AOs) as the main source of ministerial talent.

Implementing proposals put forward in a consultation paper in July 2006 (Constitutional Affairs Bureau 2006), he introduced supporting layers of politically appointed undersecretaries and political assistants in May 2008 to support policy ministers in his second term (2007–2012).[4] The introduction of further layers of political appointment not only opens up further 'political' opportunities to AOs wishing to switch track, but also in turn creates more vacancies within the AO grade for internal promotion (such as to permanent secretary and deputy secretary levels). Tung's new ministerial system of political appointments was now turned around to consolidate the AOs' power. What has emerged is a government by 'political bureaucrats',[5] which is more inclined to adopt a pro-civil service reform agenda as in the past – as evidenced by the unfreezing of civil service recruitment and a major pay raise for serving and new civil servants in 2007, the first time since 2000 and 2001 respectively.[6] What should be noted, though, is that this does not amount to a simple reversion to the self-preservation and reinvention mode of the 1980s and 1990s. New thinking in the role and functions of government has meanwhile crept in which, if sustained by a government of political bureaucrats positive about the role of the state, would help to facilitate a revisionist regime of quasi-developmentalism as the next section explains. By 2005 it seemed clear the economy had rebounded. The days of structural budget deficits have disappeared, with budget surplus once again accumulating to provide an impetus for government expansion, both in terms of generating rising expectations and an improved fiscal capacity.[7] Previous plans to privatize more government assets such as the Airport Authority, Post Office and Water Authority, and to sell government shares in Disneyland have been put aside (*Oriental Daily* 26 February 2007). At the same time, the restriction on recruitment of new civil servants has been lifted. Salaries for serving and new civil servants were raised in 2007, the first time since 2000 and 2001 respectively.

Role of the state: from non-interventionism towards interventionism

The economic success of the four newly developed East Asian economies – Singapore, South Korea, Taiwan and Hong Kong – during the 1980s–1990s was praised by the World Bank (1993) as a miracle. Among these economies, Hong Kong stood out as the exception where the government did not pursue an industrial policy in the same *dirigiste* manner as the rest and yet still achieved equally impressive results in economic growth (Wade 1990: 331–333). Such exception, however, does not mean that the Hong Kong experience was necessarily a reverse proof of a non-interventionist free-market economy. It all depends on how 'intervention' (or 'non-intervention' for that matter) is to be interpreted. Upon closer scrutiny the Hong Kong economy actually worked very differently from the textbook portrayal of a free market. Despite the non-interventionist rhetoric, the colonial government had been expanding steadily its sphere of public-policy intervention since the 1970s, and behaved increasingly as a development-oriented regime. In the absence of a political mandate to govern, the colonial rulers shied away from being an explicit *dirigiste* policy regime that characterized other East Asian economies. Inconsistencies between rhetoric and practice were often observed; if understood within the context of Hong Kong's peculiar colonial governance, they were indicative of an administrative pragmatism trying to muddle through an ambiguous policy environment where the bureaucratic elite did not have full grasp of all the political, social and economic variables.

From *laissez-faire* to positive non-interventionism: selective interventions under administrative expediency

Historically the colonial government was fiscally limited and conservative, with strong *laissez-faire* tendencies (Lo 1990: Ch. 2). The exercise of indirect rule, coupled with the cultural ingredients of 'utilitarianistic familism' and 'a minimally integrated socio-political system' within the local Chinese community (Lau 1982), also induced a dominant value system favouring family help rather than vigorous demands for social goods and services from the state. Such a regime of economic, social and political *laissez-faire* persisted until the 1960s, leading to the general perception – as played up by free-market economists like Friedman (1981: 54) and Rabushka (1976: 83) – that Hong Kong practised an almost pure form of classical capitalism where the government was limited to four basic duties and left the market to private business unrestrained by administrative interventions.[8]

In reality, Hong Kong did not pursue a dogmatic form of non-interventionism, especially from the 1970s onwards. According to Philip Haddon-Cave (1984), the then financial secretary, while the government's attitude towards the economy 'is frequently but inadequately described as being based on a philosophy of *laissez-faire*', the government stance was rather 'positive non-interventionism': though maintaining no attempt to plan the allocation of resources available to the private sector or to frustrate the operation of market forces, the government recognized a responsibility on the part of the government to respond when industries with social obligations ran into trouble and when an institution needed regulation to prevent inequitable practice. The prefix 'positive' was used to articulate a more flexible interpretation of the legacy of non-interventionism inherited from his predecessor John Cowperthwaite. Since then 'positive non-interventionism' had been held as Hong Kong's established wisdom. Many took it to mean non-interventionism, but this was just a façade. Even back in the 1970s, the government had begun to embark on various interventionist policies and measures – such as free education, public rental housing, home ownership scheme, regulating the stock market, setting up industrial estates, to name a few – when it felt the need to do so, whether for economic or social development purposes.[9]

The 1970s was also the golden era of social policy reforms (in education, healthcare, welfare, housing and labour), as well as infrastructure expansion (including large-scale transport and new town development programmes). This was partly a political response to the 1967 pro-communist riots challenging the legitimacy of colonial rule (Scott 1989), and partly a natural result of economic take-off, fuelling rising expectations and greater public demands for more public services and policy interventions. The positive non-interventionist doctrine was flexible in that it could be used to support *both* intervention and non-intervention, demonstrating the wisdom of administrative expediency. The colonial government did not adhere to any political ideology, as represented by the saying inside government: 'If it's not broken, why fix it?'. Hence positive non-interventionism was a useful weapon for the colonial officials to ward off demands from industry for subsidy, protection or bailouts, and to avoid divisive social policy debates. Leo Goodstadt (head of the Central Policy Unit in the last decade of British rule) observed that the *laissez-faire* doctrine and its like enabled bureaucrats to resist pressures of reverse capture from the privileged business and professional classes and to steer 'more acceptable boundaries between public and private interests within a political system ... based on a partnership between colonialism and capitalism' (Goodstadt 2005: 13). At the same time, not bound by any ideological dogma, the bureaucratic elite could choose to expand welfare and public services to meet changing public expectations, so long as the government coffers could afford it during a booming economy.

Though not of a Western welfare-state type, the latter-day colonial regime was active in regulative controls and had extensive direct and indirect involvement in social and community services, relying on land revenue instead of heavy taxation as the principal means of supporting these services. Schiffer (1983: 3) argued that colonial Hong Kong had developed a unique alternative model of growth between the 1950s and 1970s, with '[the economy's] successful growth ... due largely to regulatory government policies and administered prices which effectively subsidize the wage rate, thus contributing to the export-competitiveness which has powered Hong Kong's industrialization'.[10] Such an approach could be interpreted as a form of 'growth colonialism'.

From fiscally driven to politically driven state interventions: rise of political expediency and economic revisionism

After the signing of the 1984 Sino-British Joint Declaration on the future of Hong Kong, the British administration began to introduce some form of representative government. The institutions of representation (district boards, municipal councils and legislative council) in turn induced greater response to and balance of the demands from various interests for allocations and interventions within the overall needs of economic growth.[11] By the 1990s, the politics of the transition, reinforced by a growingly assertive population forced government to change tack. Financial secretary Hamish Macleod declared that positive non-interventionism had outlived its usefulness (Macleod 1992) and that he would work for 'consensus capitalism' (Macleod 1995), hinting Hong Kong had reached a similar stage to the Western capitalist welfare regime. The scene was set for a more directive state with clear objectives to intervene through public policies, services and regulations, built into a new configuration of governance characterized still by bureaucratic dominance but widening its social and political base. Indeed the evolution of the state-form throughout contemporary colonial history had demonstrated the enormous capacity of the state managers to self-reform and to actively adjust to the changing endogenous and exogenous environmental conditions. Growing political activism and social agitations, accompanied by the overall imperative of capital accumulation in an increasingly volatile and competitive global environment, had driven the government towards a revisionist regime of positive non-interventionism.

Since Macleod, successive financial secretaries had used the expressions of 'minimum intervention, maximum support' (Donald Tsang, 1995–2001), 'proactive market enabler' (Antony Leung, 2001–2002), 'big market, small government' (Antony Leung, 2002–2003), and 'market leads and government facilitates' (Henry Tang, 2003–2007), all seeking to pursue a less dogmatic application of a pro-market philosophy. After 1997, the new political architecture was partially based on the incorporation of functional (i.e. business and professional) interests. This strengthened the quest by capital and professional interests for allocative benefits from government. On the other hand limited popular participation also induced the masses to look for material satisfaction from the new government as a trade-off for acquiescence of its under-mandated rule. In the aftermath of the Asian economic turmoil, while a prolonged recession and rising fiscal problems fuelled calls for public sector retrenchment and policy reversals, casting doubt about the sustainability of the pre-existing public-service state, it had also triggered more social and labour demands for state support and intervention, even from the industrialists and small and medium enterprises. A new form of state interventionism was in the making (Cheung 2000).

Discarding positive non-interventionism: advent of a quasi-developmental regime?

In the changed policy habitat, not only were the bureaucrats previously groomed in the philosophy of positive non-interventionism forced by Tung Chee-hwa and other external actors to succumb to a more state-interventionist approach to the economy. They had also to reconsider if the past policy practices still served Hong Kong effectively. The need to enable the city to stay competitive in the new globalized economic order gradually induced an official rethinking of the hitherto less expansionist industrial policy, to contemplate the prospect of a proactive state on all fronts for the sake of maintaining the accumulation capacity of Hong Kong's brand of capitalism. Former financial secretary Antony Leung's short-lived articulation of the government's role as a 'pro-active market enabler' (Leung 2002: paras 42–43)[12] was a product of such rethinking, though he was subsequently forced to retreat to a toned-down version of 'big market, small government' when faced with a backlash from some free-market dogmatists both locally and abroad. Meanwhile, taking advantage of the new opportunities in China's fast-growing economy also demanded more active government lobbying and liaison with mainland authorities, and strategic planning to match the mainland's development. For example, in September 2006, the first-ever government economic summit on 'China's 11th Five-Year Plan and the Development of Hong Kong' was held, clearly marking a new departure in economic policy.

Still, the contentions between intervention and non-intervention remain strong and controversial. Hence, when Tsang remarked at the end of the economic summit that positive non-interventionism was no longer a relevant factor in government policy nowadays, he immediately drew an uproar in society, inviting severe criticisms from both free-market ideologues and some opposition politicians suspicious of the intentions of a more interventionist government lacking democratic mandate (*South China Morning Post*, 13 September 2006). Tsang claimed that Haddon-Cave's positive non-interventionism was used at his time to withstand the incessant pressure for government intervention, but the world had changed and so had Hong Kong (Tsang 2006a). He argued that:

> The description of Hong Kong's style of capitalism, which the HKSAR Government preferred to use in recent years, was 'Big Market, Small Government'. This means that we respond to the needs of the market and do our best to support and promote economic development within the limits of a small government. And the Government should not intervene into any sector of the market, which the private sector can sustain on its own. I also said that *our work should not be bound by a simple watchword or slogan.*
>
> (Tsang 2006a, my emphasis)

As Hong Kong's economy develops, he said, the needs of the economy change and the government has to adapt its work to suit such changing needs. Back in the 1960s and 1970s, a crucial job for the government was to invest in hardware infrastructure, including the port and industrial estates, but as the city evolves into a service economy, the government needs to put more efforts into building the software infrastructure and regulatory regimes. Globalization is another reason for a more proactive economic policy:

> ...the ability to attract and retain talents has become a defining factor in our global competitiveness. We have been proactively liberalizing our talent importation regime and further developing our education and training systems. Technological innovation and creativity are vital for a knowledge economy, and thus we are working on various initiatives such as the Science Park and the InnoCentre. Environmental issues were economic 'externalities' that did not take up much of our attention in the past, but we must address them today with gusto.
>
> (Tsang 2006a)

It seems clear that a developmental or quasi-developmental regime of some kind is rising on the horizon. This new trajectory is further reinforced by the growing need to cope with the adverse impact of the global financial tsunami that erupted in late 2008. In early October 2008 the government announced a new scheme to provide 100 per cent guarantee to bank deposits, the first such move in Asia that was quickly followed by Singapore. In the same month a Task Force on Economic Challenges led by the Chief Executive himself was set up to assess the full impact of the crisis and formulate specific options to address the challenges.[13] The supervisory framework including the Monetary Authority and the Securities and Futures Commission is to be revamped, to enhance investor protection, and strengthen the supervision of the banking, securities and insurance industries (Tsang 2008: paras 24–30). In December 2008, the government committed HK$100 billion in loan guarantees for small and medium enterprises and secured commitments from more than 100 businesses not to lay off workers for at least a year. Though still maintaining the official principle of 'big market, small government', Tsang has now sounded more positive about government interventions when he remarked repeatedly in 2007 and 2008:

> …I object to a dichotomy between the roles played by the Government and the market, whether it be a strong belief in the omnipotence of government intervention or a passionate support of the free market being sacrosanct. Both are sweeping generalizations. In striving for economic growth, complex and unique relationships exist among different sectors of our economy….
>
> (Tsang 2007c: para. 12)

> …[W]e should not see a free market and government intervention as two exact opposites. The market is not omnipotent. Intervention is not necessarily an evil. If the market fails, the government should intervene. We also need government supervision when public interests are compromised.
>
> (Tsang 2008: para. 133)

In April 2009 the Task Force on Economic Challenges identified six new economic areas for grooming as Hong Kong's priority growth sectors, in addition to existing financial services, trading and logistics, professional services and tourism. These were: testing and certification; medical services; innovation and technology; cultural and creative industries; environmental industry; and educational services (Tsang 2009). Although it is far from government picking the winners, the steering role of government in economic development is becoming increasingly prominent.

Explaining and conceptualizing Hong Kong developmentalism

Whereas the logic of minimum government was logical enough in the colonial era, the end of colony and the establishment of a SAR with a high degree of subnational autonomy in 1997 represented a new point of departure. The subsequent expansion in the state's role can be explained with reference to governance, political and economical factors.

New environment of governance, politics and economics

Unlike other colonies becoming independent, there was no 'nationalist' government per se coming to power and implementing an ambitious nation-building agenda in post-1997 Hong Kong. On the surface, the polity remained dominated by the bureaucracy inherited almost intact from the colonial regime, and as such, it would seem unlikely to question and negate past policies and practices. However, the decolonization syndrome accompanying the transfer of sovereignty had still encouraged the 'takeover' elites to pursue new social and economic blueprints so as to surpass the achievements of the previous British administration. For example, in his maiden policy address Tung Chee-hwa emphasized that 'Hong Kong has finally broken free from the *psychological constraints brought about by the colonial era*. We should have the courage to set aside past modes of thought and plan Hong Kong's long term future with *new vision'* (Tung 1997, para. 3, my emphasis).

He launched major initiatives in the areas of housing, education and industrial development, pledging a 70 per cent home-ownership target and comprehensive education reforms. He also set up a Strategic Development Commission to map out major strategic development plans, as well as a Commission on Innovation and Technology to promote industrial transformation through the application of new technology. As pointed out earlier, the new corporatist polity dominated by functional 'rent seeking' interests, the non-democratic nature of government and prolonged economic recession had together bred rising demands from all quarters for more state services, concessions and interventions.[14]

As the SAR government moves into the direction of people-based governance, it has to be more responsive to such demands. In his final days, before he abruptly resigned from office in March 2005, Tung was persuaded to set up a Commission on Poverty to formulate measures to alleviate poverty. When Tsang took over, he promised to build a harmonious society where people's general welfare would be safeguarded (Tsang 2005). He announced in his 2006 policy address the launch of a wage protection movement with voluntary participation by employers, the effectiveness of which to be monitored by the Labour Advisory Board. If a comprehensive review conducted after two years found that the movement failed to yield satisfactory results, he would accede to the labour unions' demand for minimum wage legislation (Tsang, 2006b: para. 34). By the time of his 2008 policy address, despite opposition from some business and employer organizations, he concluded that the wage protection movement had failed and announced that the government would now proceed with legislation (Tsang 2008: para. 63). He also overturned a longstanding government line dating from the colonial administration days, to accept the necessity for a fair competition law. A Competition Bill was originally expected to be introduced in the 2008–2009 legislative session (Tsang 2008: para: 61) but has subsequently been delayed.

Outside government, the quest for a Hong Kong identity somewhat akin to nascent sub-nationalism can be observed in the renewed campaign for democracy, which has gained greater momentum and strength after 1997, as well as a new movement of local awareness rooted in environmental, heritage protection, collective memory and 'Hong Kong core values' issues. Sum traced the link between identity and local politics to the Sino-British struggle over 'decolonization' during the political transition, arguing there was 'a dual struggle over the politics of identity and the social basis for a new economic and political regime in the approach to 1997' (Sum 1995: 67). An early round of identity politics surrounded the language issue, when the new SAR government decreed it would enforce the use of the mother tongue in place of English as the medium of instruction at the junior secondary level. This politically correct and pedagogically sound policy proved to be highly unpopular with schools and parents alike. Chan (2002) suggested that the school language policy was not just a pedagogical issue because 'the English language has not only become a habitus of society; it also serves to distinguish Hong Kong people from mainland Chinese'. Fung (2001) locates the identity issue within a broader cultural construct:

The return of Hong Kong to China in 1997 has led to a contraction of the political sphere, as the convergence of political structures curbed the development of local identities. The label or category 'Hong Kong people' was then appropriated with a specific meaning for the local to resist encroachment of the national. It was true that the high intensity of dominant national discourses during the political transition created a favourable atmosphere for re-nationalization. However, as soon as the political transition was over, Hong Kongers re-adhered to their own label in their struggle for cultural autonomy.

(Fung 2001: 591)

While there have been various attempts to push the local population to assimilate into the national culture and identity, leading to suggestions that indigenous Hong Kong culture is in danger of 'disappearance' (Abbas 1997), the resistance to surrendering the local identity is still visible and strong in the political, cultural and discursive arenas.

The 1 July march of 2003, where over half a million people took to the street to protest the proposed national security legislation (Cheng 2005), marked the advent of a new era of civil society mobilizations and agitations. First, there was the middle-class movement to protect the Victoria Harbour against further reclamation; then followed a series of community agitations on environmental and conservation issues. The row over the demolition of Star Ferry clock tower in December 2006 and the removal of Queen's Pier in July 2007 not only denoted the growing public sentiment in recent years against destroying landmarks of 'collective memory', it also underscored the new politics of identity to preserve the *raison d'être* of the Hong Kong system within the 'one country two systems' framework. The more the Hong Kong public embrace a strong local identity, the more demanding they become towards the government – expecting it to be proactive in protecting the Hong Kong 'sub-national' interests and furthering local welfare. The reassertion of the 'public' by the community would induce a corresponding reassertion of the state at the political level.

The economic setback, first following the 1998 Asian financial crisis, and now amidst the present global financial crisis, has imposed a mixed but rather long-lasting impact on the positioning of the state. Government is under pressure to be more proactive and interventionist in face of a more competitive global economic environment. The need for economic restructuring also requires strategically directed government actions. Government has to invest more in education, training and infrastructure development; it also has to respond to calls for a better regulatory environment. Hong Kong's position as the premier financial, shipping and trading centre needs to be strengthened. Firms and professionals expect government assistance to move into mainland China through the 'Closer Economic Partnership Agreement' (CEPA) framework first introduced between Hong Kong and mainland China in mid-2003. There is growing pressure for Hong King to integrate with Guangdong Province and the Pearl River Delta Region, especially after the promulgation by the central government of an outline plan for the reform and development of the Pearl River Delta in the coming decade (National Development and Reform Commission 2008). All these developments presuppose and demand a larger and more assertive state role, as Tsang had also alluded to in his attempt to put behind the era of positive non-interventionism.

> The very externally oriented nature of Hong Kong's economy dictates that we must adapt to global market forces…. However, our firm belief in market competition does not mean that the Government does nothing or takes a passive role. In the face of rapid changes in the world and on the Mainland [of China], we must take a proactive but at the same time pro-market approach and see how we could provide a platform and foster an environment that would best support economic development.
>
> (Tsang 2006a)

Towards development-led governance

Reading Donald Tsang's election platform for his new five-year term (2007–2012), one can detect a new Hong Kong project tantamount to some form of state-building. Under the theme of 'creating a new Hong Kong', he seeks to pursue a new open government with the civil service team as the core, a new democratic system, a new mode of economic development, and new quality of life (Tsang 2007a). His articulation of the new economic development reflects developmental thinking that calls for more government leadership and intervention:

> In the future, I will see to it that the Government substantially increases investment, with infrastructure investment as the key component, embark-

ing on various new development areas, including the development at the boundary area. Through these investments, we aim to create tens of thousands of local jobs and drive wage increases for grassroots labourers.

The Government also has a responsibility to drive Hong Kong's economic development to higher level by growing of high value-adding industries. Hong Kong should develop its own brands, its own design, its own scientific research and its own creative industries. We should further develop our financial industries and attract more quality companies to list in Hong Kong. We will also seek to become the trial platform for renminbi [China's currency] convertibility. Hong Kong must create mutual benefit for itself and the rapidly growing economy of our country, thereby bring our economy to the next level and creating greater prosperity.

(Tsang 2007b)

A 'progressive view of development' seems to be the first priority of his new term, under which focus is placed on promoting economic development, community development and social harmony at the same time. Tsang elaborates his developmental goals as follows:

…I object to a dichotomy between the roles played by the Government and the market, whether it be a strong belief in the omnipotence of government intervention or a passionate support of the free market being sacrosanct. Both are sweeping generalizations. In striving for economic growth, complex and unique relationships exist among different sectors of our economy…. [T]he Government's role is mainly to formulate policies conducive to sustainable development so that every citizen has the opportunity to share the fruits of prosperity and progress. The Government needs to balance the political, economic and social demands of different interest groups in the community, and to make progress while maintaining stability. It should take the lead at the policy-making level in certain areas such as promoting economic integration with the Mainland, taking forward cross-boundary infrastructure projects and making joint efforts to develop a world-class metropolis.

(Tsang 2007c: paras 12–13)

In his 2008 policy address, he underscored the rising uncertainties and risks to the economy, society and everyday lives, and emphasized the need for 'strong governance' (Tsang 2008: para. 15).

The trajectory towards soft developmentalism

Reviewing the city's trajectory of public sector reform and state interventions, the shift towards development-oriented governance has been gradual and evolutionary over the years, not just a matter of a sudden move resulting from political regime transition in 1997. Table 6.2 highlights the salient changes. Such a shift can be appraised against the background of the East Asian experience.

Table 6.2 Changing trajectory of role of state and public sector reform

	Dominant economic philosophy	Role of state	Public sector reform agenda
Administrative state (classical colonialism)	Laissez-faire	Self sufficiency; minimum and low-expenditure government	–
Administrative state (reform colonialism) (1970s-1980s)	Positive non-interventionism	Alternative model of growth ('growth colonialism') sustained by fiscal surplus	Bureaucrats-led reform agenda of modernization, self-improvement and localization
Transitional state	Beyond positive non-interventionism; 'consensus capitalism'	From fiscally driven to politically driven state interventions	Bureaucrats-led reform agenda to re-invent public bureaucratic power
Early post-colonial state	Towards 'proactive market enabler'	Politics-driven proactivism and strategic development	From bureaucrats-led to politics-led agenda of civil service reform and government restructuring
Quasi-developmental state?	Dumping positive non-interventionism; proactive government under 'big market, small government'	People-based and development-oriented governance; 'progressive development'	Reversion to pro-bureaucracy reform agenda under 'government by political bureaucrats' regime

The East Asian 'developmental state' has been variously described as a 'plan-rational' state (Johnson 1982), 'governed market' (Wade 1990), and 'productiv-ist' regime (Holliday 2000). Neo-Marxist literature positions the role of the state as serving the ultimate interest of the logic of capitalism, by promoting both economic growth ('accumulation') and the stability of the social and political order ('legitimation') through extensive social policy provisions and a welfare state that helps to minimize class confrontations and political challenges to the capitalist system (O'Connor 1973; Gough 1979; Offe 1984). East Asian developmentalism can be conceptualized as a strategy of state actions and interventions to promote and bolster a unique form of market capitalism with strong statist presence and steer. Inasmuch as there is a distinction between a 'hard' or 'soft' authoritarian state, there can be a difference between hard and soft developmentalism, depending on the degree of state direction, and the combination of market and non-market means. Explaining East Asian developmentalist approaches, Weiss (1998: Ch. 2) pointed to the 'transformative' capacity of the state, i.e. its capability to be insulated from undue special interests but firmly embedded in society, and to maintain effective linkages with industry and other societal/economic actors in order to ensure the happening of things through 'governed inter-dependence'. Hong Kong is moving towards a mode of 'soft' developmentalism – as compared to Singapore, for example – and its need for transformative capac-ity is as pertinent.

The question remains, though, as to whether the government possesses the necessary competence and capacity to direct and intervene economically. A steering government needs legitimacy, innovative thinking, and strong linkages with society and industry. Given the constraints imposed by the existing political system on its policy capacity (Cheung 2007), while government may aspire to be proactive, it may not always possess enough political power and strategic capac-ity, or the right administrative tools for effective intervention. Historically Hong Kong's corporate sector and even the community at large shun bureaucratic planning. Because of the slow pace of democratization the political climate is ever suspicious of government intentions and policies, thus creating a 'Catch 22' situation as illustrated by the recent controversy over discarding positive non-interventionism. Bound by the Basic Law restrictions that it should spend within the limits of revenues and keep expenditure commensurate with GDP growth (Article 107), and its own 'small government' benchmark – pitched at 20 per cent of GDP – government expansion is held in check, especially in times of economic setback when tax revenues quickly contract.

Hence the path towards soft developmentalism is not going to be straight-forward and contentions-free. The paradox is that while the shift towards some form of developmentalism seems logical and almost unavoidable, the longstand-ing conventional wisdom and social discourse of the state remain incompatible, not to mention the institutional restrictions on the state, and the lack of strong state capacity and the necessary state instruments (unlike Singapore). In the old non-interventionist days when state involvement was minimal or low, the state could rely on voluntary and non-coercive incentive instruments like the market, the family and charities. As state involvement moves towards medium and high, a mixed set of incentives and coercive instruments is required – such as subsi-dies, regulation, direct provision and the use of state organizations (Linder and Peters 1998; also Hood 1983).

Concluding remarks

Ever since the colonial era, Hong Kong has been an administrative state domi-nated by the bureaucrats. There was never any serious challenge to, not to say collapse of, the old public administration regime unlike in the Western states of the 1980s and 1990s. The market has always been the dominant ideology, though there is growing emphasis on how government can ensure the 'happening of things' through market mechanisms and overt state actions. If Western NPM is about reform for efficiency during the retreat of the state, Hong Kong NPM is now more about reform for development, looming large as a project for civil service improvement and capacity-building destined to strengthen the compe-tence of the state to spearhead social and economic development under the new 'government by political bureaucrats' regime. Inheriting an official discourse (or rhetoric) of non-interventionism rooted in the administrative expediency of a bureaucratic polity, the Hong Kong state has nonetheless evolved to become more expansionist and interventionist thanks to the politics of *responsiveness* (beginning in the late colonial period) and the politics of *representation* (since the pre-1997 transition), coupled with the need to sustain economic accumulation and development in an increasingly competitive regional and global environment. The result is a development-oriented regime only dissimilar to the typical East Asian regime in matter of degree.

Since 1997, induced by various economic, political and governance factors, the government has to both reassert the 'public' and the role of the state in economic and social management, even as it continues to emphasize the importance of 'big market' and the use of more market-oriented means – such as contracting out, service vouchers, and public–private partnership – to achieve its public policy goals. As pointed out in the discussion, there exists a paradox of 'fit' between objectives and mentality/instruments, hence the road towards developmentalism is not going to be smooth. In any case, the city is no longer the *laissez-faire* or non-interventionist regime it used to be. The real question now is *to what extent* and *by what means* the government can step in for the social and economic good and how such interventions will gain the necessary legitimacy. In terms of public sector reform, it will likely continue to chart a pro-state and pro-civil service agenda that increasingly embraces developmental and interventionist goals, rather than a civil service-sceptic and state-downsizing orientation usually associated with NPM reforms elsewhere.

Notes

* Professor Anthony B. L. Cheung is the President of the Hong Kong Institute of Education, with the concurrent title of Chair Professor of Public Administration. He writes extensively on privatization, public sector reforms, state and policy capacity, Hong Kong governance, and Asian administrative reforms.

1 By the late 1980s, the public sector was made up of: some 60 departments and agencies; a host of non-departmental public bodies and public corporations (notably the Consumer Council, Trade Development Council, Productivity Council, Export Credit Insurance Corporation, Mass Transit Railway Corporation, Kowloon–Canton Railway Corporation, Industrial Estate Corporation and Land Development Corporation (reorganized as the Urban Renewal Authority in the late 1990s); as well as tens of public or semi-public organizations heavily subvented by government (such as universities and polytechnics, schools, hospitals and social welfare organizations).

2 The backlash on the bureaucracy after the 1997 handover had resulted partly from the incompetence of the government in handling some post-handover economic and public health crises (such as bird flu and the SARS outbreak), and partly from the fiscal stress suffered by the SAR in the aftermath of the 1997–1998 Asian financial crisis.

3 Senior civil servants taking up the new political appointment have to first retire from the civil service, with the exception of the post of Secretary for the Civil Service who plays the de facto role of head of the civil service.

4 In July 2006 the government published a consultation paper proposing to create within policy bureaus a small number of positions dedicated to political affairs at deputy secretary (later renamed undersecretary) and assistant to secretary levels (Constitutional Affairs Bureau 2006).

5 In Tsang's new administration commencing in July 2007, out of the ministerial team of two senior secretaries (chief secretary, financial secretary and secretary for justice) and 12 secretaries, only six are from a non-civil service background. The rest were predominantly AOs.

6 In 2007, following the completion of a pay level survey and pay trend survey, serving civil servants and employees of subvented organizations also received a pay rise for the first time since pay reductions in 2002 and 2003.

7 According to the 2007–2008 budget speech, the government's fiscal reserves will be maintained at a level between HK$390 billion and HK$580 billion over the next five years (Tang 2007: para. 76). The fiscal situation has only become more stressful again in 2009 because of the global financial crisis.

8 The four basic duties of government were cited as: protection from violence and invasion; protection from injustice or oppression; erection and maintenance of certain public works and certain public institutions; and protection of those members of the community who could not be regarded as 'responsible' individuals (Friedman 1981: 47–53).

9 At the turn of the decade, the government even temporarily took over a few private banks that collapsed. It also set up an industrial diversification committee to find ways to help local industrialists under the pressure of regional competition; only the economic opening-up of mainland China in 1979 after the end of the Cultural Revolution provided the unexpected new opportunities for manufacturers to move their production line northwards to the Pearl River Delta, thus obviating the need for revitalizing Hong Kong's manufacturing base. Since the 1980s, building up Hong Kong as a major international financial centre allied with a regional transport hub and related manpower planning has been at the centre of government's policy agenda.

10 In terms of consumption, it was reckoned that non-market factors accounted for more than 50 per cent of a blue-collar household's normal expenditure. In production support, the government not only provided industry with infrastructure, but also supplied it with a healthier, more educated and better housed – and hence more productive and stable – workforce. Thus, despite the absence of macroeconomic planning and the subsidization of faltering industries, Hong Kong's market forces rested de facto on 'an infrastructural support system of non-market regulation of economic activities, administration of key prices, subsidization of "the social wage", interference in (and distortion of) all factor markets, and ownership of one of the two factors of production that are subject to such property arrangements' (Schiffer 1983: 31–32).

11 These institutions included the formal incorporation of industrial, business and professional interests through the functional constituency elections of the Legislative Council since 1985 and the formal incorporation of territorial popular interests through direct elections since 1991.

12 Leung envisaged the government's role to include: first, maintaining an institutional framework conducive to market development; second, providing that infrastructure in which the private sector will not invest; third, providing an appropriate environment and the resources required to raise the quality of human capital; fourth, securing more favourable market access for local enterprises through multilateral and bilateral economic and trade negotiations and participation in relevant economic and trade organizations; and fifth, considering the need to take appropriate measures to secure projects beneficial to the economy as a whole when the private sector is not ready to invest in them (Leung 2002: para. 42).

13 See Task Force membership and discussions at www.fso.gov.hk/tfec/eng/index.html, accessed 22 April 2009.

14 For example, the grassroots and labour unions demanded improved social security, employment opportunities, and a mandatory minimum wage. Regulations and interventions were called for to clean up the environment, to protect consumer interests and to ensure fair competition in the market for the sake of small and medium enterprises.

Bibliography

Abbas, A. (1997) *Hong Kong: Culture and the Politics of Disappearance*, Minneapolis, MN: University of Minnesota Press.

Burns, J. P. (2004) *Government Capacity and the Hong Kong Civil Service*, New York: Oxford University Press.

Caiden, G. E. (2007) 'Introduction', in G. E. Caiden and Tsai-tsu Su (eds) *The Repositioning of Public Governance: Global Experience and Challenges*, Taipei: Best-West Publishing Co., pp. 3–30.

Chan, E. (2002) 'Beyond Pedagogy: Language and Identity in Post-colonial Hong Kong', *British Journal of Sociology of Education* 23(2): online version.

Cheng, J. Y. S. (2005) (ed.) *The July 1 Protest: Interpreting a Historic Event*, Hong Kong: City University of Hong Kong Press.

Cheung, A. B. L. (1996a) 'Efficiency as the Rhetoric? – Public Sector Reform in Hong Kong Explained', *International Review of Administrative Sciences* 62(1): 31–47.

Cheung, A. B. L. (1996b) 'Public Sector Reform and the Re-legitimation of Public Bureaucratic Power: The Case of Hong Kong', *International Journal of Public Sector Management* 9(5/6): 37–50.

Cheung, A. B. L. (1996c) 'Performance Pledges – Power to the Consumer or a Quagmire in Public Service Legitimation?', *International Journal of Public Administration* 19(2): 233–259.

Cheung, A. B. L. (1999) 'Administrative Development in Hong Kong: Political Questions, Administrative Answers', in H. K. Wong and H. S. Chan (eds) *Handbook of Comparative Public Administration in the Asia-Pacific Basin*, New York: Marcel Dekker, pp. 219–252.

Cheung, A. B. L. (2000) 'New Interventionism in the Making: Interpreting State Interventions in Hong Kong after the Change of Sovereignty', *Journal of Contemporary China* 9(24): 291–308.

Cheung, A. B. L. (2001) 'Civil Service Reform in Post-1997 Hong Kong: Political Challenges, Managerial Responses', *International Journal of Public Administration* 24(9): 929–950.

Cheung, A. B. L. (2004) 'Public Sector Reform in Hong Kong and Singapore: Reform Trajectories and Explanations', in A. Nakamura (ed.) *Comparative Studies of Public Administration VIII: Public Reform, Policy Change, and New Public Management – From the Asia and Pacific Perspective*, Eastern Regional Organization for Public Administration (EROPA), Tokyo, Japan: Local Government Center, pp. 1–28.

Cheung, A. B. L. (2006) 'Reinventing Hong Kong's Public Service: Same NPM Reform, Different Contexts and Politics', *International Journal of Organizational Theory & Behaviour* 9(2): 212–234.

Cheung, A. B. L. (2007) 'Policy Capacity in Post-1997 Hong Kong: Constrained Institutions Facing a Crowding and Differentiated Polity', *The Asia Pacific Journal of Public Administration* 29(1): 51–75.

Civil Service Bureau (1999) *Civil Service into the 21st Century: Civil Service Reform Consultation Document*, Hong Kong: Printing Department.

Constitutional Affairs Bureau (2006) *Consultation Document on Further Development of the Political Appointment System*, Hong Kong: Government Logistics Department.

Finance Branch (1989) *Public Sector Reform*, Hong Kong: Government Printer.

Friedman, M. (1981) *Free To Choose*, Harmondsworth: Penguin Books.

Fung, A. (2001) 'What Makes the Local? A Brief Consideration of the Rejuvenation of Hong Kong Identity', *Cultural Studies* 15(3/4): 591–601.

Goodstadt, L. F. (2005) *Uneasy Partners: The Conflict Between Public Interest and Private Profit in Hong Kong*, Hong Kong: Hong Kong University Press.

Gough, I. (1979) *The Political Economy of the Welfare State*, London: Macmillan.

Gray, J. (1999) *False Dawn: The Delusions of Global Capitalism*, London: Granta Books.

Haddon-Cave, P. (1984) [1980] 'The Making of some Aspects of Public Policy in Hong Kong. Introduction to the First Edition', in D. G. Lethbridge (ed.) *The Business Environment in Hong Kong*, Hong Kong: Oxford University Press, pp. xiii–xx.

Holliday, I. (2000) 'Productivist Welfare Capitalism: Social Policy in East Asia', *Political Studies* 48(4): 706–723.

Hood, C. C. (1983) *The Tools of Government*, Hong Kong: Macmillan.

Johnson, C. (1982) *MITI and the Japanese Miracle*, Stanford: Stanford University Press.

Lau, S. K. (1982) *Society and Politics in Hong Kong*, Hong Kong: The Chinese University Press.

Leung, A. (2002) *The 2002–03 Budget*, speech by the Financial Secretary moving the Second Reading of the Appropriation Bill 2002, 6 March, Hong Kong: Printing Department.

Linder, S. H. and Peters, B. Guy (1998) 'The Study of Policy Instruments: Four Schools of Thought', in B. Guy Peters and F. K. M. van Nispen (eds) *Public Policy Instruments: Evaluating the Tools of Public Administration*, Cheltenham: Edward Elgar, pp. 33–45.

Lo, C. S. S. (1990) *Public Budgeting in Hong Kong: An Incremental Decision-making Approach*, Hong Kong: Writers' and Publishers' Cooperative.

Macleod, H. (1992) 'My Six Months Walking a Financial Tightrope', *South China Morning Post* [Sunday Edition], 9 February, Hong Kong.

Macleod, H. (1995) *The 1995–96 Budget*, speech by the Financial Secretary moving the Second Reading of the Appropriation Bill 1995, March, Hong Kong: Government Printer.

McKinsey & Co. (1973) *The Machinery of Government: A New Framework for Expanding Services*, Hong Kong, China: Government Printer.

National Development and Reform Commission, State Council (2008) 'Outline of the Plan for the Reform and Development of the Pearl River Delta (2008–2020)', December, accessed March 2009. Available at www.china.org.cn/archive/2009-01/08/content 17075239.htm.

O'Connor, J. (1973) *The Fiscal Crisis of the State*, New York: St. Martin's Press.

Organization for Economic Cooperation and Development (OECD) (1995) *Governance in Transition: Public Management Reforms in OECD Countries*, Paris, France: OECD.

Offe, C. (1984) *Contradictions of the Welfare State*, in J. Keane (ed.), Cambridge, MA: MIT.

Oriental Daily (2007) 'Hong Kong Government No Longer Keen to Sell Assets Urgently', 26 February, Hong Kong (in Chinese).

Rabushka, A. (1976) *Value for Money: The Hong Kong Budgetary Process*, Stanford: Hoover Institution Press.

Schiffer, J. R. (1983) *Anatomy of a Laissez-faire Government: The Hong Kong Growth Model Reconsidered*, Hong Kong: Centre of Urban Studies and Urban Planning, University of Hong Kong.

Scott, I. (1989) *Political Change and the Crisis of Legitimacy in Hong Kong*, Hong Kong, China: Oxford University Press.

South China Morning Post (2006) 'Tsang's Remarks Sound Warning for Market Watchdog', 13 September, Hong Kong.

Sum, N. L. (1995) 'More Than A War of Words: Identity, Politics and The Struggle for Dominance During the Recent Political Reform Period in Hong Kong', *Economy and Society* 24(1): 67–100.

Tang, H. (2007) *The 2007–08 Budget*, speech by the Financial Secretary moving the Seconding Reading of the Appropriation Bill 2007, 28 February, Hong Kong.

Tsang, D. Y. K. (2005) *Campaign Speech for Chief Executive Election*, 3 June, Hong Kong. Available at www.donald-yktsang.com/press_speeches_e.html.

Tsang, D. (2006a) *Big Market, Small Government*, press release by the Chief Executive, 18 September, Hong Kong. Available at www.ceo.gov.hk/eng/press/oped.htm.

Tsang, D. (2006b) *Proactive, Pragmatic, Always People First*, address by the Chief Executive at the Legislative Council Meeting, 11 October, Hong Kong. Available at www.policyaddress.gov.hk/06–07/eng/policy.html.

Tsang, D. (2007a) *Donald Tsang Election Platform: Policy Blueprint*, Hong Kong: Donald Tsang Election Office.

Tsang, D. (2007b) 'Hong Kong Letter', broadcast on Radio Television Hong Kong, 31 March, Hong Kong. Available at www.info.gov.hk/gia/general/200703/31/P200703300246_print.htm.

Tsang, D. (2007c) *A New Direction for Hong Kong*, address by the Chief Executive at the Legislative Council Meeting, 10 October, Hong Kong: Government Logistics Department.

Tsang, D. (2008) *Embracing New Challenges*, address by the Chief Executive at the Legislative Council Meeting, 15 October, Hong Kong: Government Logistics Department.

Tsang, D. (2009) Remarks by the Chief Executive at media session after meeting of Task Force on Economic Challenges, 3 April, Hong Kong, accessed 22 April 2009. Available at http//www.info.gov.hk/gia/general/200904/03/P200904030234.htm.

Tung, C. H. (1997) *Building Hong Kong for a New Era*, address by the Chief Executive at the Provisional Legislative Council Meeting, 8 October, Hong Kong: Printing Department.

Tung, C. H. (2002) 'Address to the Legislative Council on the Introduction of the Principal Official's Accountability System'. Available at www.info.gov.hk/gia/general/200204/17/0417216.htm.

Wade, R. (1990) *Governing the Market: Economic Theory and the Role of Government in East Asian Industrialization*, Princeton, N J: Princeton University Press.

Weiss, L. (1998) *The Myth of the Powerless State*, Ithaca, NY: Cornell University Press.

World Bank (1993) *The East Asian Economic Miracle: Economic Growth and Public Policy*, New York: Oxford University Press.

7 Reasserting the role of the state in the healthcare sector

Lessons from Asia

M. Ramesh

Introduction

This chapter compares healthcare reforms in China, South Korea, Singapore and Thailand with the purpose of drawing useable lessons about the appropriate role of the state in the sector. It argues that healthcare reforms in China and Korea offer many negative lessons for healthcare reformers, while Singapore and Thailand offer positive lessons that may be considered for emulation elsewhere. The fundamental lesson to emerge from the successful reform experiences is that a large and active state role in various aspects of healthcare provision and financing is essential for containing expenditures and maintaining access. Public ownership of providers and prospective payments are particularly effective in controlling expenditures, while direct government financing promotes equitable access. The cases also show that political economy matters: the Singapore and Thai states' strong presence in the healthcare sector is a vital reason for their superior performance.

Many governments in the region are finally realizing that their healthcare reforms are on the wrong track. While trying to reign in expenditures, they have not only created other problems, but have also, ironically, accelerated expenditure growth in the process. Far too often, policymakers are trapped in a line of thinking that offers little reason that governments will be able to effectively reform their ailing healthcare systems. Fortunately, there are countries in Asia that offer rich lessons for policy reformers. The purpose of this chapter is, therefore, to examine healthcare policy reforms in a select group of countries – China, Korea, Singapore and Thailand – for drawing useable reform ideas, both negative and positive.

In this chapter I argue that healthcare reforms in China and Korea offer many negative lessons for healthcare reformers, while Singapore and Thailand offer positive lessons that may be considered for emulation elsewhere. Chinese reforms are textbook examples of what reformers elsewhere should avoid: fee-for-service (FFS) payment system for providers without appropriate controls over them. The case of Korea shows the potential pitfalls of comprehensive national health insurance in the context of FFS payment to providers. The experience in Singapore, on the other hand, suggests the need for government control over providers for reigning in expenditures and the limitations of savings-based financing. Thailand's experiment with government-financed universal healthcare offers yet another lesson: it is possible for governments in developing countries to deliver healthcare of reasonable quality to all citizens through changes in the financing and payment systems. However, for governments to devise and implement healthcare policies that serve the general rather than sectional interests, it is essential that the state is strong and has access to strong instruments for controlling providers. The fundamental lesson to emerge from the successful reform experiences in Asia is that a large and active state role in various aspects of healthcare provision and financing is essential for containing expenditures and maintaining access.

Health policy reform in comparative perspective

China

The Chinese population had almost universal access to decent, albeit basic, healthcare until the end of 1970s. Hospitals and other health facilities were owned and financed by the government or state-owned enterprises, with prices for services and drugs set below cost to ensure affordability (Yip and Hsiao 2001). Preventive care – immunization, prenatal care, family planning, public health inspections and public health campaigns – was financed by the government and usually provided free of charge. There were three social insurance financing schemes covering almost the entire population: Government Insurance Scheme (GIS) and Labour Insurance Scheme (LIS) for the urban population, and Cooperative Medical System (CMS) for the rural population.

The healthcare status of the Chinese population rose impressively under the arrangements that existed until the late 1970s. Infant mortality rate (IMR) declined from 200 per thousand live births in 1952 to 34 in 1982, while life expectancy increased from 35 to 68 years over the same period (Blumenthal and Hsiao 2005). More remarkably, these achievements were attained at a relatively low cost: total health expenditure accounted for only 3 percent of GDP.

The institutional and economic foundations of the Chinese healthcare system were, however, undermined by economic reforms that began in the late 1970s. The government reduced subsidies for public hospitals as a part of the overall marketization of the economy which put healthcare facilities in a difficult financial situation. Their conditions were aggravated by rising costs triggered by loosening-up of government price controls. The changed financial position led public hospitals to raise revenues through the prescription of expensive, and often unnecessary, drugs, diagnostics and procedures with the objective of raising revenues (Blumenthal and Hsiao 2005). Changes to the remuneration whereby doctors' salaries were to be supplemented by bonus for the amount of revenues they raised also had the perverse effect of pressuring doctors to induce demand for clinically unnecessary services and drugs. It is conservatively estimated that as much as 30 percent of overall healthcare expenditures in China are spent on unnecessary services and drugs.

At the same time, the healthcare financing system began to collapse after the introduction of market competition, as many state-owned enterprises closed down and many more did not have the financial capacity to pay their employees' health insurance premium. In rural areas, the dismantling of collective farms during the 1980s led to the demise of the CMS, leaving the vast majority of rural population without any form of healthcare coverage. Overall, coverage under all insurance schemes together fell from 70 percent of the population in 1981 to 20 percent in 2003 (Development Research Center of State Council 2005).

Following the changes introduced during the 1980s and 1990s, total health expenditure as a percentage of GDP rose from less than 3 at the end of the 1970s to 5.6 in 2003. Out-of-pocket expenditure on health grew at a staggering average annual rate of 20 percent in real terms during the 1990s and, as a result, its share of total health expenditures rose from around 20 percent in the early 1980s to 60 percent in 2000 while the government's share declined from 40 percent to under 20 percent. Poor households were hit the hardest as a disproportionately higher percentage of them were not covered by any form of health insurance.

In the mid-1990s, the government began to gradually realize the increasing unaffordability of healthcare and its adverse political implications. In 1998, the central government launched the "Basic Health Insurance Scheme for Urban Workers" (BHISUW) specifically for urban workers. It is an individual medical savings account arrangement financed by the contribution of 2 percent of wages by the employee and 6 percent by the employer. It pays providers on a fee-for-service basis. Participation is mandatory for all government agencies and state-owned enterprises but non-compliance is common (World Bank 2004). The scheme does not cover informal sector workers and migrant workers, nor does it cover dependants of covered workers. As a result, 51 percent of urban inhabitants remain uncovered by the scheme. In August 2007, the government extended the program to informal workers in select cities on a pilot basis and has set 2010 as the target for covering the entire urban population.

In 2002, the government launched a new CMS for the rural population on a pilot basis. The scheme is funded from a government subsidy of approximately $2.50 a year and members' annual contribution of $1.25 (Blumenthal and Hsiao 2005). The plan only covers inpatient care and imposes high deductibles. The voluntary nature of the scheme and low level of public financing make the scheme unpromising notwithstanding government's optimism.

Korea

At the center of the Korean health system lies a provision system dominated by private providers and a financing system characterized by compulsory public health insurance. Ninety percent of hospital beds and a similarly high share of medical specialists are located in private hospitals in Korea (Jeong 2005).

The history of public health insurance in Korea goes back to the promulgation of the Medical Insurance Act in 1963 which provided for a voluntary insurance scheme financed from equal contribution by employees and their employers.

Without sufficient incentives or coercion, it is not surprising that the program failed to attract participation (Yu and Anderson 1992). A private member's bill providing for compulsory health insurance was passed by the legislature in 1970 but it was never implemented due to government opposition.

Breakthrough came with the adoption of National Health Insurance (NHI) in 1977 which provided for compulsory coverage for firms employing 500 or more employees. The membership threshold was reduced in phases: to 300 employees in 1979, 100 in 1981, 16 in 1983, and five in 1988. The final expansion took place when the rural self-employed were covered in 1988 and the urban self-employed in 1989. The NHI not only insures the members, but also their dependants, which is defined rather liberally: indeed around two-thirds of all insured are dependants of primary members. Only daily wage-earners with less than one month of continuous employment and the unemployed continue to be excluded from any insurance scheme.

Those not covered by NHI are eligible for Medical Aid, which is a means-tested public assistance scheme which pays for 33 to 100 percent of the individual's medical care costs depending on the claimant's level of poverty. NHI and Medical Aid together cover the entire Korean population.

Korea's universal coverage was, however, achieved at the expense of an explosion in healthcare expenditures. Under the FFS system, private healthcare providers have the incentive to over-supply treatments with a higher profit margin (Hillman *et al.* 1989). For example, Cesarean delivery rate in Korea rose from 6 percent of all births in 1985 to 43 percent in 1999 which is not surprising given that it fetches 2.7 times more FSS (Fee for Service) than normal delivery (Kwon 2003). It is such profit-maximizing behavior that underlies the ballooning of Korea's health expenditure from 2.8 percent of GNP in 1975 to 3.9 percent in 1985, to 6.0 percent in 2005.

To rein in escalating healthcare costs, the government directed its efforts at containing consumer demand through mechanisms such as increased co-payment rate and expansion of excluded services and treatments. However, these attempts were largely unsuccessful as healthcare providers exploited their market power to expand supply and substitute uninsured medical services with insured services. As a result, the proportion of out-of-pocket payments in the total health expenditure declined only slightly despite a dramatic increase in health insurance coverage. The high proportion of private payment in Korea implies that the equity gains achieved through universal health coverage are tacitly eroded by high private payments.

Realizing the limitations of measures directed at consumers, in recent years the government has begun to focus more on providers. In 1997, the Healthcare Reform Committee recommended integration of the 350 separate health insurance societies into a single national scheme, reform of the pricing scheme for medical equipment and pharmaceuticals, and separation of prescription and dispensing of drugs. The medical profession vehemently opposed reforms directed at curbing their income, especially the proposed ban on their freedom to sell pharmaceuticals which was a major source of income. Eventually the government had to agree to a 45 percent hike in physicians' fees in 2000 which showed the power of the private healthcare providers to resist policy reforms. The combination of private provision and insurance financing remains the biggest obstacle to reforms aimed at containing healthcare expenditures in Korea.

Singapore

Great Britain left Singapore with a healthcare system dominated by the public sector in hospital care and the private sector in outpatient care, and the legacy continues to this day. The cost implications of the government shouldering the bulk of the hospital care costs became evident in the early 1980s following a rise in incidence of debilitating diseases and the growing realization of population ageing. Thus started reforms that have continued relentlessly for the last two decades in Singapore (Ramesh 2008).

The provision of healthcare in Singapore is characterized by a duality whereby hospital care is provided largely by the public sector and outpatient care by the private sector: 80 percent of hospital beds but only 20 percent of outpatient clinics are in the public sector. Beds in different wards in public hospitals are subsidized by the government to varying degrees, ranging from nil in the highest class ward (A) to 80 percent of costs in the lowest class (C) wards. The government creatively uses a combination of block payments and Casemix formula to pay public hospitals – which otherwise enjoy broad management autonomy – for providing subsidized healthcare.

The National Health Plan announced in 1983 was the government's first major effort to come to grips with its rising expenditures on public hospitals. The plan initiated a range of privatization measures designed to reduce the share of expenditures borne by the government. An individual medical savings account scheme, called Medisave, was established in 1984 to enable households to pay privately for their use of hospital care. Medisave requires compulsory saving of 6–8 percent of one's monthly income, depending on age. Since savings in Medisave is one's own money, it is expected that people will spend it cautiously. Nevertheless, there are a large number of exclusions, ceilings, and co-payment requirements to curb profligate drawing on the fund.

In the same year that Medisave was established, the government announced a plan to grant greater autonomy to government hospitals in managing their operations. Operational autonomy was intended to lead to greater competition, which in turn was expected to lead to lower costs and higher standards. The arrangements have been constantly tweaked to all hospitals' management autonomy while still allowing for government supervision.

In 1990, the government established a publicly managed but voluntary health insurance scheme called the Medishield to cover hospitalization expenses towards treatment for specified "serious" illnesses. Its establishment was in response to the realization that most Medisave accounts did not have sufficient funds to pay for treatment of serious illnesses. Medishield premiums are kept low by imposing a large number of exclusions and cost-sharing requirements. As a result, those with Medishield insurance need to bear up to three-quarters of the cost of major surgery from their own pocket (Tan and Beng 1997: 300–302).

The realization that there was a segment of the population that could not afford even highly subsidized healthcare led the government to establish a public assistance scheme called the Medifund in 1993. It is an endowment trust fund built on S$1 billion contribution from the government. To prevent dissipation of the fund, only income from the fund is used to pay assistance while the principal remains untouched. To receive assistance, applicants need to pass a severe means test.

Singapore is one of the smallest healthcare spenders in the world and, more remarkably, the share of the GDP devoted to health has actually declined over the last four decades. In the early 1960s, national health expenditures formed around 4.5 percent of GDP, but then declined and hovered around 3 percent of GDP, rising to 4.2 percent in recent years. The government's share of total health expenditures exceeded 50 percent in the late 1960s, but then declined to 25 percent by the mid-1990s, and in recent years has stayed within the 33 to 35 percent range. The government's low expenditure partially reflects the efficacy of its policies as well the government's capacity to resist popular pressures.

Thailand

Thailand's healthcare system in the early 1980s was remarkably similar to what exists in China today: hospitals were owned largely by the government but were financed largely from OOP payments, with overall healthcare expenditures rising rapidly. While the government ownership of hospitals has continued, the financing function has been assumed increasingly by the Thai government. The public sector currently accounts for almost 88 percent of all hospital beds, 79 percent of all doctors, and 64 percent of total health expenditures. As a result, Thailand now has probably the most public healthcare system in the region.

Public health financing in Thailand consists of three insurance schemes: Social Health Insurance (SHI) within the Social Security Scheme (which includes old age pension, among other benefits), the Civil Servants Medical Benefits (CSMBS) and Universal Healthcare scheme (UC), and together they cover almost the entire population. SHI is a compulsory contributory social insurance scheme for workers in private formal employment. CSMB, on the other hand, is a non-contributory tax-funded program for public sector employees, including active and retired military personnel, policemen, civil servants and employees of state enterprises, and up to three dependants. CSMB pays providers on a fee-for-service basis whereas SHI and UC pay on a capitation basis.

The UC scheme (popularly known as 30 Baht scheme) was launched by the government in 2001 amidst criticisms that it portended fiscal ruin for the country. Under the scheme, people not covered by SHI or CSMB can access healthcare by paying 30 Baht (US$0.7) per visit or per hospitalization. It provides comprehensive service coverage, including treatment for catastrophic illnesses and prescribed medication. It covers nearly two-thirds of the Thai population.

UC is now almost entirely funded from the government's general tax revenues, after the military government abolished the 30 Baht payment in 2006. The annual capitation amount per subscriber that UC pays to providers is 2,089 Baht (approximately US$65), up from 1,202 Baht in 2001. Diagnostic Related Groups (DRG) formula is employed to pay providers for inpatient care to discourage providers from under-servicing patients. UC members are required to register with one primary care provider and referral is needed to access higher level services available at general and specialist hospitals.

The National Health Security Office (NHSO) functions as the purchaser of medical services on behalf of both UC and SHI schemes. As the largest purchaser of medical services in the country, it is in a position to impose prices and service conditions on providers. It is, however, only recently that the NHSO began to use its purchasing power to control providers' behavior for the purpose of lowering costs and raising service standards.

Total healthcare expenditures formed 5 percent of GDP in 1990 and 3.5 percent in 2005 (Murray *et al.* 1994; WHO 2008). It is notable that total healthcare expenditures declined despite the expansion of social insurance during the 1990s (SHI) and 2000s (UC). At the same time, the government's share of total health expenditures increased from 44 percent in 1990 to 47 percent in 1996 and eventually to 64 percent in 2005.

Lessons in healthcare reform

An important lesson from the comparative study of the three Asian countries is that public hospitals are not a hindrance to containing healthcare expenditures, notwithstanding popular beliefs to the contrary. An overwhelming majority of hospital beds in Singapore and Thailand are in the public sector and healthcare expenditures as a percentage of GDP is low in both countries and have indeed declined or remained stable. The converse is true in Korea where provision is dominated by the private sector and total health expenditures have risen rapidly. The same is broadly applicable to China as its public providers are guided by the same surplus-maximizing motives as their private counterparts. It is arguable that the dominance of private providers makes it difficult for the government to control expenditures due to lack of direct control over most providers. Public ownership, on the other hand, allows the government opportunities for directly controlling hospitals' behavior and, by extension, their expenditures, provided it has the willingness and capacity for it.

Even more important than public ownership is, however, what the government does with it. Governments in Singapore and, to a lesser extent, Thailand closely monitor the performance of their public hospitals and exercise controls as regulators and purchasers as well as owners. Public hospitals in China, in contrast, have a nearly free rein in their operations – except for the dysfunctional price controls on certain essential care which only encourage providers to substitute them with more expensive services – and so there is no reason to expect public providers to behave differently from their private counterparts. Ownership in the healthcare sector is meaningful only if the government employs its ownership rights and actively monitors and guides the performance of its hospitals so as to make them meet social needs rather than generate surplus for their managers.

The four countries also offer vital lessons regarding financing of healthcare. Voluntary public health insurance favored by many reformers and currently being tried out in China with great optimism has a dismal record in the region. Korea had a voluntary health insurance in the 1960s, and Thailand through much of the 1980s and 1990s and their experience was entirely unsatisfactory. As both Korean and Thai policymakers found out, there is an inherent problem of adverse selection with voluntary schemes whereby the healthy stay out of it and only the aged and others more likely to be sick take it up. The situation improved only after the two governments adopted compulsory insurance covering the entire population.

However, compulsory universal insurance is an enormously expensive arrangement unless accompanied by appropriate restraints. This is most vividly illustrated in Korea where insurance coverage and costs rose in tandem due to the inability of the insurance agency to curb private providers' behavior. Thailand, on the other hand, experienced no such rise after the launch of SHI and UC due to public ownership of most providers and the capitation formula by which they are paid (discussed later in the chapter).

Singapore's case highlights the limited usefulness of the individual medical savings account as a mechanism for financing healthcare. After more than two decades of high contribution rates, the average account size of Medisave accounts remains small and the scheme forms only a small percentage of total healthcare in Singapore. This is unsurprising given that most people's income is not high enough to accumulate sufficient funds in their account to pay for expensive procedures entirely from their savings. Chinese policymakers who are expanding individual medical savings accounts with much enthusiasm should bear Singapore's experience in mind and accept that there is no alternative to risk-pooling in financing of healthcare.

The Asian cases studied here also demonstrate the limited potential of out-of-pocket payments for containing healthcare expenditures. The existence of high OOP in China and Korea has done little to contain rising healthcare expenditures. This is because the volume of healthcare consumed depends not just on what patients seek but what suppliers choose to provide due to well-known market failures – especially information asymmetries – that afflict the sector. The problem is reflected in the starkest form in China where expenditures have risen and access has deteriorated despite high and rising user charges.

There is a large scope for direct government funding in the healthcare sector because there are, and always will be, people who cannot be covered by any contributory financing scheme, be it insurance or savings. Thus Korea has Medicaid for those outside the NHI net and even the Singapore government subsidizes patients that cannot afford to pay for their healthcare. Thailand has gone the farthest and provides free healthcare to the nearly two-thirds of the population not covered by SCMB or SHI. And contrary to the widespread belief that government funding leads to management profligacy, total healthcare expenditures in Thailand have declined or remained constant despite a massive increase in coverage and admission rates.

But public financing needs to be accompanied by appropriate checks if expenditure blowout is to be prevented. This is especially so when the providers are paid on a FFS basis which encourage providers to supply more services than needed and more expensive services than necessary. This is the case in China and Korea as well as with the CSMB scheme in Thailand. The behavior is not particular to private providers, as public hospitals in Thailand until the 1990s and their counterparts in China to this day are reputed to over-price and over-supply medical services.

In contrast to FFS, prospective payments, either in the form of global budget (as in Singapore and Hong Kong) or capitation payment (as in Thailand) set an outer limit to expenditures, thereby forcing providers to stay within budgetary limits. Providers unable to maintain their costs below what they receive in payment must bear the loss. Capitation payment is a superior payment mechanism because it encourages providers to sign up members and retain them while still containing expenditures. Capitation also provides incentive to providers to invest in preventive care because otherwise they will later be spending more on curative care. The main limitation of capitation is that it incentivizes providers to under-provide services so that they can pocket the difference between capitation revenues and expenditures. Capitation system therefore requires effective service contracts to ensure that providers provide necessary services while still restraining expenditures. Both Singapore and Thailand have prospective payment systems that have played a critical role in restraining their overall healthcare expenditures. Indeed they have gone further by incorporating DRG and global budget components within their payment formula to shape providers' behavior.

But public financing accompanied by a prospective payment system is not easy to achieve as it requires a tremendous amount of capacity on the part of the state. Governments find it inordinately difficult to resort to prospective payment due to opposition from those who benefit from the FFS system. Here the Thai experience is instructive: it is improbable that the government would have been able to so easily launch UC were it not for the fact that most hospitals were owned by the government. Had the sector been dominated by private providers, it is likely they would have fought against the government's program which involved greater government control and relatively small payment for their services. In Singapore too, the public ownership of hospitals makes it easier for the government to exercise close controls over the providers. This is very different from the situation in Korea where providers are almost entirely private and are able to strongly resist government efforts to contain their behavior. Chinese policymakers should bear the Thai experience in mind before going further with ceding control over their public hospitals.

Conclusion

Many countries around the world are in the process of reforming their healthcare system to address the problem of rising expenditures in the face of growing demand and rising costs. However, only a few have succeeded and many more have aggravated the problem they were intended to address. A part of the problem lies in uncritical belief in market processes as a solution to public problems. Following spectacular successes with privatization and liberalization of civil aviations and telecommunications sectors in the 1980s, followed by similar measures with regard to other service industries such as banking and brokerage, governments around the world embarked on a "third" wave of reform targeting social sectors. Governments began to scale back their direct involvement in the social sectors without appreciating the specificities of these sectors which made the experience with earlier economic reforms inappropriate and even irrelevant.

Privatization of public hospitals, greater autonomy for managers of hospitals that remain in the public sector, subsidized voluntary insurance, and larger out-of-pocket payment backed by individual medical savings accounts are a part of the larger public management strategy built on belief on competition among providers and individual responsibility on the part of consumers. Governments persist with these reforms despite lack of evidence showing that market-oriented reforms work as believed in the healthcare sector. Yet the news is not all gloomy, as many governments have indeed reasserted their role in the healthcare sector, as the cases of Singapore and Thailand show.

The Chinese healthcare reforms are an extreme example of what reformers elsewhere should avoid. The combination of a high level of operational autonomy for hospitals and fee-for-service payment arrangement has been accompanied by rising expenditures and reduced access. Recent efforts to expand insurance coverage may reduce the OOP burden of those lucky enough to have it but will only aggravate the problems of rising expenditures unless accompanied by efforts to control the providers' behavior, as the Korean experience shows.

The combination of private providers and universal health insurance has wrecked fiscal havoc in Korea. The government initially sought to contain exploding expenditures by curbing demand through high user charges but with, understandably, little effect because it was as much a supply- as demand-induced problem. It is only recently that the government turned to controlling the providers' behavior but is finding it difficult in the face of opposition from private providers who dominate the system.

Singapore was an early and enthusiastic subscriber to reform ideas based on market competition and greater individual responsibility but began to refine and in some respects scale back its efforts after the ill-effects of earlier measures became evident. While autonomy for managers of public hospitals and the reliance on OOP continued, in the late 1990s the government changed the formula by which it paid the providers so as to discourage them from surplus-maximizing behavior. It has also employed its ownership and regulatory authority to a greater degree to ensure that providers do not use their management autonomy to take advantage of consumers. Recent reforms have emphasized further refinement of provider incentives to promote socially optimal competition.

However, Singapore's healthcare system exists in an atypical context characterized by a small but exceptionally strong and capable state and so its policies would be hard to replicate elsewhere. Thailand is a more typical developing country and hence its lessons are more relevant. The Thai system is characterized by public ownership of hospitals, tax-funding for the overwhelming majority of the population, and payment of providers on a capitation basis. Public ownership and tax-financing make for an equitable system, while capitation payment helps keep costs down. Another reason for the low overall expenditures is that the healthcare available is rather basic, which encourages those who can afford better services to purchase them from private providers.

A key policy lesson to emerge from this study is that successful healthcare systems are those in which the government actively manages the relationship between providers and consumers. This may be accomplished through public ownership or through public financing. Government ownership and/or financing allows the government, as the principal, to determine what is provided and at what price. These are highly effective instruments if used in conjunction with capitation payment coupled with appropriate regulations and enforcement to prevent under-supply. But adoption of an effective prospective payment system requires tremendous political and technical capacity on the part of the state which not all governments can be assumed to possess. To succeed not only do governments need to reassert their role in the healthcare sector, they also need to build their technical, administrative, and political capacity.

Bibliography

Blumenthal, D. and Hsiao, William (2005) "Privatization and its Discontents – The Evolving Chinese Health Care System", *The New England Journal of Medicine* 353(11): 1165–1170.

Bogg, Lennart, Hengjin, Dong, Keli, Wang, Wenwei, Cai and Diwan, Vinod (1996) "The Cost of Coverage: Rural Health Insurance in China", *Health Policy and Planning* 11(3): 238–252.

Development Research Center of State Council (2005) "An Evaluation and Recommendations on the Reforms of the Health System in China", *China Development Review* (supplement).

Eggelston, K. and Hsiesh, C. (2004) "Health Care Payment Incentives: A Comparative Analysis of Reforms in Taiwan, Korea and China", *Working Paper 2004*, Department of Economics, Tufts University, Medford, MA.

Eggleston, K. *et al.* (2006) "Health Service Delivery in China: A Literature Review", *World Bank Policy Research Working Paper 39778*, Washington, DC: World Bank.

Hillman, A. L., Pauly, M. V. and Kerstein, J. J. (1989) "How do Financial Incentives Affect Physicians' Clinical Decisions and the Financial Performance of Health Maintenance Organisations?", *New England Journal of Medicine* 321(2): 86–92.

Jeong, Hyoung-Sun (2005) "Health Care Reform and Change in Public–Private Mix of Financing: a Korean Case", *Health Policy* 74(2): 133–145.

Kwon, Soonman (2003) "Payment System Reform for Health Care Providers in Korea", *Health Policy and Planning* 18(1): 84–92.

Liu, X. and Hsiao, William (1995) "The Cost Escalation of Social Health Insurance Plans in China", *Social Science and Medicine* 41(8): 1095–1101.

Liu, Yuanli (2006) "Health Care in China: The Role of Non-government Providers", *Health Policy* 77(2): 212–220.

Lui, Y., Rao, K. and Hsiao, W. (2003) "Medical Expenditure and Rural Impoverishment in China", *Journal of Health, Population and Nutrition* 21(33): 216–222.

Meng, Qingyue and Liu, Xingzhu (2006) "Reforming China's Healthcare System: Beijing's Strategy for Establishing Universal Coverage", *China Brief* 6(24): 2.

Murray, C. J. L., Govindraj, R. and Musgrave, P. (1994) "National Health Expenditures: A Global Analysis", in C. J. L. Murray and A. D. Lopez (eds) *Global Comparative Assessments in the Health Sector*, Geneva: World Health Organization, pp. 141–156.

Ooi, Elaine Wee-Ling (2005) *The World Bank's Assistance to China's Health Sector*, The World Bank Operations Evaluation Department. Available at http://lnweb18.worldbank.org/oed/oeddoclib.nsf/DocUNIDViewForJavaSearch/E37AB8730BDD15628525 6FF000592DAA/$file/china_cae_health.pdf.

Ramesh, M. (2008) "Reasserting the Role of the State in the Healthcare Sector: Lessons from Asia", *Policy and Society* 27(2): 129–136.

Tan, Teck Meng and Beng, C. S. (eds) *Affordable Health Care: Issues and Prospects*, Singapore: Prentice Hall.

Wang, G., Xu, H. and Jiang, M. (2003) "Evaluation on Comprehensive Quality of 456 Doctors in Township Hospitals", *Journal of Health Resources* 6(3): 72–74.

Wong, C. K., Tang, K-L. and Lo, V. (2007) "Unaffordable Healthcare amid Phenomenal Growth: The Case of Healthcare Protection in Reform China", *International Journal of Social Welfare* 16(2): 140–149.

Wong, Victor C. W. and Chiu, Sammy W. S. (1997) "Health-care Reforms in the People's Republic of China: Strategies and Social Implications", *International Journal of Public Sector Management* 10(1): 76–92.

World Bank (2004) *The Health Sector in China: Policy and Institutional Review*, Working Paper Report No. 34525.

World Health Organization (2008) *World Health Statistics 2008*, Geneva: WHO.

Yip, W. and Hsiao, W. C. L. (2001) "Economic Transition and Urban Health Care in China: Impacts and Prospects", paper presented at the conference on financial sector reform in China, Harvard University.

Yu, Seung-Hum and Anderson, Gerard F. (1992) "Achieving Universal Health Insurance in Korea: A Model for other Developing Countries", *Health Policy* 20(3): 289–299.

8 Reassertions of the state in Viet Nam's health sector[1]

Jonathan D. London[2]

Until the late 1980s, the Communist Party of Viet Nam (CPV) promoted the development of an entirely state-financed health system designed to eventually provide health services to all Vietnamese as a right of citizenship. But the collapse of Viet Nam's state-socialist economic institutions in the late 1980s occasioned a dramatic scaling back of these ambitions and necessitated an urgent search for new institutional arrangements to support the provision and payment for health care. In 1987, Viet Nam's government permitted limited private provision of health care and in 1989 adopted a constitutional provision that permitted public health care providers to charge fees. Low public spending on health in subsequent years appeared to reflect both the fiscal weaknesses of the Vietnamese state and state leaders' willingness to shift institutional responsibilities for health payments on to households. By the early 1990s, 80 percent of total health expenditure was estimated to be out-of-pocket. Thus, in the span of a few years, institutional responsibilities for health payments in Viet Nam had been largely shifted onto households. Access to health services beyond a basic level were now largely contingent on households' spending power.

The history of health care in Viet Nam since the early 1990s is, however, more complex and interesting than a simple story of "commodification." Viet Nam during the 1990s did indeed experience catastrophic retrenchment in the health sector, the marketization of many aspects of health care, and the ill effects of these processes. But during the 1990s and especially in the current decade, the Vietnamese state has also reasserted its power in the health sector. In this essay, I explain the character and significance of these reassertions.

The analysis is organized in three sections. In the first section, I explain how the erosion of Viet Nam's planned economy in the late 1980s affected the principles and institutions governing the provision and payment for health care. In the second section I show that, even as Vietnamese political leaders resigned themselves to allowing markets and households a greater role in health sector governance, there was from a very early stage a discernable recursive element in health policy. That is, *alongside* policies that shifted the costs of health care from the state onto households, the CPV pursued certain *redistributive reassertions* of the state. Initially, these redistributive reassertions were small and took the form of legitimacy-seeking programs targeting such key constituencies as mothers of

fallen soldiers and certain war veterans. Gradually, these redistributive reassertions have expanded in their scale and scope. Through these redistributive reassertions, the Vietnamese state has sought to renew its commitment to promoting
universal access to health services, even as the state's success in so doing has
been decidedly mixed.

In the third section, I explain the genesis and outcomes of a quite different kind
of reassertion of the state in Viet Nam's health sector. Specifically, I show how,
alongside efforts to protect certain segments of the population from ill-effects of a
commodified health system, Viet Nam's health policies have also promoted *accumulative reassertions* of the state. By accumulative reassertions, I refer to a variety
of formal and informal measures the Vietnamese state has taken that promote
state-managed health care facilities as sites of economic accumulation. I explain
how, initially, accumulative reassertions of the state amounted to little more than
tacit state approval of certain informal practices, such as acceptance of gift payments by health workers and the keeping of double and triple books. Gradually,
however, the Vietnamese state more actively promoted economic accumulation in
the health sector as a way of reducing state-run health care service providers'
dependence on the central budget. These accumulative reassertions of the state,
which the state has now sought to recast as "social mobilization," has had four
major and in some respects contradictory results. They have enabled significant
increases in revenues among some state-run health facilities, and state-run hospitals in wealthier regions in particular. They have enabled increases in staff pay,
particularly in state-run hospitals in wealthier regions; they have exacerbated
health sector inequalities, as service providers in rich regions are able to more
easily "cash in" on market opportunities; and finally, promoting economic accumulation has had the practical effect of commercializing health care, reinforcing
(perverse) incentives to place private interests of health staff before public health.
The government's recent move to promote further (and weakly regulated) decentralization in the health sector threatens to intensify these perverse incentives.

Overall in this essay, I demonstrate that reassertions of the state in Viet
Nam's health sector have responded to the different and sometimes contradictory imperatives of *market-Leninism* (London 2003, 2009).[3] In market-Leninist
regimes, Communist Parties adopt market institutions and employ market-based
strategies of accumulation while retaining Leninist principles of political organization. In Viet Nam, the subjugation of health care to market principles and out-
of-pocket payments and the social consequences of these arrangements plainly
contradicted the historically rooted, self-legitimating ideologies of the Communist Party and created pressure on the state to provide various forms of social
protection through redistribution. On the other hand, public health expenditure
remained low and the health sector's increasing dependence on resources gar-
nered through market-based accumulation reinforced the desire of health service
providers to exploit market opportunities, thereby creating pressures toward the
further commercialization and commodification of health care.

In recent years, the Vietnamese state has continued to increase public spending on health, has extended fees-free health services to all children under age six,

and has promoted the development of a national health insurance scheme that presently counts 37 million beneficiaries. As recently as 2005, however, an estimated 70 percent of total health expenditures were out of pocket and improvements in health status continues to be uneven across regions and different segments of the population.[4] Whether reassertions of the state in Viet Nam's sector will contribute to the development of a health system that meets the needs of most Vietnamese is very much an open question.

I Health sector retrenchment and its consequences

Viet Nam's health system is the product of a four-decade effort to build a comprehensive state-financed national health system; the subsequent erosion of that system in the 1980s; and the intended and unintended consequences of health policies introduced since the late 1980s. The rapid economic growth that Viet Nam has experienced since the early 1990s has permitted rapid increases in total health expenditure. But low *public* expenditure combined with other state policies have made access to health services contingent on cash payments, while spatially uneven development and weak health sector governance have contributed to sharp divergences in the costs, qualities, and distributions of health care services across different regions and segments of the population. Today, Viet Nam's health policies aim to combine state, household, and insurance sources of finance in a way that would ensure all Vietnamese access to health services.

Building a state-socialist health system[5]

Viet Nam's health policies up until the mid 1980s were "state-socialist" and universalist. Health policies were state-socialist in that they were designed to achieve a state-financed health system based on the collectivist, centrally planned economic institutions of state socialism. At all levels, health services were to be financed through a combination of transfers from the central budget and local resources. In rural areas, agricultural collectives would be responsible for financing the activities of commune-level health workers, while medicine, materials, and labour were allocated through the planned economy. Viet Nam's health policies were universalist in that they promised preventive and curative health services free of charge as a right of citizenship.[6]

The social and health outcomes of socialist universalism were mixed. On the one hand, the institutionalization of state-funded health services in Viet Nam contributed to declines in child mortality and morbidity, and gradually improved access to all types of medical care. On the other hand, the prevailing scarcity of resources severely limited the quality, scale, and scope of public health services across northern Viet Nam and across the entire country after 1975. As in other state-socialist societies, the health system in Viet Nam both reflected and reproduced state-socialist inequalities. Access to comprehensive care was a formal right of citizenship, but the actual availability and quality of services was limited: state elites and urban populations enjoyed greater access and better quality services than did rural and politically marginal masses.

Four successive decades of war (with France, the US, Cambodia, and China) placed enormous strains on the economy and the health system in particular. Large areas of the country remain unserved or underserved by the national health network. But by the mid-1980s, the CPV had overseen the development of a sprawling state-financed health system. Viewed historically, the universalist health policies that the CPV pursued in northern Viet Nam since the 1950s and on a national basis after 1975 were truly revolutionary, as they promised universal access to preventive and curative health services as a right of citizenship. However, the consequences of Viet Nam's poor economic performance and wars severely diminished the amount of public resources available for investment in health. Indeed, the fiscal foundations of Vietnamese state socialism were on the verge of collapse.

Health care and state-socialist involution

The erosion of state-socialist economic institutions in Viet Nam during the 1980s emasculated budgetary resources for health and hobbled the functioning of the state in virtually all its aspects. Declining state revenues and the dissolution of state-socialist economic institutions eviscerated the fiscal foundations of universalist health provision. Budgetary transfers to hospitals at the provincial and district levels shrank. As agricultural cooperatives failed or dissolved, so too did the financial bases of the CHS. Clinics and hospitals struggled to function while health workers' morale plummeted. In many areas, hospital workers went months without wages and had to resort to various improvisational strategies to make ends meet.

In 1987, to alleviate financial strains on the health system, the CPV sanctioned the private provision of health services as well as the limited private sale of pharmaceutical drugs.[7] In 1989, the CPV (acting through the rubber stamp National Assembly) granted the government formal constitutional authority to introduce user fees. This resulted in the Prime Minister's Decision No. 45, which formally permitted the 'collection of partial expenses' (*thu một phần kinh phí*) in public (i.e., state-run) clinics and hospitals.[8] However, the continuation of the dire fiscal situation meant that conditions in the health sector deteriorated, further limiting the quality, scale, and scope of state-financed health services and gradually affecting their utilization as seen in Figure 8.1.

Whether and to what extent declines in utilization are due to the poor quality of services or the introduction of user fees remains the subject of debate. What was clear was that the health sector faced a catastrophic failure of public financing and that the collapse of state socialism would require new institutional arrangements for health finance.

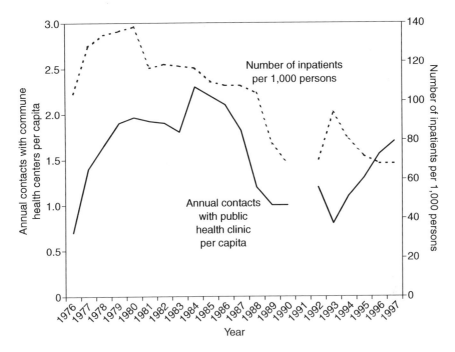

Figure 8.1 Utilization rates at public health facilities, 1976–1998 (source: adapted from MOH, World Bank (1993, 2001)).

Health policies after 1989 and their outcomes

What emerged after 1989 was a largely ad hoc and at times incoherent patchwork of policies whose principal thrust have been to reduce the state's financial responsibility for health care while at the same time seeking to maintain the state's leading role in its provision. More specifically, the most salient features of Viet Nam's health policies since 1989 have been low public expenditure, the consequent shifting of financial responsibilities for health payment from the state onto households, and sustained efforts to frame this shifting of financial responsibilities in a rhetoric of state-led social mobilization. Combined with weak health sector regulation and spatially uneven economic growth, these policies contributed to the increasing subordination of health care and health to the logic of markets.

Low public expenditure

The most significant attribute of health policies in Viet Nam since 1989 has undoubtedly been the state's low public spending on health. This was unavoidable, as the fiscal crisis that Viet Nam encountered in the late 1980s drained the state of financial resources. However, through nearly two decades of rapid economic growth and continuous increases in revenue, public health spending in

Viet Nam has not increased markedly as a proportion of GDP, as state expenditures on other social policy fields such as education have (Figure 8.2).

The fiscal weakness and incapacities of the Vietnamese state in the early 1990s certainly prevented the possibility of a swift return to a state-financed system. And economic growth and increases in the scale of the state budget meant that there have been significant absolute increases in public health expenditure. However, public health expenditure has remained low as a proportion of GDP relative to other sectors and has not been sufficient to address the country's health needs.

Internationally, Viet Nam's *public* spending on health remains quite low in per capita terms. As of 2007, this accounted for roughly 6 percent of the central budget, whereas it represents 18.8 percent in Cambodia, 17.1 percent in Thailand, and 10 percent in China.[9] As of 2006, public health spending on health in Viet Nam (from the state budget) accounted for roughly 18 percent of total health expenditure, while total public expenditure (comprising budget, insurance, and foreign aid) accounted for 31 percent of total health expenditure. By the mid-1990s, Vietnamese households were shouldering an estimated 80 percent of the total costs of health services through out-of-pocket payments. Today, by all estimates, over 60 percent of total health expenditure is out of pocket. Total per capita health spending was US$46 by 2006. As recently as 2006, government health expenditure declined, with 2006 outlays only amounting to 86 percent of 2005 figure, in real terms.[10] The significance of future increases in public health expenditure will need to be assessed against increases in the costs of care, particularly as Viet Nam in 2007–2008 experienced an inflation of over 30 percent (London and Ufford 2008).

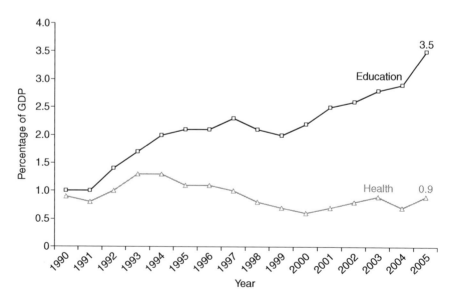

Figure 8.2 State education and health spending as a percentage of GDP (source: GSO).

Some implications of low public spending

The main implication of this shift was that access to health services beyond a basic level would become – in principle and in practice – increasingly contingent on households' ability to mount out-of-pocket payments. The dependence of health treatment on cash payments tends to contribute to inequity in the accessibility of health services. The health system favors wealthier, urban-based population segments that have better access to better facilities. The poorest population segments (poor and "near-poor") remain vulnerable in the face of high, privately borne costs of care.

Health care in Viet Nam is proportionately more expensive for the poor. Tipping (2000, cited in Segall and Associates, 2002) has used 5 percent of income as a benchmark for "affordable health care." Research published in 2000 found that among households who reported illness, spending on health care amounted to 22 percent of poor households' income, compared to only 8 percent for the non-poor (Segall and Associates 2002). Data suggested that by 2004, such conditions persisted, as is suggested in Table 8.1.

As Table 8.1 shows, although the poorest quintile of households' expenditure on health amounted to only 30 percent of that of the richest quintile, health expenditure for poor households consumed over 40 percent of household income (MOH 2005: 23). The high costs of treating illness frequently forces poor households to borrow money from neighbors, sell assets, or seek loans from moneylenders, with the result that many households descend into the health poverty trap – arriving back home from illness weaker, poorer, and in debt. Data from the 2006 Viet Nam Households Living Standards survey suggest these trends have persisted, but could not be quoted for this publication.

It is also important to recognize that low public spending on health also means low wages in the health sector. Indeed, until recently, health sector workers were among the worst paid of all state workers in Viet Nam. With respect to recurrent versus capital expenditures, recurrent expenditures account for roughly 75 percent of the annual health budget. Data indicate that in the period from 1991 to 1993 salaries and wages in the health sector increased from 16 to 28 percent of state budget health expenditure and from 36 to 47 percent during the period 1998 to 2000 (Sea Change 2006). (This reflects salary increases for state workers.) Low wages, in turn, have contributed to low morale, and have also contributed to the proliferation of informal "gift" payments to doctors, a further source of inequity.

Weak health sector governance has compounded Viet Nam's problems in the health sector. Viet Nam's health sector has always functioned in a more decentralized manner than its formal organization would suggest. But in the transition to a market economy, the MOH was also slow to adopt appropriate governance functions and remains particularly weak with respect to information, planning, monitoring, and strategy (Fritzen 2007). The government's overall move towards decentralization continues to shift the locus of financial discretion away from the center. The share of total public expenditure from the budget spent by local

Table 8.1 Average annual per capita expenditure/inpatient care by income expenditure quinti e (2004)

Expenditure group	Average annual per capita expenditure on inpatient care ('000s of VNĐ)	Percentage of those who must pay over VNĐ 1 million	Average annual per capita income	Inpatient costs as a proportion of income (%)
Poorest	511.1	12.1	1,262	40.5
Near-poor	744.8	16.8	1,922	38.8
Average	794.0	18.7	2,459	32.3
Better off	1,152.9	23.1	3,336	34.6
Richest	1,865.3	37.9	7,359	25.3

Source: MOH (2005: 23).

governments has increased over the years to an estimated 48 percent in 2005, while the figure for the health sector hovers around 80 percent (SRV and World Bank 2005). The MOH's ability to regulate a highly decentralized health system is among the most important question marks in the evolution of Viet Nam's health policies. As it stands Viet Nam's health system exhibits many of the attributes of health systems in poorly regulated market economies.

Ideological adjustments

The increasing contingence of health care on cash payments poses special problems for a Communist Party. In the early 1990s, CPV ideologues justified departures from socialist principles by emphasizing the limited financial powers of the state. Since the early 1990s, Party ideologues have developed a rhetoric of rationalizing cost-shifting under the heading of 'socialization' *(xã hội hóa)*. As a long-time health official and one of the coiners of the concept "socialization" expressed in a manual for commune level officials:

> The concept of socialization should be understood as an effective and planned cooperation of activities of all social forces following a national direction and a strategy aiming to resolve a social problem ... For each community, family, citizen, socialization is understood as a process of response to and participation in the leaders' mobilization movement, then becoming a process of active and conscious activities for the sake of improving their own quality of life ... Socialization is understood as a "social solution" of highly inter-sectoral characteristics, with the participation of many social forces.
>
> (Đam 1997)

With some emblematic flourishes, the CPV has promoted "socialization" as a collective mass-mobilization response to "the new situation." Indeed, in its most recent English language publications, Vietnamese state agencies translate socialization as "social mobilization," though "socialization" not "social mobilization" is still used in Vietnamese. The rhetoric of socialization is evocative of that from mass mobilizations of Viet Nam's wartime and immediate post-war years. The Party line on "socialization" has become an entrenched feature of health policy in Viet Nam. It is lauded as the "correct policy" and is invoked to justify many things, from the need for people to "contribute" fees, to exhorting state-owned enterprises to contribute charitable donations, to the need to promote the privatization of certain aspects of the public health system. As we will see later, these terms "socialization" and (now) "social mobilization" have also become standard rationale deployed by the state to justify its need to promote economic accumulation within state-run health facilities.

II Redistributive reassertions of the state

From the time the CPV began to liberalize Viet Nam's health sector, it has also taken steps to protect various segments of the population through a variety of redistributive means. It has done so in three principal ways: through "safety-net" programs designed to ensure access to health services for certain segments of the population; through efforts to salvage and gradually expand the national network of state-run and state subsidized health providers, including commune health stations and state hospitals; and through the gradual development of a national health insurance system. As I will show, these redistributive reassertions of the state in the health sector have addressed different and at times even contradictory state imperatives and their impacts on the health of Vietnamese people have been mixed.

Safety nets: protecting the poor and vulnerable while protecting
legitimacy

Since 1989, Viet Nam has developed a system of safety nets designed to protect certain segments of the population from the vagaries of a marketized health system. Initially, these safety nets appeared mainly to be legitimacy seeking, as they offered protection for the CPV's most valued political constituencies and only a limited array of disadvantaged groups. Only several years later, in 1993 and 1994, did the state initiate measures specifically targeting the poor, and these measures did not take effect until the late 1990s. With expanding state revenues, the CPV has called for the gradual expansion of these safety-net programs. In 2005, the state began a program offering health services to all children under the age of five. Current plans are to eventually merge these safety nets into the national health insurance system, which is addressed later in this section.

When the CPV decided to permit the collection of user fees in 1989, it had major concerns about the potentially adverse impacts of fees. Fees contradicted Article 61 of the 1980 Constitution not to mention a tenet of state socialism. Some localities even refused to consider collecting fees, at least at the beginning. There were reasons for concern. Fees-for-services threatened not only to undermine the health and wellbeing of the population, but also to alienate several of the Party's key political constituencies. Hence, the Prime Minister's Decision No. 45 not only permitted the collection of fees, but dictated that fee exemptions or reductions be extended to ten different qualifying groups, which included members of certain political "priority groups" (such as certain veterans and mothers of certain fallen soldiers, as well as children and orphans).

The fee exemptions and reductions listed in Decision 45 had their limits. First, the granting of exemptions remained dependent on the discretion of local Party cells and hospital administrators. Second, the list of those eligible was quite limited and conspicuously made no mention of "the poor." Perhaps most fundamentally, even at this early stage, the exemptions and reductions granted covered only a portion of the actual expenses incurred by those seeking treatment. Given the list of beneficiaries eligible for fee reductions and exemptions, it is hard not to conclude that the first round of fee exemptions and reductions were largely or at least significantly legitimacy-seeking measures.

But in 1993 and 1994, the scale and scope of the state's health sector safety nets increased, as the state took measures to extend fee exemptions and reductions to the poor. In 1993, the government introduced its Hunger Eradication and Poverty Reduction program (HEPR). The HEPR was actually a set of programs designed to ameliorate the widening gap between high- and low-growth regions and between richer and poorer segments of the population by extending exemptions for health, education, and other services to government-designated poor communes and individuals falling below the state-set poverty line. In 1994, the government introduced Decree 95 (of 1994), which stated that those certified by local authorities as officially poor would be exempted from fees, with charges to be covered by the regular budget of the local public health provider. Administering the HEPR program was a massive undertaking. It was not until 1998 that the government even specified the institutional arrangements for the implementation of these programs.

By the end of 1998, the state had established HEPR boards in 6,958 communes (out of 7,515 at the time), and local authorities commenced their poverty-accounting efforts – using government criteria to identify "poor" households in each commune. The government issued a number of additional policies intended to identify and assist especially needy (usually "remote" and "especially difficult") areas and ethnic minority groups. This included Decision 135, which stipulated medical fees exemptions for entire "poor" villages. However, the total value of fee exemptions granted by hospitals during the period 1998 to 2000 amounted to less than 4 percent of hospital expenditures during the same period. Decisions to grant exemptions again remained subject to the discretion of individual hospitals contingent on the availability of funds, and criteria determining who was "officially" poor were not consistently applied (MOH 2005).

Viet Nam's continuous economic growth and increasing government revenues permitted gradual expansions of the fee exemptions schemes. The first of these occurred in 1999, when the Council of Ministers issued Circular 5, which stipulated health insurance for all households certified as "hungry" as well as those households in the 30 poorest percentile of the poor in any given locality (not including those localities under Program 135). Funding for this program was, in principle, to be met by a combination of national and local budget sources, as well as "contributions" from "social and economic organizations." While local funding arrangements were mandatory – their actual scale and impact depended heavily on the finances of localities (MOH 2005).

In 2002, the government expanded this same model in the form of Decision 139 and Circular 14 which, in addition to setting a new criterion of eligibility for fee exemptions and reductions (in part, in accordance with a new poverty line), also stipulated that all provinces must establish "health care funds for the poor." Decision 139 also clarified the government's intent to phase out fee exemptions and reductions by drawing the poor into the national health insurance program, analyzed further below. By 2002, all provinces had established a Health Care for the Poor Fund and Management Board, and by 2004, there were some 13.1 million beneficiaries, accounting for 16 percent of the entire population. By one estimate, in 2004, the total funds committed for Decision 139 was VNĐ717.7 billion, or roughly US$43 million (Trần 2005).

Perhaps the most ambitious fees exemptions scheme of all was announced in March of 2005, when the government issued Decree 36, granting all children less than six years of age free medical treatment.[11] Some foreign observers regarded this exemption scheme as an example of a "delusional" state policy, in that it is one the state could not possibly afford (Harvard 2008). Nonetheless, the policy has been carried out. In 2005, household surveys in three provinces showed over 80 percent of children had been issued such cards. People surveyed in the research reported their appreciation of the policy in principle, but complained that without referrals they could only get treatment at the CHS, where equipment and doctors were regarded as inferior, that the paperwork required was excessive, and that when using the cards at hospitals they were subject to long waits (Phan 2006).[12] When asked in an interview in 2008 whether this policy was indeed delusional, a senior member of the National Assembly Committee on Budgetary Affairs acknowledged the difficulties, but said the policy would remain as a "goal."[13] Gradually, funding for this program has increased, whereby hospitals are reimbursed VNĐ130,000 per child treated (as of 2008), though the policy only provides treatment for common and basic maladies and there is effectively no guidance for addressing more costly treatments. Many hospital staff claim to be experiencing difficulties owing to delays and red tape in the reimbursement process (MOH-HPG 2008).

Overall, fee exemptions and reductions, though they have grown in scope, still only reach a limited proportion of the population. Across provinces, districts, and communes, there remains wide variation reported in the accuracy and efficacy of poverty accounting, with numerous reports of patronage involving the arbitrary designation of certain communes and certain households. Existing safety-net programs also generally fail to capture economic migrants. Perhaps most fundamentally, fee exemptions cover only one component of the costs of health services, and poor persons have a hard time making up the large gap between formal fees and other costs, such as transport, medicines, food, lodging fees for relatives, and informal payments. Despite these limitations, the scale and impacts of fee exemptions has grown over time and represent a significant reassertion of the state's role in the health sector.

Salvaging and strengthening the state-run health network

The collapse of state-socialist institutions in the late 1980s placed the financial viability of the state-run health sector into question. Since the late 1980s, public health expenditure has remained low as a proportion of GDP and low in comparison with other countries. However, Viet Nam – first with foreign donor support and later on its own – has effectively preserved and strengthened the state-run health network, and state health providers remain the most important providers of health services. Many of the improvements in the country's health status since 1989 may be linked to the state's maintenance of a basic floor of health services – primarily through the continued public finance of commune health stations and public hospitals.

The commune health stations (CHS) were always a core element in Viet Nam's national health system. In the early 1990s, however, the CHS were facing acute shortages owing principally to an absence of local sources of financial support. In 1994, Viet Nam's Prime Minister issued Decision 58, which permitted use of the central budget (through province budgets) to pay and or supplement salaries for three to five CHS staff per commune. Though most of this supplemental funding came into the budget from foreign donors, Decision 58 is credited with improving the income and morale of CHS workers and perhaps even rescuing the primary health system of the country. Notably, no such policy support was given to primary care providers in China (Đang *et al.* 2006).[14]

In addition to stabilizing salaries, the state moved to increase the numbers and coverage of the CHS, with some success. In 1993, 800 communes in Viet Nam still lacked a CHS and 88 communes lacked both a CHS and a health worker. By 2004, 98 percent (or all but 149) of communes had a CHS and at least one health worker, while 67.8 percent of communes had a doctor. By 2002, 93 percent of communes had a trained midwife, and 90 percent of hamlets (below the commune level) had at least one active health worker, who were paid as low as VNĐ100,000 (US$5.50) per month (MOH 2005). The central government also reasserted its role by specifying funding norms. In 2002, Circular 2002 required all CHS to maintain a basic operational budget of no less than VNĐ10 million per year, not including wages or funds for health for the poor. It also established a range of compulsory funding norms for the CHS, with the local People's Committee to be held accountable in the case of any shortfalls (Đang *et al.* 2006). By 2006, Viet Nam counted some 10,672 state-run clinics at the commune and precinct level (GSO 2007: 559).

Beyond primary health care, Viet Nam's state has continued to expand and upgrade its network of public hospitals, which now exceeds 1,000 in number. The scale and functions of Viet Nam's hospitals fall into three main groups, corresponding to secondary, tertiary, and quaternary levels of medical care.[15] Viet Nam's 597 district-level hospitals provide the most basic level of hospital care and constitute the secondary level of services provision in the country's health system. On average, district level hospitals have fewer than 80 beds (MOH 2000). Viet Nam's 324 province-level hospitals constitute the tertiary level of health. Province-level hospitals and large urban hospitals are administered by Provincial and City Health Departments, respectively. They range from 300 to 500 beds in size. Providing services at the quaternary level of care along with standard outpatient services are Viet Nam's 31 centrally managed hospitals. These are the largest and most technically sophisticated hospitals and average over 500 beds. Almost all are located in Viet Nam's largest cities.

In terms of utilization, district hospitals are the most common site of treatment for Viet Nam's large rural population and for the rural poor. District hospitals, however, vary widely in their sophistication and in the quality of services provided. Unevenness in the quality of district hospitals tends to be reinforced by continued uneven development across localities, combined with a fiscal system which, though redistributive in important respects, fails to compensate for the greater need of poor localities and their populations.

Provincial hospitals serve the curative and outpatient needs of both local and regional populations. In comparison to district hospitals, province-level hospitals have seen faster growth in services utilization and many show serious signs of congestion. Hospitals at the central level are the most congested in part because they offer (or are perceived to offer) the highest quality and most sophisticated services. In addition to handling the most complex medical procedures, Viet Nam's centrally managed hospitals are the preferred location for treatment by Viet Nam's increasingly wealthy urban populations.

Although Viet Nam's public spending on health has remained low, the state has evidenced a commitment to gradually expanding the number and upgrading the quality of its public hospitals. In 1989, Viet Nam had 774 hospitals (MOH 1991). By 2008 there were 1,119 (MOH-HPG 2008). In 1994, the MOH initiated a program to upgrade medical equipment in the country's hospitals and, by 2000, most central and province-level hospitals were – according to state standards – "adequately equipped," while roughly 60 percent of district hospitals had x-ray machines and 92 percent had ambulances (Đang *et al.* 2006). Viet Nam's public hospitals are easily the most important site for medical treatment. While the number of private doctors in Viet Nam is increasing, the number of private hospitals remains small. As of December 2007, Viet Nam had 74 private or "non-public" hospitals, with some 5,600 beds, accounting for roughly 3 percent of the national total (*Tài Chinh Tháng* ibid.).

Health insurance

Evidence of the CPV's early concern with the impacts of commoditizing health was also visible in the Party's early expressed intent to develop a national health insurance system. Indeed, the same government decision that permitted the collection of fees for services in 1989 and the listing of those who were to receive exemptions and reductions also made deliberate mention of the need for the development of a health insurance system. Initially, the Party viewed health insurance principally as a mechanism for mobilizing resources for the health sector in a climate of acute scarcity (Axelson 2007). Only later did health insurance policies indicate the ambition of building a stable mechanism of health finance for the entire country.

Since the early 1990s, the state has made concerted efforts to make the health insurance system more coherent and unitary, though with limited results. In September 1994, voluntary health insurance for school children (six years old until university) was introduced through Circular 14 (Ministry of Education and

Training [MOET] and Ministry of Health [MOH], 1994), and by the 1995/96 school year, about half of provincial health insurance offices had established school health insurance.

Two features of health insurance in Viet Nam during the 1990s were particularly noteworthy: First, membership was on an individual basis: dependants were not covered and are not covered up until the present. This runs contrary to international best practices in health insurance and has probably contributed to the low uptake of health insurance by several population groups. Until recently, the national health insurance program left large segments of the population unprotected; the introduction of a new poverty line in 2005 will expand the numbers eligible for the national targeted program (Health Care Fund for the Poor), while proposed revisions to that program will make qualifying "near-poor" persons eligible for subsidized health insurance. Still, health insurance covers individuals, not households. The actual administration of health insurance poses practical problems for poor beneficiaries and Viet Nam's growing population of economic migrants are left uninsured.

Second, until the late 1990s, the poor were not covered by health insurance and tens of millions of rural people were largely left out of the scheme. Notably, Decree 299 did not include provisions for covering the poor and vulnerable. Provinces were instead encouraged to set up their own support systems for these groups (ibid). Like fee exemptions, Viet Nam's health insurance policies have had a significance corporatist element: a government ordinance issued in 1995 stipulated health insurance would be granted to certain veterans and mothers of certain fallen soldiers through the compulsory insurance scheme. As Axelson notes, the poor would eventually become covered by health insurance through polices introduced in 1999 and 2002, as would dependants of three groups: dependants of military officers in active service (Decree 63 in 2002), beneficiaries of the Health Care Fund for the Poor (Decision 139 in 2002), and dependants of policy officers in active service (Decree 63 in 2005). But these later developments came only after 2002, the period in which the state began to be more assertive in the pursuit of health insurance.

Since 2002, the government of Viet Nam has been more assertive in its approach to health insurance. Health insurance is compulsory for workers in the formal sector and represents an increasingly important mechanism for health payment, even as the budget remains, by far, the largest source of funding for hospitals and other public providers of health services in Viet Nam. By 2006, roughly 40 percent of Viet Nam's population was covered by health insurance (MOH HPG 2007). Yet 50 percent of Viet Nam's population may be qualified as "near-poor": poor enough to be severely impacted by catastrophic health costs but not "poor enough" to qualify for free health insurance.

Viet Nam repeatedly states its aim of achieving universal coverage of the population by 2010, though in recent months it has hardly mentioned this target, and has instituted policies that seem to take a step back. Recent developments in the health insurance scheme evidence confused priorities and unresolved issues. A health insurance ordinance rolled out in 2004, promised benefits that were

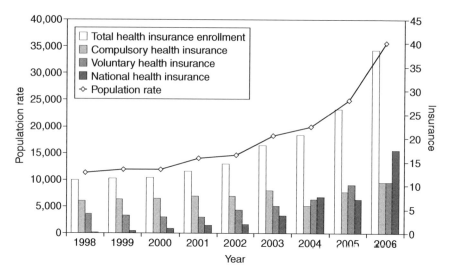

Figure 8.3 Health insurance enrollment, 1998–2006 (source: Nghiem Tran Dung (2007)).

later deemed financially unsustainable, while a subsequent decision rolled back benefits but also increased the price of subscription, pricing out rural households. A more recent government decision raised the cost of voluntary health insurance while reducing coverage. These more recent decisions appeared to lead to a decline in voluntary enrollment, particularly among the poor. The debate about whether to make the health insurance scheme compulsory remains unresolved as of mid-2008.

III Accumulative reassertions of the state

In the wake of state socialism, Vietnamese health policymakers had to find new institutional arrangements to govern the financing of health services. On the one hand the state's low public expenditure on health has shifted many of the burdens of health finance onto households. On the other hand, it has created powerful incentives within the health sector to maximize budgetary and non-budgetary sources of revenue through both licit and illicit means. While the government has taken a number of significant steps to protect the population from the pernicious effects of fees-based public services, it has simultaneously taken steps to promote economic accumulation within the public sector, so as to reduce public service delivery units' reliance on public finance. This "reassertion" of the state amounts to an effort by the state to improve the financial performance of public-service delivery units by promoting the commercialization of those units' operations.

Accumulation in the health sector: from cost recovery to commercialization

In their pursuit of state goals, states need resources and revenue in particular. Viet Nam's efforts to bolster its "extractive" capacity has taken many forms, though doing so at local levels of governance (versus at ports and in industrial parks) has proven difficult. These reassertions of the state include the expansion of "cost-recovery" mechanisms, the legalization of private provision of health services within or loosely connected to nominally public health facilities, and the autonomization of public hospitals aimed at the expansion of revenues. These formally sanctioned accumulative reassertions of the state exist alongside and in combination with other forms of accumulation within the health system, including unsanctioned but institutionalized forms, such as "gift payments" to medical staff and informal arrangements whereby hospitals lease equipment from their own staff. These payments have been tolerated by the state, largely because most doctors relied on such payments for the lion's share of their incomes. In Viet Nam, privatization of health service delivery has occurred largely (though not exclusively) within the formal shell of nominally public service providers.

Another illustrative example of autonomous accumulation in the health sector occurred in response to the 2005 policy on health care for children under the age of six. Although some provinces already had similar policies in place on a small scale, the introduction of this national decree led to an explosion in the number of patients in the public health system, particularly in hospitals (*Tài Chính Tháng* May 2005). At the Central Pediatrics Hospital, for example, average outpatient numbers soared from between 600–700 per day to some 1,000–1,200 per day after the Decree's introduction. The hospital's 530 beds, already overloaded before the decree, were after the decree facing some 900 patients. For hospital staff, the volume of work doubled while salaries remained constant. Nurses responsible for administering injections of various kinds saw an increase from 15–20 patients per day to roughly 50 per day. Pediatrics hospitals in Ha Noi and Ho Chi Minh City quickly devised strategies to recover costs by offering "policy" and "non-policy" streams for patients, whereby the latter received preferential treatment in special rooms and even new wards under the rubric "Services on Demand," in exchange for fees. This tiered arrangement for higher and low or no-fee paying users is quickly developing into an institutionalized feature of health care provision, and is in some respects actually being promoted by the state, as I will argue below.

I believe the state's reassertions in the sphere of accumulation have emerged in response to the state's weak extractive and allocative capacities and functions to achieve and maintain the subjective legitimacy of key political constituencies within the state and among important international constituencies, including international financial institutions, supranational trade organizations, and foreign investors.

The financial autonomization of hospitals

Since 1989, the state has gradually but unmistakably promoted "cost-recovery" and other methods to finance services. But the most decisive movement toward an accumulative reassertion has come more recently, in a decision by the CPV (and its state) to embrace autonomization of public services, including health services. As is often the case with decentralization and autonomization schemes, this one was conceived largely without consideration of its health sector impacts.

At the center of the discussion are two government decrees – Decree 10 (effective in 2004) and its replacement, Decree 43 (effective in 2006). The stated aims of these decrees are to improve the quality of public services by conferring greater financial and managerial autonomy to public service delivery units. Specifically, the decrees grant service delivery units greater discretion over service organization, the allocation of financial resources, and the management of personnel. The decrees encourage public service delivery units to finance service upgrades and "resolve" staff wage costs through the development of alternative non-budgetary sources of revenue. To this end, the decrees also encourage service delivery units to adopt a "business model of management" so as to more energetically "mobilize financial resources from society." Decrees 10 and 43 represent an historic shift in the formal principles and institutions governing the provision and payment for public services in Viet Nam's hospitals.

Decrees 10 and 43 are likely to affect all aspects of health service delivery and all segments of Viet Nam's population. That said, a major focus of this section is whether and how Decrees 10 and 43 will affect the quality and accessibility of hospital services in Viet Nam, particularly for poor and near-poor segments of the country's population. Skeptics of decentralization fear that Decrees 10 and 43 will promote the commercialization and commodification of health services, resulting in the worsening of health sector inequalities – a development that would be at odds with the stated principles of the Communist Party of Viet Nam. By contrast, defenders of Decrees 10 and 43 suggest that by reducing hospitals' overall reliance on the central budget, the decrees will free up scarce budgetary resources, which can then be channeled to those in greatest need.

It bears emphasis that Decrees 10 and 43 do not merely amount to the "legalization of existing practices," even if their implementation does formally accommodate certain forms of institutionalized de facto decentralization and autonomization. Instead, Decrees 10 and 43 actively promote autonomization as a reform strategy. The decrees represent an attempt at reform through autonomization and commercialisation, and the implementation of the decrees will give local health service delivery units a direct role in deciding the direction and substance of health care reforms.

While Decrees 10 and 43 do not amount to the outright privatization of services, the thrust of Decree 43 is unmistakable: to reduce the burden on the central budget and encourage units to develop new forms of income, in the interest of upgrading the quality and range of services as well as covering staff pay. The emphasis on transitioning to a commercial model of governance is a striking reminder of how far Viet Nam has come from central planning. On the other hand, formally stated aims do not ensure positive outcomes and formally stated principles do not guarantee adherence to principles. Indeed, if there is a "dark cloud" hovering over the implementation of Decrees 10 and 43 in Viet Nam's health sector, it is international experience with similar measures, in which principles such as accountability, transparency, and responsiveness were cast aside.

Without effective systems of monitoring, regulation, and information sharing, decentralization by decree can ironically eventuate in a situation of "bottom up" decentralization, to the extent that lower levels of government become mainly concerned with "beating" the system (Painter 2006). Studying responses to decentralizing decrees therefore requires cognizance of both formal and informal dimensions of decentralization. It may also result in the further and formalized development of a tiered system in which health services for the rich and poor become split (IHSP 2008). The autonomization of health service delivery currently underway in Viet Nam may well counteract some of the redistributive reassertions described above.

The autonomization of public services and health services in particular is a central-state initiative that responds to the weak extractive capacities of the Vietnamese state and the (misguided) faith in decentralization. The redistributive impulse in Vietnamese health policy could not address a more fundamental issue facing the health sector and all other social sectors: the need for additional economic resources. Given the political and budgetary priorities of the Vietnamese state and its limited extractive and allocative capacities, the answer would not be the budget. Instead, the "solution" would be autonomization: allow public service providers to generate their own resources. So does financial autonomization represent a reassertion of the private in the public's clothing? Certainly, it is an odd type of privatization, whereby the state (and Party and individuals associated with both) seek to generate and exploit the benefits of commoditized health services and mitigate the political risks, with mixed success both with respect to improving the quality and equity of services and protecting the Party's legitimacy.

There is already evidence that many hospitals have been effective in increasing off-budget revenues through various forms of business ventures, including separate hospital wings for "services on demand," "build-operate-and transfer" arrangements for constructions and, (especially) for-profit ventures whereby hospital staff and outside partners invest in diagnostic and other equipment. Certainly this kind of "socialization" can contribute to upgrading hospital facilities while at the same time privileging those with the means to afford cash payments for access to more expensive (for-profit) services.[16]

Conclusion

In the wake of state socialism, the CPV adopted policies designed to shift institutional responsibilities for health finance onto the population. Public health spending has been low. But rapid economic growth during this period permitted sustained increases in total health spending and improvements in health status.

Still, the cost-shifting policies that the CPV maintained after 1989 have helped commodify health in Viet Nam and make access to health services beyond a basic level contingent on out-of-pocket payments.

In addition to cost-shifting, Viet Nam's health system since 1989 has experienced two reassertions of the state. "Redistributive reassertions" included fee exemptions programs, as sustained commitment to providing a floor of basic health services through the finance of commune health centers, district hospitals, and the development of a national health insurance system. Being small in scale during the 1990s, in recent years these redistributive aspects of health policy have grown and are now important institutionalized features of Viet Nam's health system. The gradual expansion of targeted "safety-nets" programs and the national insurance scheme represent a welfare and external legitimacy-enhancing redistributive reassertion of the state. While this redistribution has its limits, it is non-trivial. Unlike in many countries, Viet Nam today possesses a preventive health outlet in literally every local jurisdiction of the country. And, in the last five years, targeted programs have expanded in scale and scope and the insurance scheme designed to protect the Vietnamese from the harshness of the "new situation" has gradually been scaled-up.

Indeed, while the CPV has not accorded health budgetary priority, it would be inaccurate to conclude that the CPV is not concerned with development of the health sector. A recent example is the Party's Resolution 46 of 2005, which criticized "poor management" in the health sector and expressed concern about the political consequences of a health system that is widely perceived to be inequitable. There are also indications that the Party has come to appreciate the merits of more public spending: in 2008, the National Assembly stated its intent to devote at least 10 percent of the national budget for health (*Kinh tế Nông Thôn* 2006).

Another response to catastrophic retrenchment has been an *accumulative reassertion* of the state. Viet Nam's adoption of fees for service principles in the early 1990s formally sanctioned cost-recovery in the health sector. Various informal and illicit forms of accumulation also exist. But recent years have seen efforts by the central state to promote greater accumulation with the state health sector. The autonomization of public hospitals is a strategy by the state to address its own weak extractive capacities and reduce hospitals' overall reliance on scarce public sector resources. Alternatively, the incentives that autonomization introduces into hospitals threatens to undermine principles of equity and transform "public" health services into private profit centers.

In any context, the reassertion of the state in the delivery of public services is likely to respond to quite diverse and sometimes contradictory state imperatives. Viet Nam's health sector is a case in point. A discussion of "reasserting the state" in Viet Nam's health sector leads us to the conclusion that the state's reassertions embodied contradictory responses to the realities of a commodified health system in a decentralized society with limited state capacities. Viet Nam's health sector is very much in the process of becoming. Just what it is becoming remains unclear. Whether and to what extent a combination of modest redistribution, health insurance, and state-sponsored market-based accumulation strategies within the "public" health sector actually promote social equity and public health remains to be seen.

Karl Polanyi's famous concept of "double movement" referred to the subjugation of social life to markets and the subsequent need for state intervention to protect human life from being destroyed (Polanyi 1944). Reassertions of the state in contemporary Viet Nam's health sector represent a contemporary instance of a Polanyian "double movement," albeit in the context of a market-Leninist regime.

Notes

1 Forthcoming in *Policy & Society* (2008).
2 City University of Hong Kong. Please direct correspondence to jonathan.london@ cityu.edu.hk.
3 The journalists Nicolas Kristof and Cheryl WuDunn (1994) were first to use the term *market-Leninism* in a published work. I arrived at the term independently in the mid-1990s and have sought to specify its conceptual, theoretical and practical meaning.
4 World Bank (2008) *Health Financing and Delivery in Viet Nam: The Short- and Medium-Term Policy Agenda.*
5 For a lengthier analysis, see London (2003).
6 As stipulated in the constitution of 1980.
7 This was permitted by the Ministerial Circular No. 30.
8 Decision 45 was issued by the Council of Ministers on 24 April 1989.
9 WHO.
10 MOH-HPG (2007) *Joint Annual Health Review 2007.*
11 Decree 36 NĐ-CP, 17/3/2005.
12 The same research suggested the proportion of children that had been issued the health cards was overstated. In one province in the south, for example, local authorities reported 96 percent of children had been issued cards, whereas independent research found only 84 percent had.
13 Interview with the National Assembly's Committee on Finance and Budget, May 2008.
14 Formerly, localities were responsible for paying local health workers' wages at the commune level.
15 Preventive health services, such as commune health stations, represent the primary level of care.
16 Viện Chiến lược và Chính sách y tế. Đánh giá tác động của việc thực hiện tự chủ tài chính bệnh viện đối với cung ứng và chi trả dịch vụ y tế. Nguyen Khanh Phuong and Jonathan London principal authors (IHSP 2008).

Bibliography

Axelson, Henrik (2007) "The evolution of health insurance policy in Vietnam," Workshop on Key Health Insurance Policy Issues, sponsored by the Joint Health Policy Initiative (JHPI), Hanoi.

Bryant, John (1998) "Demographic Change in North Vietnam," *Population and Development Review* 24(2): 235–69.

Council of Ministers (1989) *Quyết định số 45/HDBT của Hội đồng Bộ trưởng 24/4/1989 về việc thu một phần viện phí y tế* (Edict No. 45 was issued by the Council of Ministers, on 24 April 1989).

Council of Ministers (1992) *Nghị định số 299/1992/HĐBT về ban hành điều lệ bảo hiểm y tế* (Decree 299 in 1992).

CPV (2005) *Nghị quyết số 46-NQ TW của Bộ Chính trị, về công tác bảo vệ, chăm sóc và nâng cao sức khỏe nhân dân trong tình hình mới* (Resolution 46. Standing Committee of the Politburo, Socialist Republic of Viet Nam).

Đam Viet Cuong (1997) "Socialization of Health Care Activities in Viet Nam," *Implementation of Socialization of Health Care Activities for the People at the Commune Level*, Hanoi: Communist Party of Viet Nam Central Committee for Science & Education, Ministry of Health: UNICEF.

Đang *et al.* (2006) *Ensuring Health Care for the Rural Poor in Viet Nam and China: A State or Market Approach?* Hanoi: Medical Publishing House.

Fritzen, Scott A. (2007) "Reorienting Health Ministry Roles in Transition Settings: Capacity and Strategy Gaps," *Health Policy* 83(1): 73.

GSO (2007) *Viet Nam Statistical Yearbook*, Hanoi: General Statistics Office, p. 559.

Harvard University (2008) "Choosing Success: The Lessons of East and Southeast Asia and Vietnam's Future: A Policy Framework for Vietnam's Socioeconomic Development, 2011–2020," Harvard Vietnam Program, John F. Kennedy School of Government.

Hoang Dinh Cau (1965) "The Training of Medical and Health Workers in the Democratic Republic of Vietnam," *Vietnamese Studies* 6: 42, 58, cited in Bryant, "Demographic Change in North Viet Nam."

IHSP (2008) *Đánh gia tác động của việc thực hiện tự chủ tìa chính bệnh viện đối với cung ứng chi trả dịch vụ y tế* (Assessing the Impact of the Implementation of Financial Autonomization with Respect to the Provision and Payment for Health Services), Nguyễn Khánh Phương, Jonathan London *et al.,* Institution of Health Strategy and Policy: Ministry of Health.

Kinh tế Nông Thôn (2006) "Đại biểu Quốc hội đề nghị tăng đầu tư cho y tế cơ sở. Available at www.kinhtenongthon.com.vn/printContent.aspx?ID=10919.

Kristof, Nicolas D. and WuDunn, Cheryl (1994) *China Wakes: The Struggle for the Soul of a Rising Power*, New York: Times Books/Random House.

London, Jonathan D. (2003) "Viet Nam's Mass Education and Health Systems: A Regimes Perspective," *American Asian Review* 21 (June).

—— (2009) "Viet Nam and the Making of Market-Leninism," *The Pacific Review*, 22(3): 373–97.

London, Jonathan D. and van Ufford, Paul (2008) *Food Prices, Vulnerability, and Food Security in Viet Nam: A UN Perspective*, Vietnam: UNICEF.

Merli, M. Giovanna and London, Jonathan D. (2002) "Mortality in North Viet Nam Since 1945," unpublished paper presented at meetings of Association for Asian Studies, 4–7 April, in Washington, DC.

MOH (1991) *Health Statistics of Viet Nam, 1986–1990*, Hanoi: Department of Health Statistics and Informatics.

MOH (1994) *Thông tư số 14/1994/TTLB-BGDĐT-BYT ngày 19/9/1994 về việc hướng dẫn thực hiện bảo hiểm y tế tự nguyện cho học sinh* (Circular 14), Hanoi: Ministry of Education and Training (MOET) and Ministry of Health (MOH).

MOH (2000) "Bao Cao: Tinh Hinh Thuc Hien Cong Tac Y Te Nam 1999 va Phuong Huong Ke Hoach Nam 2000" (Report: The Situation of Health in 1999 and Planning Orientations for the Year 2000), unpublished report, Hanoi: Ministry of Health.

MOH (2005) Các Giải Pháp Tài Chính Y Tế Cho Người Nghèo" (Health Financing Measures for the Poor), unpublished research report, Hanoi: Ministry of Health.

MOH (2008) 55 Năm xây dưưungj và phát triển ngành y tế Việt Nam. Available at www. moh.gov.vn/homebyt/vn/portal/InfoList.jsp?area=58&cat=1443.

MOH-HPG (2007) *Joint Annual Health Review 2007*, Hanoi: Ministry of Health.

MOH-HPG (2008) *Joint Annual Health Review 2008*, Hanoi: Ministry of Health.

MOH, MOF (2002) *Thông tư số 14/2002/TTLT-BYT-BTC ngày 16/12/2002 hướng dẫn tổ chức khám chữa bệnh và lập, quản lý, sử dụng, thanh quyết toán Quỹ khám, chữa bệnh cho người nghèo theo Quyết định số 139/2002/QĐ-TTg* (Circular 14/2002).

MOLISA, MOH, MOF (1999) *Thông tư số 05/1999/TTLT-BLDTBXH-BYT-BTC ngày 29/1/1999 hướng dẫn thực hiện việc khám chữa bệnh miễn nộp một phần viện phí đối với những thuộc diện quá nghèo quy định tại Nghị định 95/CP ngày 27/8/1994* (Circular 95/1999).

National Assembly's Committee on Finance and Budget (2008) interview, May.

Nghiem Tran Dung (2007) Health Insurance Department, Hanoi: Ministry of Health, March, p. 17.

Painter, Martin (2006) "From Command Economy to Hollow State? Decentralisation in Vietnam and China," *The Australian Journal of Public Administration* 67(1): 79–88.

Phan Hồng Vân, Trần Văn Tiến, Khương Anh Tuấn, Hoàng Thị Phượng (2006) Đánh giá kết quả thực hiện chính sách khám chữa bệnh miễn phí cho trẻ em dưới 6 tuổi tại Ninh Bình, Đà Nẵng và Tiền Giang, Số ra ngày 15/08/2006 (Số 12006).

Polanyi, Karl (1944) [1957] *The Great Transformation: The Political and Economic Origins of our Time*, Boston: Beacon Press, by arrangement with Rinehart & Company, Inc.

Prime Minister (1998) *Quyết định số 135/1998/QĐ-TTg ngày 31/7/1998 của Thủ tướng Chính phủ phê duyệt chương trình phát triển kinh tế – xã hội các xã đặc biệt khó khăn miền núi và vùng sâu, vùng xa* (Decision 135).

Prime Minister (2002) *Quyết định số 139/2002/QĐ-TTg ngày 15/10/2002 về việc khám, chữa bệnh cho người nghèo* (Decision 139, Health Care for the Poor).

Sea Change Partners (2006) "Vietnam's Health Workforce in Transition: Problems, Policies and Prospects," unpublished report prepared for The World Bank Office, Hanoi, May.

Segall, Malcolm and Associates (2002) "Economic Transition Should Come with a Health Warning: the Case of Vietnam," *Journal of Epidemiology and Community Health* 56(7): 497–505.

Socialist Republic of Viet Nam (1994) *Nghị định 95/1994/NĐ-CP ngày 27/8/1994 về việc thu mộ phần viện phí* (Decree 95).

Socialist Republic of Viet Nam (2002) *Nghị định số 10/2002/NĐ-CP ngày 16/1/2002 về chế độ tài chính áp dụng cho đơn vị sự nghiệp có thu* (Decree 10 effective in 2004).

Socialist Republic of Viet Nam (2002) *Nghị định số 63/2002/NĐ-CP ngày 18/6/2002 quy định về khám bệnh, chữa bệnh cho thân nhân sỹ quan tại ngũ* (Decree 63/2002).

Socialist Republic of Viet Nam (2005) *Nghị định số 36/2005/NĐ-CP ngày 17/3/2005 của Chính phủ quy định chi tiết thi hành một số điều của Luật bảo vệ, chăm sóc và giáo dục trẻ em* (Decree 36 NĐ-CP, 17/3/2005).

Socialist Republic of Viet Nam (2005) *Nghị định số 63/2005/NĐ-CP ngày 16/5/2005 ban hành Điều lệ bảo hiểm y tế* (Decree 63/2005).

Socialist Republic of Viet Nam (2006) *Nghị định số 43/2006/NĐ-CP ngày 25/4/2006 quy định quyền tự chủ, tự chịu trách nhiệm về thực hiện nhiệm vụ, tổ chức bộ máy, biên chế và tài chính đối với đơn vị sự nghiệp công lập* (Decree 43 effective in 2006).

Socialist Republic of Vietnam and the World Bank (2005) "Vietnam Managing Public Expenditure for Poverty Reduction and Growth: Public Expenditure Review and

Integrated Fiduciary Assessment, Volume 1. Cross-Sectoral Issues," A Joint Document of the Socialist Republic of Vietnam and the World Bank, prepared with the support from Like Minded Donor Group, Hanoi.

Tài Chính Tháng (Finance Monthly) (2005) *Thực hiện chủ trương khám chữa bệnh miễn phí chi trẻ em dưới sáu tuổi: Căng thẳng chuyện 'đầu tiên'?* May, No author.

Trần thị Chung Chiến (2005) Về tình hình thực hiện các chính sách chăm sóc sức khỏe cho người nghèo ở Việt Nam Tap chi Chinh Sach Y te Số ra ngày 15/12/2005 (Số 9).

UNICEF, United Nations Children's Fund (2008) unpublished policy brief on "Impacts of the Food Price Crisis on Viet Nam's Children."

World Bank (1993) *Viet Nam: Transition to Market.*

—— (2001) *Vietnam: Growing Healthy, A Review of the Health Sector.*

9 Reasserting the public in public service delivery

The de-privatization and de-marketization of education in China

Martin Painter and Ka Ho Mok

Introduction

The processes of economic reform and growth in China are bringing with them huge social and economic transformations. The economic reforms started in the late 1970s have unquestionably enabled some social groups to become wealthy but the same processes have also widened the gap between the rich and the poor, as well as intensifying regional disparities (Keng 2006; Weil 2006; Yao *et al.* 2004). The most recent *China Human Development Report 2005* indicates that the gap between the rich and poor in China has been widening: the richest 10 per cent of urban dwellers controlled 34 per cent of urban wealth while the poorest 10 per cent held a mere 0.2 per cent. Commenting on the urban–rural income gap, the United Nations noted that China had perhaps the highest income disparity in the world (UNDP 2005). At the same time, forms of protection and security that were associated with the command economy have been undermined and replaced by new modes of welfare provision and new kinds of citizen entitlements. For most, access to benefits is no longer connected with stable membership of local work units but is increasingly the product of other factors: self-reliance or community self-help; a history of compulsory contributions linked to employment; or a claim based on 'ability to pay'. In this context, fundamental issues are only now beginning to be raised about the role of the state in social provision in a 'socialist market economy'.

Under state socialism the role of the state in social provision and protection was limited and ambiguous, because much of the responsibility for collective welfare devolved directly on the shoulders of the productive, wealth-generating sector (state-owned enterprises, collectives and other production units) rather than on the state budget proper. This responsibility was largely devolved to the work unit – the *danwei* – which performed vital social support roles. In the command economy, the state claimed its legitimacy from successfully managing and directing the key productive sectors of the economy, which in turn provided for those members of society who were directly engaged in them. But with the nexus between the state and workplaces fractured as a result of marketization, new questions about the role of the state in social provision have emerged.

In embracing the market economy, China has also embraced contemporary ideas and strategies of neo-liberalism, not only in reforming the economic sector but also public sector management and social policy delivery (Wong and Flynn 2001; So 2006). In many sectors, market-leaning policy instruments have been used to reform and restructure service provision (Min 2004; Mok 2006a). This has imparted a growing 'privateness' to China's social policy sector, the commodification of some public goods and a process of 'individualization of social rights' (Shi *et al.* 2005; Mok 2006b; Wong 2002). Recent re-focusing of leadership attention in China on the quality and accessibility of health and other public services has acknowledged the need to resolve some of the tensions of these growing inequities. Pronouncements by the Chinese leadership on the need for building a harmonious society have been linked with improved services such as health and education for the poor. The state's responsibility for regulating and assuring the conditions for collective welfare – work safety, the environment, the provision of affordable health care, unemployment relief and so on – have risen to new prominence on the policy agenda.

This chapter sets out to describe and appraise some recent policy responses that aim to cope with the more harmful consequences of marketization. The case of education is presented within a wider context of state restructuring – in particular, what we call 'dual decentralization' (Painter 2008) – and its accompanying debates about the role of the state in providing public goods in post-socialist China. The chapter first explores the wider background of privatization and marketization in China's case. It notes that governance processes have lagged far behind what is required to regulate and monitor new, decentralized forms of service provision. The lack of accountability mechanisms through which bottom-up political voice might be expressed is one dimension to this governance crisis, but in this chapter we pay more attention to systems of regulation, management and financing. We conclude the chapter by exploring and appraising some recent efforts to address flaws in these systems in the case of education.

State restructuring and dual decentralization

Rocca (2003: 14–15) refers to the phenomenon of 'societalization' of the traditional unified, centralized socialist state, which has stepped back from the project of transforming society from 'above' or 'outside' but instead has 'pushed into the market' and become entangled in dealing with the societal consequences of marketization. Public officials, acting at first from *within* the state, are exercising new economic and political roles *beyond* the state as they participate in and benefit from the dispersal of the state's resources into the market economy. Informal and illegal uses of state power and resources by state actors to facilitate economic accumulation beyond the state are accompanied by (and usually take advantage of) official programmes of state restructuring which have created new social and economic institutions formally and legally 'at a distance' from the state. As well as legislating for various forms of corporate business organizations, legal personality has also been endowed on a new range of social organizations under state sponsorship and regulation, many of them performing 'state-like' functions. In the process, the state has created a complex array of state-cum-societal 'hybrids'. This process has its pragmatic side, as well as being part of a deliberate process of state restructuring and economic reform. For instance, it arose in part as a strategy for 'downsizing', or shedding large parts of the over-staffed and under-resourced bureaucracy inherited from the command economy. In preference simply to making large numbers of staff redundant, state agencies looked to ways to generate new kinds of local employment through creating various 'para-state' or non-state activities and organizations that (hopefully) could be self-sustaining. In some cases, this took the form of setting up enterprises with the use of state assets and employees, with a view to returning profits (Duckett 1998); in others, the activity is concerned with 'community construction' or neighbourhood support systems (Benewick *et al.* 2004).

There are other dimensions to the 'de-centring' of the Chinese state during the reform era. Decentralization was also a process of growth in the responsibilities and powers of sub-national government. In China, sub-national expenditures rose from about 45 per cent of the total prior to the economic reforms in the 1980s to close to 70 per cent. Thus, decentralization in China is at one and the same time about dispersing power vertically *within* the state and dispersing power horizontally *away* from the state. The command economy essentially merged administrative and economic power under central state control, so the transition process involves both dissolving the merger and also downsizing the centre. Administrative and economic reforms are intertwined processes in which this 'dual decentralization' is the core element. This is illustrated in Figure 9.1, which correlates these two forms of vertical and horizontal decentralization with processes of economic and administrative reform respectively, producing a four-fold distinction between different kinds of decentralization: 'local autarky'; administrative deconcentration; privatization or socialization; and 'cellularization'.[1]

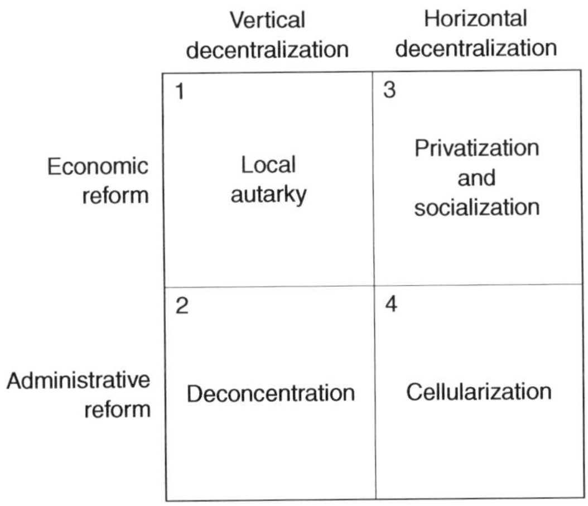

	Vertical decentralization	Horizontal decentralization
Economic reform	1 Local autarky	3 Privatization and socialization
Administrative reform	2 Deconcentration	4 Cellularization

Figure 9.1 Dual decentralization in the transition economy.

The first quadrant – local autarky – describes the situation where economic policy is decentralized such that regional or local economies are increasingly free to operate autonomously in competition with each other. Economic decentralization has been a common developmental strategy in China both before and after marketization. Economic decentralization has been a self-reinforcing process, as it has enabled local state actors to build their local power bases through control of state assets during the marketization process, often using their power to enrich themselves and their families in the process. Because local state actors are now also businessmen and capitalists, they occupy new resource bases to resist the central state.

Quadrant 2 contains a range of types of administrative decentralization, including administrative delegation or vertical specialization of administrative functions, as well as various forms of political devolution and fiscal decentralization that accompany the delegation of local power and authority.[2] Quadrant 3 involves the divestiture of assets or the handing over of production and distribution activities to the for-profit and the not-for-profit private sectors. If there is not private sector or 'third sector' involvement to begin with, the state or its agents may play an active role in creating one. Finally, Quadrant 4 describes a process of 'cellularization' by which functions of government are hived off into disaggregated, 'para-state' entities that stand alone and at some degree of arm's length from the state's authority.[3] Cellularization often accompanies marketization and is frequently characterized by high levels of informality and corruption. Some of the resulting organizational forms are 'hybrids' which blur a clear distinction between state and market, or public and private. Indeed, the struggle over the creation of such distinctions (including the institutional forms that define these boundaries) is one of the key features of the transition process (Rocca 2003).

Vertical administrative and fiscal decentralization in China has been subject to extensive analysis (for example, Wong 1997; World Bank 2005b), but less attention has been given to the implications of horizontal decentralization for state capacity and for mechanisms of public accountability (but see Lam and Perry 2001; Lo *et al.* 2001; and World Bank 2005a). We argue that marketization and cellularization are accompanied by high levels of informalization, which is undermining the accountability, integrity and legitimacy of public sector service delivery to the point where a vicious cycle of declining state capacity may have been set in train.

The crisis of the public sector and dual decentralization

Economic decentralization accompanied by deconcentration of administrative powers in modern China dates back to the mid-1950s, with decisions to implement formal power-sharing with the provinces over project approval, control of enterprises and collection of revenues (Schurmann 1968: 195–6). Despite occasional reversals, decentralization has continued apace, as much a result of bottom-up as of top-down forces (Libertahl 1992; Bernstein and Lu 2003). In China, local governments with enhanced revenue autonomy strove to expand their revenue base through investment in and diversification of local production, accompanied by local protectionism (Shirk 1992: 82–4). However, the unitary nature of the state under principles of democratic centralism has been maintained. The significance of the vertical decentralization in the reform era was that it afforded local party-state officials new opportunities to wield political power and accumulate economic resources. Accompanying this was a rapid growth in employment in local bureaucracies of nearly 80 per cent between 1978 and 1987 (Shirk 1992: 85). These local bureaucratic empires were buttressed by new forms of bureaucratic rent-seeking (Lu 2000). While the formal taxing capacity of local governments seems not to have kept up with the growth in staff and activities (Mountfield and Wong 2005: 97), a plethora of new fees, charges, levies and fines were imposed, many of them of 'off-budget' and of dubious legality (Bernstein and Lu 2003: 107–9). These sources of revenue were tapped through the use of local discretionary powers; were retained by the local bodies that collected them; and were available to reward local officials with jobs, bonuses and other benefits (Bernstein and Lu 2003: 84–6; Gong 2005; Wedeman 2000). The development of extra-budgetary financing arrangements was both a response to tensions in the vertical decentralization process and also a significant development in the process of horizontal decentralization. The growth of off-budget activity may be seen as a form of cellularization, as it created opportunities for autonomously managed, informal 'fringe' activities involving extra staff, topping up of salaries, opportunities for 'moonlighting' and spawning of new administrative entities. New 'para-state' administrative forms (discussed in more detail below) have emerged in parallel with the informalization of local finances and the growing recourse to alternative sources of local government revenue.

To appreciate the growing significance of this 'para-state' sector in China, we need to place it in the context of the inherited structures of the socialist state. China's hierarchically organized administrative system had three components: administrative agencies (central ministries and the administrative departments of both central and local governments); service delivery units;[4] and enterprises. Here, we focus mainly on the second category. China had over one million service delivery units employing nearly 30 million in 2002, or 41 per cent of the public sector workforce. Sixty per cent of China's professional classes worked for them; they owned two-thirds of 'non-commercial' state assets; and they absorbed about one-third of the recurrent expenditures of all governments (World Bank 2005a, 1–2). In the past, the way these organizations were staffed and managed differed little from administrative agencies: the same terms and conditions of 'civil service' employment and pay scales applied to them and party control and management was exercised in the same way as in the departmental system. They were also likely to be funded (at least in part) from the state budget. Their service functions were diverse, but the largest sectors were education and health. Supervision of service delivery units rested with administrative departments at central, provincial or local levels. Sixty-five per cent of their employees were affiliated with county and township governments. The control and management of service delivery units was a matter of vital interest to local governments and the heads of their departments, as many were repositories of significant state assets, important instruments of patronage and (increasingly) significant sources of revenue.

With the increasing decentralization to local government and the growing reliance on extra-budget and off-budget financing, the autonomization and marketization of service delivery units through user charging became a way of generating revenue in order to meet the growing demands for local service provision. According to official statistics, about half of the revenue of service delivery units in China by 2002 was raised through fees (World Bank 2005a: 3). Thus, service delivery units during the reform era have become increasingly cellularized at the same time as some of their production processes have been socialized or marketized. These developments were encouraged by administrative reform policies to increase the degree of autonomy and flexibility enjoyed by service delivery units. Early 'experiments on a vast scale' (Cheng 2001: 322) allowed for more flexible systems of recruitment and remuneration; separation from government departments; delegation of enhanced management autonomy; and better utilization of assets and revenue-raising through setting up affiliated companies and 'social organizations'. Increased powers to levy fees or set charges and to borrow money for investment were accompanied by new regulations permitting retention of surplus revenues; investment and incentive schemes for employees; and flexible remuneration packages. Regulations have been revised to permit some professional employees to provide fee-paying services to clients while in their official positions.

These coupled 'cellularization-marketization' processes have been a mixture of both informal, bottom-up stratagems and top-down encouragement. The bottom-up pressures came in part from managers trying to make ends meet and in part from chronically under-paid employees seeking new income-earning opportunities. Thus, an important parallel development has been the part-privatization of the remuneration of many public employees (such as teachers and health workers) and civil servants. Salary supplements, bonuses and in-kind benefits derived from extra- and off-budget sources provided a growing component of rewards, dependent not on efficiently performing official duties so much as on being able to take advantage of whatever income-generating activities were to hand. Local, 'cellular' systems of loyalty and dependency based on access to and control of these revenue sources developed in competition with centrally regulated, standardized rewards, resulting in a highly fragmented, localized employment system, rather than a unified one. The outcome has been the clouding of a clear conception of the public service roles of the civil servant and other state employees, particularly in service delivery areas where fees and charges are a growing source of revenue.

In sum, public service delivery units have been increasingly decoupled from their supervising departments in terms of operating norms and organizational forms (while at the same time remaining inter-dependent with them because of their economic value as sources of jobs and revenue). In addition, local governments have been encouraged to expand local service delivery by collaborating with non-government 'social organizations'. This has resulted in a special category of 'civilian-run non-enterprise organizations' or *minban feiqiye danwei* (as discussed later, *minban* are prominent in the education sector). Here, the phrase 'non-enterprise' does not mean that these organizations do not in some senses operate in the market: they may rely on private financing and invariably derive their revenue from marketing their services and charging fees; indeed, they spearhead the marketization process in some areas of public service delivery.

China's reform trajectory towards administrative decentralization and marketization results in a set of both deliberate and unintended outcomes that, together, constitute a deep ambiguity about the scope and nature of 'the public sector' in post-socialist China. This has come to be acknowledged in various attempts to counter some of the worst consequences of marketization with respect to legality, quality of service, accessibility and equity. This process of 'reasserting the public' in China has several critical elements: first, a search for new conceptions and definitions of the appropriate roles for the state in public service provision and regulation; second, a search for new modes of 'public interest' regulation of privatized or socialized non-government forms of service provision; and third, a search for new forms of state capacity in a system of government that is both increasingly 'vertically' decentralized and also increasingly horizontally fragmented and cellularized. In the next section, we elaborate on some of the problematic aspects of marketization of social provision by looking more closely at experience in the education sector. We then turn to the government's responses to these problems, that is their attempt to 'bring the state back in'. In the conclusion, we return to the broader themes raised in the discussion to this point.

Dual decentralization in education: fees and charges

As early as 1985, the CCP issued the *Decision of the Central Committee of the Chinese Communist Party of China on the Reform of the Educational System* which marked the beginning of a process of educational reform, and gradually aligned the educational system with the newly emerging market economy. The documents called for the devolution of power to lower levels of government and a reduction in the rigid governmental controls over schools (CCCCP 1985). Since then, the state has started to diversify educational services, allowing and encouraging the non-state sector to establish and run educational institutions. Meanwhile, the state has deliberately devolved responsibility and power to local governments, local communities and other non-state actors by providing a necessary framework for educational development (Hawkins 2000; Ngok and Chan 2003).

With the emergence of self-financing students and non-state education providers (including private and foreign ones), China's education has undergone diversification, marketization, privatization, commodification and decentralization (Borevskaya 2003; Mok 2000; Ngok and Chan 2003). In the process, the contribution of the state budget to education expenditure has remained quite static and (by international standards) low (Table 9.1). Most recently, the State Council of the People's Republic of China has openly recognized insufficient government funding being allocated to education. In this connection, the 11th Five Year Plan (2006–2010) calls on governments at all levels to make the development of education a strategic priority and 'to commit to a public education system that can be accessed by all' (cited in Li 2007). While the contribution of the state budget has not kept pace with demand, local governments and individual education institutions have funded growth by seeking to increase student intakes and raising tuition fees. The additional revenues both finance educational developments and provide the means to improve teachers' incomes. At the same time, the scramble for students and revenue has led to abuses, such as over-charging (Yang 2004). In addition to over-charging, some schools impose 'miscellaneous' charges such as accommodation fees, supplementary class fees, uniform fees and so on.

The structural change in the financing of education in China is most obvious in higher education. Now, all university students have to pay tuition fees and the user-pays principle has been made the foundation of Chinese education, with the result that parents and families are bearing a heavier financial burden for education (see Zhu 2005; Dai 2005; Li 2007). According to Wang (2007) China now faces a new equity issue in education, especially when students have to pay at least 7,000 *yuan* annually for higher education (equivalent to 35 years of income of ordinary peasants in rural China). Hence, the most recent yearbook compiled by the Chinese Academy of Social Sciences reports that spending on education was ranked sixth on a list of serious public concerns by Chinese citizens in 2006, with school bills gobbling up more than 10 per cent of the average household budget (Yu *et al.* 2007). As Cummings (1996) suggests, education under the influence of traditional Asian values is a matter beyond the individual but of concern to the whole family. A tertiary student in China is obligated to carry the hopes of an entire family. This is a deeply rooted traditional value, which has

Table 9.1 Public education expenditure in China

Year	Gross domestic product	Government appropriation for education	Percentage (%)
1992	2,663.8	72.9	2.74
1995	5,847.8	141.2	2.41
1999	8,206.8	228.7	2.79
2000	8,946.8	256.3	2.86
2001	9,731.5	305.7	3.14
2002	10,517.2	349.1	3.32
2003	11,739.0	385.1	3.28
2004	15,987.8	446.6	2.79

Source: NBSC (2005).

Note
Government appropriation for education includes the expenditure of central and local governments on education.

formulated a strong mindset favouring learning and education commonly shared among Chinese people no matter whether they live in rural or urban areas. Nonetheless, Yin Jianli, a researcher with Beijing-based NGO Western Sunshine Action, recently points out that 'the initial elation of a university offer quickly turns into frustration for many rural families because supporting a college student can plunge them into dire straits' (quoted from Li 2007: 8).

Dual decentralization in education: multiple providers

In late 1993, the *Programme for Reform and the Development of China's Education* stipulated that the national policy was actively to encourage and support social institutions and citizens to establish schools according to laws and to provide the right guidelines and strengthen administration (CCCCP 1993). Article 25 of the *Education Law* promulgated in 1995 reconfirmed once again that the state would give full support to enterprises, social institutions, local communities and individuals to establish schools under the legal framework of the People's Republic of China (PRC) (SEC 1995). In short, the state's attitude towards the development of non-state-run education can be summarized by the phrase 'active encouragement, strong support, proper guidelines, and sound management' (*jiji guli, dali zhichi, zhengque yindao, jiaqiang guanli*). Under such a legal framework, educational providers have proliferated, particularly when the Chinese state in an effort to expand capacity encouraged all democratic parties, people bodies, social organizations, retired cadres and intellectuals, collective economic organizations and individuals subject to the Party and governmental policies, actively and voluntarily to contribute to developing education through various forms and methods (Wei and Zhang 1995: 5). In 1998, there were around 50,000 *minban* education institutions at various levels, recruiting approximately 10.66 million students; in 2004, these numbers had risen to 70,000 and 17.69 million respectively (*China Education Yearbook* 1999; 2005).

The creation of a hybrid public/private education provider sector is not confined to the growth of purely 'third sector' institutions or to the emergence of purely for-profit establishments in the private sector. In addition, many public schools in China have undergone a process of privatization and marketization by which they are no longer entirely public in nature but are classified as *gouyou minban* (state-owned and people-run) (Mok 2005: 224–5). *Gouyou minban* means that schools remain under government ownership but the proportion of finance from the private/non-state sector is increased, mainly through charging tuition fees, while the schools acquire a high level of autonomy. The proliferation of publicly owned but privately run institutions, coupled with the growing legitimization of fee-charging, were the instruments for achieving the policy objectives of expanding enrolment rates in education at all levels (Mok and Ngok 2008; Lin 2004; Lin *et al.* 2005; Shi *et al.* 2005; Shanghai Research Institute of Educational Sciences 2005).

In the higher education sector, *gouyou minban* institutions are named 'second-tier colleges' and are extension arms of public (national) universities. Similarly, these colleges are run as self-financing entities and operate in terms of market principles. The *gouyou minban* institutions serve as revenue-generating projects, especially in the context of reductions in government funding; at the same time they create a market in education services, as they compete for students. These features have given rise to ideological debates about the legitimacy of the rising for-profit nature of 'public' education and the increasingly entrepreneurial activities of 'public' educational institutions. Despite these ideological debates, the extension of *minban* education has become an inexorable trend in China, particularly with the increase in the number of 'quasi *minban*' institutions. Recent statistics show that over 1,000 public schools had applied this 'privatized' running mechanism by 2004 (Lin and Chen 2004: 46). By 2005, there were 344 second-tier colleges throughout China, enrolling 540,000 undergraduate students (Chen and Yu 2005: 167).

Growing inequality

Not surprisingly, with the increasing reliance on user charges, the declining levels of state support and the scramble for revenue by education institutions, there has been an increased level of concern among both citizens and policy makers over growing inequalities. In the era of the planned economy, the Chinese institution *hukou* (household registration system) was the key determinant of the opportunity for receiving education. *Hukou* system was established in 1958 and it determined where one could live and what benefits one was entitled to enjoy. While primarily a means to control population mobility, *hukou* system has also crucially determined the different life chances of the people living respectively in urban and rural areas (Liang 2001). People living in urban areas have enjoyed better social services and welfare provision provided by their urban work units systems. Even in the post-Mao era, the *hukou* system still imposes institutional constraints for rural migrants to enjoy equal schooling and higher education opportunities, despite the fact that many of them have been allowed to remain in urban China for work and residence. Being regarded as temporary immigrants or 'floating population', these new urban immigrants cannot obtain similar social status to their urban counterparts because they are still classified as rural citizens without an urban *hukou* registration.

The Ministry of Education has promulgated the *Temporary Regulations Concerning the Education of Children of the Floating Population*, which stipulates that children from temporary migrant families should be primarily enrolled in local schools. However, local governments are reluctant to finance education for children of migrant residents, meaning that the latter may have to bear the full financial burden of local schooling (Liu *et al.* 1998). Where local schools in cities accept temporary migrant children, their parents have to pay the education endorsement fee (*jiaoyu zanzhu fei*) (Cao 1997). In the face of these discriminatory provisions, migrants are particularly vulnerable to abuses such as overcharging. Such institutional and financial barriers have disadvantaged temporary migrant children in terms of educational opportunities: they are less likely to be enrolled in school than their urban (and even rural) counterparts (Wang and Zuo 1999).

Economic reform and development in the last 30 years has significantly improved the livelihood of those living in the coastal areas. Nonetheless, the same social and economic transformations have also intensified the coastal–inland disparity. This has resulted in a concentration of education opportunities in socio-economically prosperous regions in the eastern coastal area. Putting the current developments of private/*minban* education into perspective, it is clear that the people living in the eastern coastal areas of China have disproportionately experienced the success of economic growth in the last two decades and many of them are willing and have the financial ability to pay for these educational services. Educational inequality also exists in forms of urban–rural and regional disparities in public expenditure. This is because the government concentrated development funds on coastal areas and cities as distinct from inland provinces and the countryside. According to official statistics, 214,913 million *yuan* were allocated to the coastal region, constituting 55.8 per cent of the educational budget.[5] Regarding non-governmental financial resources, 36,361 million *yuan* were generated in the region, representing about 67.2 per cent of the total. However, the population of the coastal region constitutes only 41.4 per cent of the total population (MOE 2004).[6] Another important indicator showing inter-province inequity is the number of students per 100,000 inhabitants. The national average is 1,420. In Beijing the figure was 6,204 in 2003 compared with only 985 in Anhui in the same reporting year. Comparing the household consumption expenditure of three relatively wealthy regions in China (Beijing, Shanghai and Tianjin) with three relatively poor regions (Guizhou, Guangxi and Gansu) in terms of the number of students per 100,000 inhabitants, we find that the average rate of the three most wealthiest is 4.6 per cent but that of the three poor regions is only 0.9 per cent in terms of the number of students per 100,000 inhabitants. When comparing the financing situation between these places, the total non-governmental financial resources devoted to education of the three wealthy regions was 3.45 billion *yuan* in 2004, but by only 800 million *yuan* in the three poor regions (see Table 9.2) (MOE 2004).

Recent studies have suggested that educational inequalities are larger the higher the level of schooling (Qian and Smyth 2005; Rong and Shi 2001). Given that there is no university in the rural area of China, students from villages are eligible for applying for admissions to university nationwide (Zhong 2006). However, a study indicates that students from rural areas are considered inferior to those from urban areas (Wang 2005a). For example, students from urban areas in Guangdong occupied 72.2 per cent and 89.9 per cent of places in the key universities led by central ministries and *minban* vocational college respectively, even though there is a relatively even allocation of places in the normal public universities and public vocational colleges (see Table 9.3) (Wang 2005b: 11).

As noted at the outset, the Chinese government has recognized the growing concerns over unequal access to good quality education and of the burdens being experienced by families as they seek to provide their children with the

Table 9.2 Non-state educational contributions in selected regions (2003)

Region	Social organizations and individual	Donations and fund raising	Total
National	25,901	10,459	36,360
Beijing	624	522	1,146
Tianjin	477	21	498
Shanghai	1,315	491	1,806
Jiangsu	2,204	229	2,433
Gansu	186	57	243
Anhui	452	241	693
Guangxi	251	97	348
Guizhou	150	58	208

Source: MOE (2004).

Note
Unit: million *yuan*

Table 9.3 Allocation of places of study (%) in Guangdong (2003)

	Overall	Key universities led by central ministries	Normal public universities	Public vocational colleges	Minban vocational colleges
Students from urban areas	60.7	72.2	50.6	48.0	89.9
Students from rural areas	39.3	28.8	49.4	52.0	10.1

Source: Wang (2005a).

opportunity to participate in China's growing affluence. They are also sensitive to the growing criticism of abuses such as over-charging, criticism that is part of a wider backlash against abuses of power by state and party officials. In the next two sections we look at the measures being taken to redress some of the problems linked with the autonomization and privatization of education. The main responses to date are in the form of curbs to over-charging; curbs on the creation of high-fee, high-status selective schools (known as 'transformed schools'); and structural and financial reforms to the school education system. In the conclusion, we turn to a broader question: in what form is the state being 'brought back in'?

Curbs on over-charging

To cope with the over-charging practices in the education sector, the central ministries launched a fixed-amount (lump-sum) payment method (*yi fei zhi*) for education fees in 2004. This payment method was initially introduced to help students from poverty-stricken counties but later it was implemented more universally. Under the new provisions, schools can only charge a fixed education fee, which would cover all miscellaneous items. At the same time, provincial governments are made responsible for determining the payment level in their jurisdictions. The lump-sum amount set by the provincial governments may vary among different localities within the same province (China Education and Research Network 2004). As is commonly the case with the introduction of new regulations in China, the major question is whether the measure is being effectively implemented. According to a survey conducted by the Agricultural University of China, the malpractice of over-charging fees has not been completely terminated even after the launch of the fixed-amount payment method. For instance, a peasant family needed to pay 680 *yuan* to send its child for studying in a junior secondary school in 2005 even after the county government in 2004 had set a fixed amount of 330 *yuan* (*China Youth Daily* 14 July 2006).

Curbs on 'transformed schools'

As described earlier, government policy has allowed some public schools to transform into state-owned and people-run (*guoyou minban*) institutions (also known as transformed schools (*gaizhi xuexiao*)). These 'transformed schools' enjoy more autonomy in deciding the level of tuition fee and admission of students. Therefore, they can charge higher tuition fees for those students who are not within the catchment area. As many parents in China are willing to pay more for better education for their children, many prestigious public schools set up their *minban*/private extensions or collaborate with *minban*/private institutions to enrol these students. As well as paying a higher tuition fee, parents of these children must also pay a large 'selection fee' (*ze xiao fei*). Well-established secondary schools with a strong reputation and for which there is high demand from parents have used the transformation policy to set up profit-making entities. For example, Shunchang Secondary School, a public senior secondary school in Fujian, developed a collaborative project with Jinqiao Secondary School, a newly established private school, in 2003. Under the collaborative arrangements, new senior secondary students of Shunchang would automatically be transferred to Jinqiao, and Shunchang would provide teachers (thereby offering their staff new income-earning opportunities). In return, Jinqiao would pay Shunchang an amount of 50 million *yuan* as a lump-sum investment plus 6–15 per cent of the school fees as a dividend payment annually (*21st Century Business Herald*, 11 October 2004). The practice of 'prestigious school running *minban* school' (*mingxiao ban minxiao*) or 'school-within-a-school' (*xiao zhong xiao*) has been criticized as abusing the transformation policy. Other *minban* schools have difficulty in competing with transformed schools – that is, the stated aim of diversification of education delivery has been thwarted.

In response to these practices, the central government started to draw back from and modify the 'transformed school' policy in 2006. Article 22 of the revised *Compulsory Education Law* does not allow local governments to change the public nature of public schools. The central government also issues instructions to close down some transformed schools if they do not have an independent status.[7] Meanwhile, to prevent unequal allocation of resources, the law also prohibits local governments and schools to classify individual schools and classes as 'key schools' and 'key classes' (MOE 2006a, 2006b). Again, whether these measures will be fully implemented remains a problematic issue.

Structural and financial reforms to school education

Since the promulgation of the *Compulsory Education Law* in 1986, China has implemented a universal, nine-year compulsory education system. Junior secondary education has been universalized for 73 per cent of the national population and steps have been taken to universalize senior secondary education in many urban areas and economically developed coastal regions. Nevertheless, compulsory education has not been implemented evenly across the country. This is because the project lacks full government funding. However, education and science has become one of the central government's strategic development directions, as a result of which education has received a higher priority for development when compared to other policy areas in the 11th Five Year Plan (2006–2010) during the Fifth Plenary Session of the 16th Central Committee of the CCP. In response to growing educational inequalities, the central government has re-emphasized the importance of providing basic education to citizens and accordingly has begun to provide relatively more funding to the state school sector. With a continual increase in state funding to elementary education in recent years, the net enrolment rate of primary school children grew to 99 per cent in 2005, while the gross enrolment rate of junior secondary schools reached 95 per cent (China Education and Research Network 2006).

The consolidation of nine-year compulsory education in rural areas has been given high priority. This, along with the policy goal of achieving full literacy among middle and young age groups, is termed 'two basics' (*liangji*). To narrow regional disparities in achieving the 'two basics' in the population, the central government initiated a four-year project costing 10 billion *yuan* in 2004. The project aims to facilitate 410 regions at county-level to achieve 'two basics' by 2007. According to the objectives, the rate of 'two basics' population will increase to 85 per cent, while the enrolment rate of junior secondary education will rise to 90 per cent in 2007. Meanwhile, the illiteracy rate among the middle and young age groups is planned to drop to below 5 per cent, by promoting adult literacy to a 6 million population (MOE 2007).

In 2003, the State Council launched the *Decision on Strengthening Education in Rural Region*, in which the government introduced new measures to achieve the stated goal of free basic education, namely waiving tuition and textbook fees and providing subsidies to students studying in boarding schools (*liangmian yibu*) (State Council 2003). Under new arrangements in 2005, the central and local governments would share the responsibilities of funding school education in rural regions. For the funding for tuition and miscellaneous items, the ratio of central input to local input is 8:2 and 6:4 for the western and central parts of China respectively. The ratio for the eastern provinces would be calculated based on the financial situations of individual provinces. For the funding of textbooks, the central government would bear those of the central and western regions, while local governments in eastern regions received no subsidy. The policy of waiving tuition and miscellaneous fees of students from rural areas began in the western part of China in 2006 and was expanded to the central and eastern parts of the country in 2007 (State Council 2005). The exemption policy will benefit about 150 million households with school-age children in rural areas (*People's Daily* 5 March 2007). Moreover, the central government also plans to set up a standard level of public financial input into rural compulsory education by 2009 and the required standard will be implemented by 2010 (State Council 2005).

In addition, the central government has committed to fully subsidize teacher education so as to enhance the quality of teachers, especially in rural regions. The vacancy rate for school teachers in rural regions is as high as 43 per cent. Meanwhile, the qualifications of about 310,000 school teachers is below the national standard, while about 500,000 provisional teachers do not have any relevant training. Among this group of provisional teachers, 76 per cent are working in rural areas in western and central China. To enhance the quality of the teaching profession, Premier Wen Jiabao announced the provision of free teacher education in 2007 in order to attract more young people to join the profession. Six major institutions of teacher education under the Ministry of Education will provide free education and accommodation to their future teachers and will provide subsidy to their living cost beginning in 2007. Furthermore, the government is encouraging teachers working in urban schools to move to rural schools by offering concessional terms of enrolment in postgraduate studies (*People's Daily* 5 March 2007; CNCSAA 2007).

Conclusion

We have examined some of the coping strategies employed by the Chinese government to address the problems generated from the privatization and marketization of education. Two types of response are evident: first, efforts to address some of the 'market failures' of the privatized education system through regulatory and financial reforms; and second, measures to restructure the respective roles of central and local governments. At the same time, the central government is beginning to articulate a set of principles about the 'welfare' role of government in assuring certain basic minimum standards and redressing inequalities. In the process, with the higher levels of financial support for the provision of school infrastructure afforded to rural local governments and those in the western provinces; tougher regulation of fees and charges; and curbs on further *minban* transformations, the pace of privatization is being slowed and the state's role as basic provider, as well as regulator and guarantor, is being reassessed.

Is this change a fundamental reversal or a pause? In our view, it is the latter, the aim being to redress some of the most obvious flaws of dual decentralization without fundamentally reversing it. Thus, re-centralization in the form of asserting a new role for central government is not so much a process of taking back powers from local government as it is a matter of taking on a greater share of their financial burden in achieving centrally mandated standards – that is, the centre is simply handing over more money (whether it thereby actually gains or loses power is a moot point). The setting of tougher standards is a major step in redefining the role of the public sector but it remains to be seen if the standards are enforced. Nonetheless, with the recent moves of the state to bridge the gap between social policy formulation and public finance provision, a trend of reasserting of the 'public' in public policy delivery has evolved (Ngok 2008; Ngok and Wen 2008).

The role of the centre as basic standard-setter, partial funder and overall regulator in the marketized system is fundamentally a market-conforming and supportive role. The state is now, in effect, intervening in order to try to make the market work more effectively. In terms of provision as distinct from funding and regulation, the school education system is now highly diversified, with multiple public and private actors playing different roles in different places (Mok and Ngok 2008). At the same time, it is a highly 'governed' market, albeit with numerous distortions as a result of measures by local governments to make use of their market power to garner rents. In this context, we should not underestimate the difficulties in overcoming the vested interests now embedded in the sector. Local governments, school managers, teachers and many parents (especially those who can afford to pay) have a stake in this system. Fundamentally challenging its form through tough pro-competitive regulations, or imposing tougher regulations to stamp out abuses and improve equity, threaten to create tensions between central and local governments, as well as with school managers and governing bodies. Even in regulating against malpractice it is questionable whether the central government has the capacity to prevent resistance and evasion by local actors who benefit from the system through their use of local discretionary powers (Bernstein and Lu 2003; Gong 2005).

In this regard, the attempted reassertion of the state in education should not be understood as a fundamental shift away from the market-oriented model but as an attempt to cope with some of the failings of that model through a mix of regulation, financing and residual direct provision. Aside from whether or not these instruments of 'market correction' will work to achieve equity, quality and universality, an important question for the future direction of regulation is whether the government will be a successful 'pro-competitive' regulator in the education sector or whether it will remain captured by the vested interests of the providers. In this connection, we hypothesize that having presided over and stimulated the autonomization and marketization process, it is arguable that the degree of decentralization – both horizontal and vertical – that resulted has seriously weakened the regulatory capacity of the central state. (Mok and Ngok 2008; Ngok and Guo 2007). Thus, whether or not the reassertion of state-ness in education will succeed in promoting accessibility, quality, legality and equality in the education sector is still subject to debate. In this connection, de-privatization and de-marketization is less a matter of reversal-cum-reconstruction in the context of new thinking about the limits to privatization and marketization strategies, but more an exercise in 'damage control' by which private and para-state organizations operating in the market are subject to new forms of regulation and some direct measures of subsidy are introduced to address the plight of the very poor. However, heightened public investment in the rural and non-coastal areas is introducing a potentially contradictory 'dual-track' system in which marketization may only be delayed: the incentives and legal framework for marketization will likely see the private sector grow in these parts of the country, just as it did in the coastal regions, as more funds are injected into the system.

But with a very strong political will of the Chinese Communist Party to adopt the 'scientific approach to development' (*kexue fazhanguan*) and the call for 'people-centred development', which is comprehensive, coordinated and sustainable, for the promotion of overall harmonic development of economy, society and human beings, we can safely anticipate that the present Chinese regime has attempted to bring the 'welfare' back into public service delivery. Judging from what has been achieved in the 29th Olympic Games organized by the Beijing Government and the post-earthquake crisis management in Sichuan directed by the central government, we may come to believe that the attempted reversal from the market to the state in public service delivery would succeed with a very strong political determination of the party-state in China. It is clear that the present Chinese authorities have tried to address the tensions and contradictions between rapid economic growth and worsening social inequalities. However, in the case of education, we have argued that any attempted reversal from the market-driven approach to a more state-centred, welfare-based approach would exceed the capacities of the state. Tensions and contradictions in education policy provide just one case among many others in contemporary China of a core political dilemma: how to uphold socialist ideologies in a neo-liberal policy setting, in order to preserve the legitimacy of the CCP regime.

Notes

1 Although we limit the second category on the vertical axis to 'administrative' reform, it could also include measures that might be considered as 'political' reform; however, political devolution as an issue is strictly constrained in China by the principles of democratic centralism under the leadership of the Communist Party.

2 The various terms used in discussions of these forms of decentralization do not have precise, agreed meanings – deconcentration, delegation, devolution and so on are often defined differently and rarely can be specified without overlap (but see Turner and Hulme 1997: 152–6). The use of 'deconcentration' here seeks to capture a dimension of unintended dispersal as well as deliberate delegation or devolution of power and authority.

3 The term 'cellular' has a particular connotation in debates on Chinese politics (Liberthal 1992: 11; Shue 1994: 68–70; Agelasto 1996: 275–6). It often refers to the extent to which local economic and political units were able to block the upward flow of information and to cushion themselves from the effects of vertical commands, particularly in rural China. Bernstein and Lu (2003: 88) argue that post-reform fiscal and political changes have further 'cellularized' power in China. The term is used here somewhat more narrowly to connote a process of horizontal structural fragmentation and autonomization on the fringes of the state.

4 In Chinese, the term commonly employed for these bodies is *shiye danwei*. The terms used in English vary: 'institutional units' (Cheng 2001); 'public service units' (World Bank 2005a); or 'service organizations' (Lam and Perry 2001).
5 Coastal region here includes Beijing, Tianjin, Hebei, Liaoning, Shanghai, Jiangsu, Zhejiang, Zhejiang, Fujian, Shandong, Guangdong, Guangxi, Hainan.
6 Non-government financial resources here refer to input from social organizations and individuals and donations.
7 Independent status consists of possession of a separate legal identity; a separate campus; independent finance; and independent admissions and qualification-awarding mechanisms.

Bibliography

21st Century Business Herald (2004) 11 October.
Agelasto, Michael (1996) 'Cellularism, *Guangxiwang* and Corruption: A Microcosmic View from Within a Chinese Educational *Danwei*', *Crime, Law and Social Change* 25(3): 265–88.
Benewick, Robert, Tong, Irene and Howell, Jude (2004) 'Self-governance and Community: A Preliminary Comparison between Villagers' Committees and Urban Community Councils', *China Information* 18(1): 11–28.
Bernstein, Thomas P. and Lu, Xiaobo (2003) *Taxation without Representation in Contemporary Rural China*, Cambridge: Cambridge University Press.
Borevskaya, N. (2003) 'The Private Sector in the Chinese Educational System: Problem and Prospects', *Far Eastern Affairs* 31(4): 89–107.
Cao, H. (1997) 'Where to put their school desks?', *China New Digest* 315: 3–6.
Central Committee of the Chinese Communist Party [CCCCP] (1985) *The Decision of the Central Committee of the Communist Party of China on the Reform of Educational Structure*, Beijing: People's Press.
Central Committee of the Chinese Communist Party [CCCCP] (1993) 'The Programme for Educational Reform and Development in China', *Zhonghua Renmin Gongheguo Guowuyuan Gongbao* 2: 58–66.
Chen, C. G. and Yu, Q. Y. (2005) *Zoujin dazonghua: 21 shiji chu Guangzhou shi gaodeng jiaoyu fazhan yanjiu* (Towards Massification: Research on Higher Education Development in the Early 21st Century), Guangzhou: Jinan daxue chubanshe.
Cheng, Siwei (2001) 'Strategic Directions and Policy Implementation for Reforming China's Institutional Units', *Studies on Economic Reforms and Development in China*, Oxford: Oxford University Press, pp. 319–46.
China Education and Research Network (2004) 'A Government Official's Answers to Questions on Lump-sum Payment Method'. Available at: www.edu.cn/20040531/3106852.shtml.
China Education and Research Network (2006) 'The Educational Development during the 10th 5-Year Plan. Available at: www.edu.cn/news_1461/20060228/t20060228_164200.shtml.
China Education Yearbook 1998 (1999) Beijing: People's Press.
China Education Yearbook 2004 (2005) Beijing: People's Press.
China Higher Education Student Information (2007) Available at www.chsi.com.cn.
China National Center For Student Assistance Administration [CNCSAA] (2007) *Introduction to the Policies of Financial Assistance to Tertiary Students*, Beijing: CNCSAA.

China Youth Daily (2006) 14 July.

Cummings, W. (1996) 'Asian Values, Education and Development', *Compare* 26(3): 287–304.

Dai, J. L. (2005) 'Resident's Life: Moving towards the Society of Overall Well-to-do Level', in B. Ren (ed.) *2005 Blue Book of Zhejiang*, Hangzhou: Hangzhou Publishing House.

Duckett, Jane (1998) *The Entrepreneurial State in China. Real Estate and Commerce Departments in Reform Era Tianjin*, London: Routledge.

Gong, Ting (2005) 'Corruption and Local Governance: The Double Identity of Chinese Local Governments in Market Reform', paper presented to the Fourth International Convention of Asian Scholars, 20–24 August, in Shanghai.

Hawkins, J. N. (2000) 'Centralization, Decentralization, Recentralization: Educational Reform in China', *Journal of Educational Administration* 38(5): 442–54.

Keng, C. W. (2006) 'China's Unbalanced Economic Growth', *Journal of Contemporary China* 15(46): 183–214.

Lam, Tao-Chiu and Perry, James L. (2001) 'Service Organizations in China: Reform and its Limits', in Peter Nan-Shong Lee and Carlos Wing-Hung Lo (eds) *Remaking China's Public Management*, Westport, CT: Quorum Books, pp. 19–40.

Li, R. (2007) 'Casualties of the Rush to Profit from Schooling', *South China Morning Post*, 27 January.

Liang, Z. (2001) 'The Age of Migration in China', *Population and Development Review* 27(3): 499–524.

Liberthal, Kenneth G. (1992) 'Introduction: The "Fragmented Authoritarianism" Model and its Limitations', in Kenneth G. Liberthal and David M. Lampton (eds) *Bureaucrats, Politics and Decision Making in Post-Mao China*, Berkeley: University of California Press, pp. 1–30.

Lin, J. (2004) 'China: Private Trends', *International Higher Education* 36: 17–18.

Lin, J., Zhang, Y., Gao, L. and Liu, Y. (2005) 'Trust, Ownership, and Autonomy: Challenges Facing Private Higher Education in China', *The China Review* 5(1): 61–82.

Lin, T. and Chen, Y. (2004) 'The Plights and Outlets of Public Primary School and Middle School in the Course of Institution Changing', *Forum on Contemporary Education* 5: 45–9.

Liu, C., Taibin, L. and Jun, L. (1998) 'A Case Study of Migrant Sponsored School in Western Shanghai', in S. Zhang, W. Le, C. Xu and C. Song (eds) *The Floating Population in Shanghai: Current Situation and Future Prospects*, Shanghai: East China Normal University Press.

Lo, Carlos Wing-Hung, Lo, Jack Man-Keung and Cheung, Kai-Chee (2001) 'Service Organizations in the Environmental Governance System of the People's Republic of China', in Peter Nan-Shong Lee and Carlos Wing-Hung Lo (eds) *Remaking China's Public Management*, Westport, CT: Quorum Books, pp. 41–63.

Lu, Xiaobo (2000) 'Booty Socialism, Bureau-preneurs and the State in Transition: Organizational Corruption in China', *Comparative Politics* 32(3): 273–94.

Min, W. F. (2004) 'Chinese Higher Education: The Legacy of the Past and the Context of the Future', in P. Altbach and T. Umakoshi (eds) *Asian Universities: Historical Perspectives and Contemporary Challenges*, Baltimore, MD: The John Hopkins University Press.

Ministry of Education [MOE] (2004) *China Educational Finance Statistical Yearbook 2004*, Beijing: Zhongguo Tongji Chubanshe.

Ministry of Education [MOE] (2006a) *Compulsory Education Law*, Beijing: MOE.

Ministry of Education [MOE] (2006b) *Implementation Opinion on the Works of Controlling Overcharging in Education,* Beijing: MOE.

Ministry of Education [MOE] (2007) 'Two Basics' Project in Western China. Available at: www.moe.edu.cn/edoas/website18/level2.jsp?tablename=1798.

Mok, K. H. (1996) 'Marketization and Decentralization: Development of Education and Paradigm Shift in Social Policy', *Hong Kong Public Administration* 5(1): 35–56.

Mok, K. H. (2000) 'Marketizing Higher Education in Post-Mao China', *International Journal of Educational Development* 20(2): 109–26.

Mok, K. H. (2005) 'Riding over Socialism and Global Capitalism: Changing Education Governance and Social Policy Paradigms in Post-Mao China', *Comparative Education* 41(2): 217–42.

Mok, K. H. (2006a) *Education Reform and Education Policy in East Asia,* London: Routledge.

Mok, K. H. (2006b) 'The Growing Prominence of the Privateness in Higher Education: Challenges for Higher Education Governance in China', unpublished paper currently under review by Compare.

Mok, K. H. and Ngok, K. L. (2008) 'One Country, Diverse Systems: Politics of Educational Decentralization and Challenges for Regulatory State in Post-Mao China', *China Review* 8(2): 169–99.

Mountfield, Edward and Wong, Christine P. (2005) 'Public Expenditure on the Frontline: Toward Effective Management by Subnational Governments', *East Asia Decentralizes: Making Local Government Work,* Washington, DC: World Bank, pp. 85–106.

National Bureau of Statistics of China [NBSC] (2005) *China Statistical Yearbook 2005,* Beijing: Zhongguo Tongji Chubanshe.

Ngok, K. L. (2008) 'A Study of Social Policy Expenditure of China in the Context of Public Policy Pattern Transformation', *Chinese Public Policy Review* 2: 42–68.

Ngok, King Lun and Chan Kin Keung, David (2003) 'Towards Centralization and Decentralization in Educational Development in China: the Case of Shanghai', in Ka Ho Mok (ed.) *Centralization and Decentralization: Educational Reforms and Changing Governance in Chinese Societies,* Hong Kong: Comparative Education Research Centre, The University of Hong Kong and Kluwer Academic Publishers.

Ngok, K. L. and Guo, W. Q. (2007) 'The Quest for World Class Universities in China: Critical Reflections', *The Journal of Comparative Asian Development* 6(1): 21–44.

Ngok, K. L. and Wen, Z. Y. (2008) 'The Development of Social Policy in China: 2004–2007', *Chinese Public Policy Review* 2: 213–31.

Painter, M. (2008) 'From Command Economy to Hollow State? Decentralization in Vietnam and China', *Australian Journal of Public Administration* 67(1): 79–88.

People's Daily 5 March 2007; 7 September 2004.

Qian, X. L. and Smyth, R. (2005) 'Measuring Regional Inequality of Education in China: Widening Cost – Inland Gap or Widening Rural–Urban Gap?', *ABERU Discussion Paper* 12: 1–12.

Rocca, Jean-Louis (2003) 'The Rise of the Social and the Chinese State', *China Information* 17(1): 1–27.

Rong, X. L. and Shi, T. J. (2001) 'Inequality in Chinese Education', *Journal of Contemporary China* 10(26): 107–24.

Schurmann, Franz (1968) *Ideology and Organization in Communist China* (second edition), Berkeley, CA: University of California Press.

Schweickart, D. (2006) 'China: Market Socialism or Capitalism? accessed on 8 February

2007. Available at www.solidarityeconomy.net/2006/11/01/china-market-socilism-or-capitalism.

Shanghai Research Institute of Educational Sciences (2005) 'The Causes, Implications and Trends of the Policy of Transformation in Public Schools', *Education Development and Research* 8B: 16–23.

Shi, Q. H. *et al.* (2005) 'Affiliated Colleges and Private Education Development in China: Take Independent Colleges as an Example'. Available at: www.ocair.org/files/presentations/Paper2003_04/forum2004/ChinaHE.pdf.

Shirk, Susan (1992) 'The Chinese Political System and the Political Strategy of Economic Reform', in Kenneth G. Liberthal and David M. Lampton (eds) *Bureaucrats, Politics and Decision Making in Post-Mao China*, Berkeley, CA: University of California Press, pp. 59–91.

Shue, Vivienne (1994) 'State Power and Social Organization in China', in Joel S. Migdal, Atul Kohli and Vivienne Shue (eds) *State Power and Social Forces: Domination and Transformation in the Third World*, Cambridge: Cambridge University Press, pp. 65–88.

So, W. Y. (2006) 'Privatisation', in C. Tubilewicz (ed.) *Critical Issues in Contemporary China*, London: Routledge; Hong Kong: Open University of Hong Kong Press.

State Council (2003) *Decision on Strengthening Education in Rural Region*, Beijing: State Council.

State Council (2005) *Notice on Deepening the Financial Mechanism for Rural Compulsory Education*, Beijing: State Council.

State Education Commission [SEC] (1995) *Education Law*, Beijing: State Education Commission.

Ta Kung Pao (2006) 25 April.

Turner, Mark and Hulme, David (1997) *Government Administration and Development: Making the State Work*, Houndsmill, Basingstoke: Macmillan Press.

United Nations Development Programme [UNDP] (2005) *China's Human Development Report 2005*, Washington, DC: United Nations Development Programme.

Wang, F. and Zuo, X. (1999) 'Inside China's Cities: Institutional Barriers and Opportunities for Urban Migrants', *The American Economic Review* 89(2): 276–80.

Wang, X. (2005a) 'Implications of Social Stratification for Higher Education Enrolment', *Jiangsu Higher Education* 3: 47–9.

Wang, X. (2005b) 'A Study on Higher Education Enrolment in Guangdong: A Survey on a Number of Higher Education Institutions in Guangdong', *Higher Education Exploration* 3: 11–13.

Wang, Y. B. (2007) 'China's Higher Education on a Overpass of 4 fold Transitions', paper presented to the video seminar series of 'Universities and Ideas', 30 April 2007, in Zhejiang University, Hangzhou China.

Wedeman, Andrew (2000) 'Budgets, Extra-budgets and Small Treasuries', *Journal of Contemporary China* 9(25): 489–511.

Wei, Y. T. and Zhang, G. C. (1995) 'A Historical Perspective on Non-governmental Higher Education in China', paper presented to the International Conference on Private Education in Asia and the Pacific Region, at University of Xiamen, Xiamen.

Weil, R. (2006) 'Conditions of the Working Classes in China', *Monthly Review* 58(2), accessed on 8 February 2007. Available at http://canadiandimension.com/articles/2006/07/29/596.

Wong, Christine E. (ed.) (1997) *Financing Local Government in the People's Republic of China*, Hong Kong: Oxford University Press.

Wong, Linda (2002) 'Individualization of Social Rights in China', in Sally Sargeson (ed.) *Collective Goods, Collective Futures in Asia*, London: Routledge, pp.162–78.

Wong, L. and Flynn, N. (eds) (2001) *The Market in Chinese Social Policy*, Basingstoke: Palgrave.

World Bank (2005a) *China; Deepening Public Service Unit Reform to Improve Service Delivery*, Report No. 32341-CHA, Poverty Reduction and Economic Management Unit East Asia and Pacific Region, Washington, DC: World Bank.

World Bank (2005b) *East Asia Decentralizes: Making Local Government Work*, Washington, DC: World Bank, pp. 1–24.

Yang, D. P. (2004) 'The New Development Paradigm and China's Education', in X. Yu *et al.* (eds) *Analysis and Forecast on China's Social Development 2005*, Beijing: Social Sciences Academic Press.

Yang, D. P. (2005) 'Towards Social Justice: Education in 2005', in X. Yu *et al.* (eds) *Analysis and Forecast on China's Social Development 2006*, Beijing: Social Sciences Academic Press.

Yang, R. (1997) 'The Debate on Private Higher Education Development in China', *International Higher Education*, Fall, 1–4.

Yao, S. J., Zhang, Z. Y. and Hanma, L. (2004) 'Growing Inequality and Poverty in China', *China Economic Review* 15(2): 145–63.

Yu Zin *et al.* (eds) (2007) *Bluebook of Chinese Society 2007*, Beijing: Social Sciences Academic Press.

Zhong, X. (2006) 'Analysis of the Reasons about the Impartiality Deficiencies in China's Higher Education', *Journal of Jiangsu Polytechnic University* 7(3): 41–4.

Zhu, Q. F. (2005) 'Social and Economic Indicators: Analysis and Assessment', in X. Yu *et al.* (eds) *Analysis and Forecast on China's Social Development 2006*, Beijing: Social Sciences Academic Press.

10 Public planning with business delivery of urban public transport

Paul A. Barter

Introduction

This chapter highlights a trend for a set of 'public–private partnerships' or 'hybrid models' to increasingly be seen as best practice in public transport for a wide range of international contexts. In particular, most interest here is in the models in which a public agency takes responsibility for the excellence of an integrated system and delegates delivery of efficient services to business enterprises under service contracts, often with competitive tendering.

Rising interest in such approaches might not seem to be a case of 'reasserting' the role of the public sector. In fact, opposition in some countries has involved characterising such reforms as 'privatisation'. However, with a more global perspective, the emergence of public sector agencies taking the lead on detailed system planning can actually be seen to mark the defeat of a long-standing push for deregulation. It represents a triumph for public planning over more purely market-led arrangements. Furthermore, the starting point for such reforms outside the West has generally not been public monopoly but the lightly regulated private provision of public transport. It should thus be seen as very much an assertion of a vital role for the public sector. I term this approach, 'proactive planning with service contracting' rather than simply 'service contracting' (which is more familiar in the literature) in order to emphasise that well-focused and ambitious public sector planning is seen here as a vital aspect of the model, which should not be understood simply in terms of its approach to contracting out.

Also of interest here is the question of how widely applicable the more ambitious approaches to proactive planning with service contracting will prove to be in low-income cities. Case studies examined here provide cause for cautious optimism. A surprisingly diverse and international range of cities with a wide range of income levels have been adopting such approaches, although their starting points and pathways for these reforms have varied enormously. Which reform trajectories are feasible is clearly also an important question for would-be regulatory reformers.

In the section below I provide an overview of the regulatory trends over many decades, culminating in a push for deregulation followed by disappointment and a recent search for alternatives. Then, I highlight a number of illustrative cities which provide a picture of diverse starting points and trajectories towards an ambitious approach to public sector planning combined with private sector operation of public transport services. This is followed by a synthesis of lessons learned.

Before proceeding further it is important to define what is meant by the term, public transport. As used here, it refers to passenger transport services which are available to the general public and which are run regularly (or semi-regularly) on fixed (or semi-fixed) routes. It is equivalent in common usage to the North American term, transit. The word 'public' in public transport need not imply state ownership, nor even public sector management or planning. With this conception of public transport, taxis are excluded but 'jitney' style services by minivans are included. In some cities, shared taxis can straddle a grey area at the boundary between taxi service and fixed-route public transport.

The push for deregulation and its historical background

Great international diversity in actual regulatory arrangements and ownership structures, particularly in developing countries, can make it difficult to generalise about trends in this sector. Nevertheless, it is meaningful to discuss some major tendencies that have swept the industry. The most prominent example in this section is the push for deregulation starting in the 1970s. Along with privatisation, this was the most widely noted trend in public transport arrangements until quite recently (see for example, Gómez-Ibáñez and Meyer 1993). At its most ambitious, this agenda involved calling for deregulation of prices and services and the removal of barriers to entry in public transport markets. It was especially apparent in the high-income English-speaking countries as well as through parts of the international development assistance bureaucracy, most notably the World Bank. However we will also see that this agenda was not purely the well-known neo-liberal one.

Typology of regulatory and industry structure options

Before discussing the historical trends it would be useful to briefly explain the range of regulatory options as they are understood in this chapter. The following typology is adapted from those used by Bayliss (2000) and Meakin (2002) and is informed by Vasconcellos' (2001) insights on cycles of public transport regulation. Unconventionally, my key criteria in arranging the options is not the extent of competition, nor ownership arrangements, but the extent to which the state takes responsibility for service outcomes. This leads me to frame my categories differently, such as making an unusual distinction between 'passive franchises', 'proactively regulated franchises' and 'proactive planning with service contracts'. Glover (2007) suggests public sector responsibility as a definition of 'public transport'. I see this as an untenable definition but he is right in highlighting the importance of whether or not government takes responsibility for outcomes.

Public monopoly

Services are owned, planned and operated by a publicly owned enterprise. An urban region may have several of these state-run operators. There may be some private involvement in the form of management contracts or contracting out of certain other very specific tasks. In theory at least, the state takes total responsibility for the outcomes here. However, state-owned operators vary widely in their organisation, management efficiency and performance.

Proactive planning with service contracts

Services are planned by a state agency and procured from independent businesses (either private or state-owned) under service contracts. It is usually routes or bundles of routes that are the subject of contracts. The public sector agency takes primary responsibility for the planning of the network and for many of the service outcomes. A symbol of this is that system marketing and its public identity are created by the public sector coordinating agency, while the operators' identities remain in the background. In the most ambitiously integrated systems the payment approach is often 'gross-cost', which means payment for bus kilometres run, sometimes in combination with other incentive payments, and the operators are limited in the tactical choices available to them. However, some variations use 'net-cost' contracts, in which operators keep fare payments, and these usually involve the state taking somewhat less planning responsibility, less ambitious integration of the system, and require more tactical freedom to remain with the operators. Most focus in this chapter is on the more ambitious approaches above.

Franchises (well-regulated)

Operators are given the right to serve a route or a whole area but with some obligation to do so in a comprehensive way and to meet service standards in return for exclusivity and discretion over many tactical details of service. Competitive tendering or other direct competitive pressures may or may not be present but the obligations are enforced effectively. Responsibility for outcomes is shared, and this may be symbolised by both the public sector regulator and the private sector operators having prominent public identities. Hong Kong, Singapore (until 2009) and many Brazilian cities have such systems in practice. Franchising the right to serve logical areas may be somewhat more effective than route by route.

Passive franchises

Operators are given the right to serve routes, usually with some simple service obligations and at least some exclusivity. Examples mentioned later include Kuala Lumpur and Seoul in the past. On paper, such systems can be similar to service contracts or the well-regulated franchises above. However, the public sector fails to take active responsibility for planning of the route network as a whole. A related problem is that it often fails to adequately enforce obligations under the contracts. As a result, the network will often be a set of long-established routes, or merely be those proposed by operators. Incumbents often remain in place indefinitely with licence renewals becoming routine and lacking any requirement for competitive tendering. Regulation tends to focus on fares and on protecting the incumbents from 'unfair' competition.

Deregulation

As used here this term refers to a set of arrangements in which the state has little direct influence over service outcomes. Almost always, it is the vehicle rather than the route that is the subject of licensing. Most typologies distinguish several variations. The most extreme form involves vehicle licensing with little or no barriers to entry or exit. Simple quantity limits may be added to this, but still with no obligation to provide service. Some basic features of quality may also be enforced. Effective deregulation may also exist if franchises for routes or areas lack exclusivity or allow for sub-contracting and do not impose any obligation for comprehensive service. Interestingly, deregulated services do not always have deregulated prices in practice.

A related but distinct dimension is the issue of how contracts to serve a route or area monopoly are awarded. This can be done in various ways, some involving more explicit competition than others. Options include competitive tendering, performance-based contracts, negotiated renewable contracts, or some hybrid of these (Houghton and Hensher 2005).

Deregulatory push in Western cities and its background

Debate over deregulated versus planned on-street public transport services extends as far back as the mid-nineteenth century, when horse-drawn versions of what we would now call buses became common on the streets of London and Paris, initially in an unregulated (and chaotic) manner (Gómez-Lobo 2007). By the early twentieth century, rail-based public transport (trams, urban rail and suburban rail) became the main motorised modes of transport in Western cities. These tended to settle into localised monopolies formalised as 'franchises'. However, from the 1920s they began to face competition from free-wheeling petrol or diesel-fuelled buses operating initially in a relatively unregulated environment (see for example the account of London's experience in Rimmer 1986). This led to increasingly successful calls to restrict on-road competition and for coordination across modes (Van de Velde 2003).

Then, as car ownership increased through the middle of the century, the financial position of public transport operators was further eroded through direct competition especially for off-peak and non-radial trips, due to congestion impacts on service, and through the emergence of urban development patterns poorly suited to public transport (see, for example, Hall 1977 for accounts of these trends in several major cities). Together with fare regulation, such trends led to the deterioration of service and/or bankruptcy for many public transport companies, followed by municipal or state takeovers in most Western cities by the 1960s.

However, disappointment with the subsequent performance of state-run public transport was a factor behind a push for privatisation and deregulation from the 1970s. This dovetailed with the wider mood in policy-related professions. For example, many transport economists questioned earlier justifications of public monopoly. Mees (2000) provides a critical review of this intellectual push. In 1986, a dramatic reform privatised and deregulated bus services and fares in Britain with the exception of those in London and Northern Ireland. This much-studied reform created open entry in the bus industry but required operators to give advance warning of changes in timetables or routes. Public transport professionals elsewhere watched with interest.

Paths to deregulated public transport in market economies of the South

Public transport industry arrangements in the developing world were, and continue to be, highly diverse. The focus of the review here will be countries with market economies that are, or were until recently, developing countries (the 'South'). We can find almost every possible combination of public sector and private roles, often with more than one approach coexisting in a single city. Nevertheless, some widespread trends can be observed which have both commonalities with and differences from those of the West.

The early twentieth century public transport story in the large cities of the market-oriented parts of the South was often similar to that of the West, although rail and tram investments were generally on a smaller scale. This and rapid urban growth resulted in a large role for buses in mixed traffic by the 1960s (Barter *et al.* 2003). Experiences diverged from those of the West from the middle of century. Formal sector or corporate public transport enterprises generally thrived only in the large cities where demand for their services was 'thick'. In smaller cities and towns, motorised travel played a smaller role and was often dominated by informal taxi-like modes and later by unregulated atomistic public transport operations (see below). Unlike the West, relatively few cities in the South had public monopolies my mid-century, although some post-independence governments did later follow that trend (Gwilliam 2000).

Others used franchises to grant some exclusivity to the operators of established routes in return for fare regulation. Although the literature promoting deregulation devoted more energy to highlighting the evils of public monopoly, in practice the route franchising approach also has a poor record of becoming moribund and inefficient (with regulatory capture often implicated). Operators under such route licences often face crippling fare controls and their networks tend to become frozen in place with no effective mechanisms or incentives for the network to be improved (Gwilliam 2000).

Many, perhaps even most, cities in the South have at various times seen 'free-enterprise' public transport industries develop without effective regulation and with fragmented ownership. These often arose into a vacuum (as in small cities) or with the failure of incumbent franchised or route-licensed bus systems (or earlier tram systems) to expand or extend service rapidly enough (Cervero 2000). Deregulation in the South thus usually emerged by unplanned attrition, in the form of initially illegal bus or van services. In some cities, such as Delhi, a partial opening of entry occurred in response to the failings of the public monopoly operator (Mehta 2002). Another pathway to fragmented and unregulated service was often seen in Latin America, involving informal subcontracting by route licensees to atomistic small players (Vasconcellos 2001; Estache and Gómez-Lobo 2005). There were also examples of deliberate deregulation reforms, most famously in Santiago. Some of these predated Britain's, although their starting points were diverse, including regulated private franchises and public monopolies.

There was also a countertrend for some governments to seek to create or bolster large corporate public transport enterprises without necessarily national-ising. Singapore in the early 1970s was a prominent example with an enforced consolidation and the imposition of 'professional' management. This created a single operator (later two) under what amounted to an area franchise. Some Brazilian cities also consolidated their bus industries in the same period (Vasconcellos 2001).

The policy agenda for deregulation in the South was promoted not just by neo-liberal policy thinking but also by the 'discovery' and defence of the informal sector in development studies and related fields. This school of thought displayed suspicion of central control and of the imposition of formal-sector corporate organisational models in the then conventional approach to public transport, with its allegedly modernising agenda, technological fixations and proneness to capital intensive projects (Rimmer 1986). Singapore's reforms, and similar 'modernising' policies elsewhere in Southeast Asia, were thus criticised by admirers of 'unincorporated' small operators in deregulated contexts such as in Rimmer (1986). These sentiments resonated with neo-liberal appeals for deregulation (see Roth and Wynne 1982, or for a critical review Mees 2000).

Many developing cities have faced regulatory instability. Some have come full circle more than once as they pass through one of the characteristic cycles of regulation in which each relatively easy option breaks down or is rejected in turn (Vasconcellos 2001; Gómez-Ibáñez and Meyer 1993). Deregulated systems also often prove unstable because their troubling outcomes provoke attempts at regulation.

Widespread disappointment with deregulation

By the end of the 1990s the push for deregulation had lost its momentum, both in the West and the South. Britain's deregulation experience was an important influence and has been much reviewed. The reform allowed greatly reduced

public subsidy, lowered costs per bus kilometre, and led to increased bus kilometres. However, it also saw drops in passenger numbers faster than the earlier
trend (and in contrast with London), increased real fares and loss of coordination
(White 1995; Mackie *et al.* 1995). Importantly, criticism has been based not just
on the expected 'pro-planning' concerns but also on disappointment with the
robustness of competition itself (Mackie *et al.* 1995).

British-style deregulation was not taken up elsewhere in the West, except for
New Zealand and certain deregulated niches such as airport shuttles in the
United States (Cervero 1997; Transportation Research Board 2001). In
automobile-dependent Australia and the USA one reason for this may be that
public transport had withered so badly that there seemed little hope of it thriving
as a business with open entry. For Europe the explanation lay more in the desire
to preserve and strengthen integration, as we will see later.

Experiences in the South with deregulated (or never regulated) bus or van services have also been problematic, although it should be acknowledged that they
have not always been decisively inferior to regulated alternatives, such as public
monopoly systems or ossified route franchise systems. Such systems still deliver
high levels of public transport service in many cities, despite their problems. Nevertheless deregulated competition in the market clearly has unfortunate (and now
predictable) results. These include: oversupply with bus congestion on key routes;
high fares (where there is fare deregulation); failure to serve low-demand locations
and times; racing dangerously for passengers; waiting at terminals until full before
departing; and many others (Estache and Gómez-Lobo 2005). It also aggravates
the declining fortunes of any public monopoly or franchised services, which often
labour under stricter regulation, fare control or service obligations. Moreover, vigorous competition in the market rarely seems to last long. Routes tend to become
informally regulated by route associations or other business entities which, lacking
state-backed enforcement powers, often use intimidation and regulate in their own
interests not the public interest (Vasconcellos 2001).

Disappointment with unregulated buses in both Britain and the South has
eroded the promotion of deregulation by the policy establishment, at least for
large cities (see, for example, World Bank 2002). It has also prompted a theoretical reassessment (Gómez-Lobo 2007; Estache and Gómez-Lobo, 2005). This
reassessment is helping to clear up some long-running confusion. Bus systems
are not natural monopolies in the sense that, if left to themselves, ownership
does fragment. However, government-imposed barriers to entry are indeed
useful and theoretically justifiable.

It should be noted that the end of the push for deregulation has not automatically meant the end of unregulated or ineffectually regulated public transport in the
South. Reform of such systems is no simple matter. How then can cities in the
South with deregulated public transport gain better control and better outcomes?
State-run monopolies are unlikely to provide a lasting solution. Many route franchise systems are also in need of reform, having often become passive, without active
planning and with moribund entrenched operators. Fortunately, various cities have
been finding ways forward. These are discussed in the next section.

The rise of proactive planning with service contracting

This section highlights a surprising range of cities that have been making transitions to strongly and ambitiously planned public transport with services procured under service contracts of some kind. Some may find it surprising that this trend extends to various countries of the global South, where both deregulated, fragmented systems and moribund route-licence ('passive franchise') systems have been reformed. In the West it is public monopolies that have been transformed.

The regulatory approaches now most commonly recommended to low-income developing cities (large ones at least) are hybrid models. Some are in the 'proactive planning with service contracting' category while many fall into the 'franchises' category, often with a new determination to use effective contracting mechanisms to avoid the problems of what this chapter calls the 'passive' approach to franchises. Best practice thus now usually calls on the state to take at least some significant responsibility for the system as a whole and calls for private provision via some kind of contracting-out mechanism, usually with competition for the market or at least its threat (Meakin 2002; Gwilliam 2005; Bayliss 2000).

Can the 'proactive planning with service contracting' approach be used in low-income cities? There are concerns that it may require more institutional capacity than is realistic for most developing countries. In fact, there are such concerns even over the less ambitiously planned systems and the less intensively managed contracts of the franchise approach. In discussing options for cities in the South, Estache and Gómez-Lobo (2005) broadly endorse a range of hybrid options including service contracts, but they comment that, in the absence of strong institutions these options may not be possible, in which case deregulation may be superior to a public enterprise approach. Örn (2005) endorses more strongly a planned and coordinated service-contracting approach for developing cities but does not see any feasible pathway towards it from a starting point of unregulated public transport. On the basis of Jamaica's failure to achieve a direct jump from deregulation to what he calls a 'coordinated system with managed competition' he suggests that public monopoly probably needs to be an intermediate stage.

A brief review below of a series of cases will provide grounds for optimism that ambitious versions of proactive planning with service contracts may be more widely applicable than has been assumed. Surprisingly diverse cities have been converging on such options via a number of different pathways.

European cases

Public monopoly was the 1980s starting point for most European cities. Those that have so far responded ambitiously to the push for competition and private participation have adopted not Britain's deregulation option, but procurement approaches that retain strong public control. A key factor in this choice appears to have been a heightened commitment to public transport network integration that gathered momentum in the 1980s and 1990s.

Systems that had come under public ownership during the middle of the twentieth century nevertheless often remained quite fragmented under an array of public agencies or governments at several levels. Following the pioneering example of Hamburg, various cities across central and northern Europe formed regional public transport alliances in which a small but strong coordination agency takes responsibility for public transport planning in consultation with operators and political leadership (Glover 2007). Services operated by various state or municipality owned enterprises, and sometimes some private companies, were now procured under contracts by the alliance agency. This allowed integration of ticketing, marketing, information, schedules, physical facilities and network layouts across whole urban regions (Mees 2000).

These new regional arrangements proved compatible with a service contracting model for privatisation and competition. London was a pioneer in Europe. Its buses had been exempted from the 1986 deregulation but had still been required to introduce private participation and competition. London did so through competitive tendering while retaining central control under a state-owned agency. The results are widely regarded as successful, with both efficiency gains and increases in patronage. It experimented with different approaches to tendering and service contracts and eventually settled on gross cost contracts (Hensher 2003). By the 1990s, Scandinavian cities were at the vanguard of regulatory reform in European public transport. An empowered public sector agency dedicated to the excellence and integration of the system as a whole procured service delivery from businesses using service contracts with competitive tendering (Van de Velde 2003; Hidson and Müller 2003).

Curitiba

These shifts in Europe were predated by events in Brazil where Curitiba was a pioneer in the 1960s and 1970s of a step-by-step shift towards proactive planning and coordination with service-contract procurement. The city has been widely praised for its pioneering use of bus rapid transit (BRT) and for integrating land use patterns with its busway-based development spines (Cervero 1998). Less well known is its sustained success in bringing its privately operated bus system under efficient public regulatory and planning control (see, for example, Hook 2005; Vasconcellos 2001).

In stark contrast to the European examples, Curitiba's starting point was a fragmented and little regulated bus system. In the 1950s the city's bus industry had been regulated via route licences without strong exclusivity or oversight. The result was essentially a deregulated situation because of informal sub-contracting to even smaller operators and fragmentation of ownership. In 1962, enforced consolidation of the industry reduced the number of companies from more than 300 to ten and established a more robust franchise ('concession') contracting approach with stronger enforcement (Hook 2005). A shift from route licences to area contracts was a further improvement (Poole *et al.* 1994).

Further steps went with the 1974 introduction of the first BRT lines. A closed BRT approach was adopted with only dedicated high-capacity buses running on the busways themselves. These were to be run by the incumbent operators. As Hook (2005) explains, with contracts due for renewal, the threat of competitive tendering was vital in order to prod operators into investing in higher capacity buses suited to the trunk routes. A dedicated public transport planning agency was created and took on powers for detailed tactical planning of an 'Integrated Transport Network' as a whole. This agency is somewhat insulated from short-term political influence (Cervero 1998). This was a big step towards the pro-active planning with service contracting approach and was followed by a series of innovations over the next two decades that created a highly integrated system, with free transfers, efficient feeders, and payment for service kilometres (gross-cost contracts) with centralised fare collection by 1987 (Hook 2005). By then the system had many of the key features of the service contract approach, although so far without regular competitive tendering (Hidalgo *et al.* 2007).

Bogotá

Bogotá, capital of Colombia, has recently become famous for its dramatic urban transport and public space transformations in the late 1990s. Like many other Latin American cities, Bogotá's pre-reform bus system was effectively a deregulated one, since its route licence arrangements allowed informal sub-contracting to a multitude of tiny firms competing on the road, with the usual problematic results (Estache and Gómez-Lobo 2005).

The centrepiece of the changes was the Transmilenio BRT system, which is widely regarded as the pinnacle to date of BRT planning. It deserves as much attention for its innovations in regulatory design and its industry restructuring in a challenging context (Hook 2005). Bogotá's public transport transformations have not involved a city-wide reform. Rather, each corridor was addressed in turn as the Transmilenio BRT system expanded. A lean public agency plans and manages the system and makes the service-related tactical decisions. Contracts with operators on the trunks are gross-cost. A sophisticated monitoring system, including the use of GPS, ensures buses run as required. Each trunk route also has integrated feeder buses. An innovative feature of contracts is that each trunk route was allocated to two concessionaires, which share the service kilometres on that route. This allows 'fines' for poor performance to be in the form of reducing the services allocated to the offending concessionaire (and shifting them to its rival). This provides for ongoing competitive pressures in real time (Hook 2005). The planning agency also reserves the right to reduce service if overall patronage drops.

Just as crucial, was the approach to the transitions in each corridor. Incumbent players were assured of a share in the new system but under conditions. Large numbers of old buses were required to be scrapped. The new consortia were encouraged to form joint ventures with international companies. This process of engaging with the actors in the traditional bus industry has been a challenge at every expansion of the system. Large parts of the city remain outside the reformed Transmilenio arrangements and the power of incumbents continues to threaten the reforms (Gilbert 2008).

Political deliberation issues were also made explicit in the design of Transmilenio. One key to success was that, as in Curitiba, the public transport changes were part of a larger package that included high-profile improvements to the city's public spaces. Contractual and market designs involve several protections against short-sighted political interference (Hook 2005). In fact, a new administration in 2007 is seen as hostile to the busways and their expansion (Gilbert 2008).

Seoul

In 2004, Seoul implemented dramatic changes to gain better control of its bus system with a proactive planning and service contracting approach and, at the same time, to shift to a highly hierarchical, integrated route network design (Pucher *et al.* 2005). The approach appears to have been consciously inspired by both European and Latin American precedents (Kim Gyeng-chul, pers. comm. 19 June 2007).

Government efforts on public transport during the 1970s to 1990s focused on rail and neglected buses, which were organised under passive route-franchise-based regulation. Nevertheless, the bus system thrived until the mid-1980s in a context of very low car ownership (Kwon 1981). However, from the late 1980s the bus system suffered increasingly from traffic congestion and competition from cars, rail and taxis. By 1994 it was reported that most of the 97 companies within Seoul were marginal or running at a loss (Liu 1994). The regulatory system was not capable of renovating the network of routes.

By the early 2000s a sense of crisis triggered a search for new lower cost approaches to improving public transport (Pucher *et al.* 2005). After long preparation by a team at the Seoul Development Institute, Seoul embarked in 2004 on a rapid jump to its 'semi-public' approach with ambitious network integration. This involved metropolitan government control over a highly hierarchical network with service procured from the private operators under gross-cost contracts (Pucher *et al.* 2005; Kim 2007).

Benefits claimed so far include impressive increases in bus speeds, reductions in accidents, and an upward trend in bus passenger numbers without a drop in subway use. Operating subsidies initially rose but comparisons are difficult because service levels were also dramatically increased and bus deficits should be set against avoided expenditure on metro/subway extensions (Pucher *et al.* 2005). The early public response was disastrous but soon turned positive. And, like Bogotá, Seoul's reforms went hand in hand with dramatic improvements to much-loved public places (Kim 2007).

Kuala Lumpur

A large proportion of the public transport system, both rail and bus, in the Kuala Lumpur region has recently come under state ownership, reversing a long-standing emphasis on privatisation in Malaysia. This may have set the scene for a shift towards a more proactively planned overall system combined with service contracting.

In the early 1970s, Kuala Lumpur had nine 'stage bus' companies, which operated under passive route franchise agreements hampered by tight fare controls (Rimmer 1986). In 1975 a partial deregulation, under a World Bank project, introduced individually owned minibuses with a jitney style of operation. Stage buses remained but without exclusivity on many routes. Problems from on-road competition quickly emerged. The minibuses were demonised for unruly on-road behaviour and then phased out in the mid-1990s (Barter 2004). Meanwhile, the moribund route-based vehicle licensing framework for stage buses remained in place, resistant to reform (Sabariah 2001). An attempt at consolidating several companies did little to improve matters. Meanwhile, transport in the metropolitan area became increasingly dominated by cars, motorcycles and expressways (Barter 2004).

Despite this, significant urban rail investment took place in the 1990s, creating five different systems (Barter 2004). However, the privatised model proved financially untenable. By 2004, two light rail systems had been brought under government ownership and privatisation of the suburban rail system had been cancelled. A large proportion of the bus industry was also brought under state ownership.

This created an opportunity. A steering committee based in the Ministry of Finance (which now owned much of the system) decided to 'increase in the level of integration of different modes of public transport' and 'to significantly improve regulation and enforcement of public transport services' (Ravindran 2007). In late 2004 a new public transport company, RapidKL, was created.

Although RapidKL is a state-owned operator it has apparently been framed with an eye to further reform. The government's financial instrument, Syarikat Prasarana Nasional Berhad, not RapidKL, owns the public transport assets. Integration is central to RapidKL's performance indicators under an operating agreement with government (Westra 2007). RapidKL has also been granted an Operator Licence which gives it the flexibility to deploy its buses efficiently throughout its network (Ravindran 2007).

Some obvious short steps from the current arrangement could create a hybrid procurement model. Instead of being seen as an operator as it is now, RapidKL could become the lean state-owned agency that takes responsibility for proactive planning of an excellent, coordinated system while contracting out its services to private operators. It would need to be empowered to control all public transport services in the region, not just those it already runs. If these steps were taken then Kuala Lumpur's trajectory would provide an interesting twist on Örn's suggestion that public monopoly is a necessary intermediate step.

However, major challenges remain. Three rail systems and several bus operators remaining outside the integrated system. These bus operators compete directly in the market with RapidKL. Furthermore, little attention has been paid so far to situating the reforms within a package of other urban improvements. Kuala Lumpur's wider car-focused transport policy settings and urban context make this a hostile environment for public transport (Barter 2004).

Santiago de Chile

Santiago has in 2007 made the leap to a proactively planned system with service contracting for its enormous bus system under a single dedicated public sector agency, Transantiago. This has also introduced an integrated, highly hierarchical network. Somewhat like Seoul, it did do so with a major shake-up implemented over the whole system at once. Unfortunately, the early 'teething problems' of Transantiago were extreme, to the point of severely harming the political standing of the government.

Santiago's public transport has been a testing ground for many of the regulatory fashions of the last 30 years. Estache and Goméz-Lobo (2005) use the city to illustrate key trends in bus regulation, as does Gwilliam (2005). In 1979, under the right-wing Pinochet government, deregulation occurred, then fare deregulation in 1983. This replaced the previous system in which a state-run operator coexisted with private operators running on route licence monopolies. Unwise fare control and the moribund route-based franchising system had resulted in serious under-provision of services.

The results of deregulation included extreme bus industry fragmentation, fare increases of approximately 100 per cent, oversupply with underutilised buses, safety problems and bus congestion with severe air pollution on the main corridors where services converged. Between 1979 and 1990 the number of buses (increasingly they were minibuses) rose from just over 5,000 to almost 14,000. However, services did improve in some important ways with expansion to new areas, many new routes and much reduced waiting times (Estache and Goméz-Lobo 2005).

In 1991, there was a shift to route contracts with a competitive tendering process that also served to set fares. This applied to routes passing through the city centre, which were 77 per cent of routes (Gwilliam 2005). These changes helped but problems re-emerged because of weak control that permitted creeping deregulation via sub-contracting to very small operators, and because of the incentives that operators and drivers faced under the net-cost fare arrangements (Gwilliam 2005).

In 2003 Chile's government embarked on an ambitious plan to revamp Santiago's bus network and fare system into an integrated and centrally controlled system, along with the metro rail system, under an authority called Transantiago. The final phase of the reform took place in early 2007. Bus service is now procured under competitively tendered net-cost service contracts (Graftieaux 2006).

Initial results were disastrous (although they have reportedly been improving in 2008). Even before the early 2007 implementation, commentators warned of important risks in the design (for example, Gwilliam 2005 and Graftieaux 2006). Some sources of difficulty relate to failings of the public sector implementation of the reform and these might bring comfort to sceptics of state planning (Hidalgo *et al.* 2007). However, other problems arise from an unwillingness to grasp the full extent of planning responsibility that needs to be taken on by the planning agency in order to pull off a highly integrated system. In seeking to exploit market processes, aspects of the regulatory design retained more discretion and risk in the hands of the operators than in most other planned service contracting approaches discussed in this section (Graftieaux 2006). Any further reforms to improve Transantiago seem more likely to increase the capacity to plan and control the system rather than revert towards more market-oriented options.

Others to watch

Several other cities are relevant to the arguments here and are worth mentioning briefly. For example, several Australian cities, most prominently Perth and Adelaide, have been successfully using service contracts (Hensher 2003). At the same time, they have also increased somewhat the emphasis on integration in their system planning. This has reportedly facilitated lower costs and rising patronage. These experiences should be of interest for other highly car-dependent cities, such as those in the United States. Arguably a model compatible with excellent integration is even more crucial for low-density areas than elsewhere (Mees 2000).

Singapore's earlier story has already been mentioned. It has announced as part of its Land Transport Master Plan 2008 that it will make a shift from its well-regulated area franchise approach for its bus system towards the service contract approach with greater public sector responsibility for planning of the route network. Tranches of routes will become contestable. These changes arose from a desire for service planning that is more customer-focused and well integrated than is currently possible with only service standards as the main tool under the franchise approach. Singapore's decision may be of interest in Hong Kong and other places with well-regulated franchises but which wish to be more ambitious in striving for system integration and excellence.

Indore in northern India has since 2006 been gaining media attention for the 'Indore City Transport Service'. This was introduced into a city that had no formal sector bus system, but has a wide array of taxi-type services and unregulated minivan services. According to its website, the new system seems to use a service contract approach and to have proactive planning by a public sector agency that has been empowered to focus on system excellence. The heart of the system is a 'special purpose vehicle' owned by both state and municipal governments. It plans the system but tenders out 70 per cent of its services to operators. These retain their on-board ticket revenue but the City Transport Service handles sales of season-passes which have been emphasised heavily. These passes are customer friendly and provide revenue that can be disbursed to operators in ways that reward good service. Other cities in India are reported to be taking an interest in Indore's model.

A variety of pathways

We have seen that cities in a variety of contexts have been adopting similar 'proactive planning with service contracting' approaches to the regulation and structuring of their public transport services. They have been doing so from various starting points and via a number of different sets of reform trajectories.

Figure 10.1 displays regulatory reform pathways for cities mentioned in this chapter. It portrays these trajectories on a matrix of the regulatory options from earlier in this chapter versus the extent to which excellent integration is achieved. As mentioned earlier, these regulatory options are arranged according to the degree to which the public sector takes responsibility for outcomes.

The European paths contrast with those in most other cities, with the most common shift being from public monopoly to service contracting. Kuala Lumpur is creating a public monopoly but in a framework that suggests that this may be an intermediate step towards a service contracts model. However, none of the others have used public monopoly. Most had starting points as deregulated/ unregulated systems or had passive franchise systems with little government planning. They have shifted to proactively planned service contracting via other intermediate steps or directly. Curitiba had several steps. Bogotá made a dramatic leap from a rather unregulated state to an ambitious hybrid model, but has been doing so corridor by corridor. Seoul and Santiago both made heroic metropolitan-wide reforms very rapidly. Singapore had a long period (more than 30 years) under the 'intermediate step' of a well-regulated franchise system but has recently announced a shift towards more proactive public sector planning and coordination and a more service contracting approach to procurement of the services.

Synthesis and conclusions

This story presented here seems to be one of an industry successfully discovering the appropriate role for the public sector. It would be misleading to imply that there are no more problems nor dilemmas. Nevertheless, I have drawn attention to the fact that many recent success stories in urban public transport have been associated with strong public sector planning and control, either ongoing or reasserted. For many, this has gone hand in hand with both competition (for the market) and a role for political deliberation and accountability mechanisms. This ambitious public sector planning has involved the creation of dedicated agencies that have been empowered to coordinate the system at a metropolitan scale. The most successful cases have devoted their ability to do proactive planning to seek excellence via ambitious levels of network integration.

In the West, a shift towards this model is often seen as 'privatisation'. However the international and historical perspective provided in this chapter

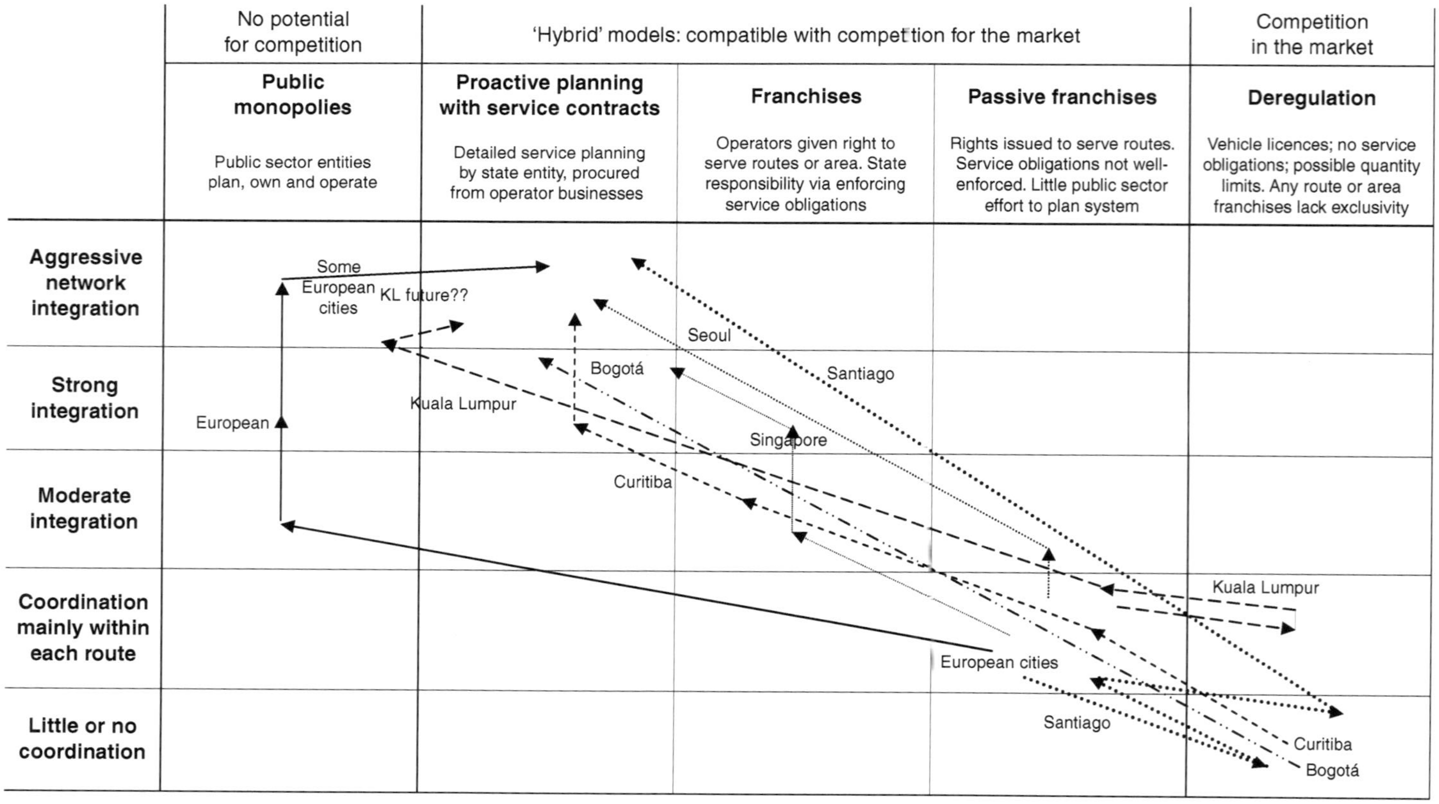

Figure 10.1 Pathways of regulatory arrangements versus network integration in urban bus systems.

Column headers:

No potential for competition
- **Public monopolies**: Public sector entities plan, own and operate
- **Proactive planning with service contracts**: Detailed service planning by state entity, procured from operator businesses

'Hybrid' models: compatible with competition for the market
- **Franchises**: Operators given right to serve routes or area. State responsibility via enforcing service obligations
- **Passive franchises**: Rights issued to serve routes. Service obligations not well-enforced. Little public sector effort to plan system

Competition in the market
- **Deregulation**: Vehicle licences; no service obligations; possible quantity limits. Any route or area franchises lack exclusivity

Row labels:
- Aggressive network integration
- Strong integration
- Moderate integration
- Coordination mainly within each route
- Little or no coordination

Labels on plot: Some European cities, KL future??, European, Kuala Lumpur, Bogotá, Curitiba, Seoul, Singapore, Santiago, Kuala Lumpur, European cities, Santiago, Curitiba, Bogotá reveals that proactive planning with service contracts should be better understood as a retreat from deregulation. More generally it is a response to the poor results seen whenever the public sector fails to take responsibility for overall system outcomes, such as under passive approaches to franchising. Recent European Union directives will give the model of proactive planning with service contracts a further boost in Europe. It will be interesting to see if it can also succeed in North America where such reforms have so far been very limited.

Questions of pathways were also addressed. Although some had suggested that public monopoly may be a necessary intermediate step for developing cities, we have in fact seen a surprising range of cities taking more direct paths towards this effective combination of public and private roles.

The question remains of how widely proactive planning with service contracting can be applied, especially in the South. This review suggests that it may be possible in more developing country contexts than has previously been assumed. It will be important to watch those cities in the South that have adopted this model. Most of the cases discussed here were in middle-income or high-income contexts with reasonable prospects for mustering sufficient institutional capacity. However, we have also seen that this approach is now spreading to India where the case of Indore seems promising. However, it is not yet well documented. Indore's bus system, and other Indian cities that may emulate it, will need to be studied to see if this model will prove to be an enduring and successful one for such low-income contexts. This would have important implications for public transport across the South.

References

Barter, P. A. (2004) 'Transport, Urban Structure and Lock-in in the Kuala Lumpur Metropolitan Area', *International Development Planning Review* 26(1): 1–24.

Barter, P., Kenworthy, J. and Laube, F. (2003) 'Lessons from Asia on Sustainable Urban Transport', in N. P. Low and B. J. Gleeson (eds) *Making Urban Transport Sustainable*, Basingstoke: Palgrave-Macmillan.

Bayliss, D. (2000) *Competition in Urban Public Transport*, Final Report. Halcrow Fox – UK, Review Paper for the World Bank's Urban Transport Policy Review. Available at http://siteresources.worldbank.org/INTURBANTRANSPORT/Resources/uk_competition_bayliss.pdf.

Cervero, R. (1997) *Paratransit in America*, New York: Praeger Publishers.

Cervero, R. (1998) 'Creating a Linear City with a Surface Metro: Curitiba, Brazil', *The Transit Metropolis: A Global Inquiry*, Washington, DC: Island Press, Chapter 10.

Cervero, R. (2000) *Informal Transport in the Developing World*, Nairobi: United Nations Centre for Human Settlements.

Estache, A. and Gómez-Lobo, A. (2005) 'Limits to Competition in Urban Bus Services in Developing Countries', *Transport Reviews* 25(2): 139–158.

Gilbert, A. (2008) 'Bus Rapid Transit: Is Transmilenio a Miracle Cure?', *Transport Reviews* 28(4): 439–467.

Glover, L. (2007) 'Integrated Management of Sustainable Urban Passenger Transport Systems in Dispersed Cities: A Review of Successful Institutional Interventions, Governance and Management of Urban Transport', Melbourne: GAMUT Centre. Available at www.gamutcentre.org/media/recent publications/Integrated_Transport_FINAL_ REPORT_14 Feb 2007.pdf.

Gómez-Ibáñez, J. A. and Meyer, J. (1993) *Going Private: The International Experience with Transport Privatization*, Washington, DC: The Brookings Institution.

Gómez-Lobo, A. (2007) 'Why Competition Does Not Work in Urban Bus Networks', *Journal of Transport Economics and Policy* 41(2): 283–308.

Governance and Management of Urban Transport (2007) Melbourne: GAMUT Centre. Available at www.gamutcentre.org/media/recent publications/Integrated_Transport_ FINAL_REPORT_14 Feb 2007.pdf.

Graftieaux, P. (2006) 'Transmilenio and Transantiago', presentation to a Brown Bag Lunch, *World Bank Infrastructure Network*, 21 September. Available at http://go. worldbank.org/NM0Q4YKTY0.

Gwilliam, K. M. (2000) *Public Transport in the Developing World – Quo Vadis?*, Discussion Paper TWU-39, Transport Division, The World Bank.

Gwilliam, K. M. (2005) 'Bus Franchising in Developing Countries: Recent World Bank Experience', in D. A. Hensher (ed.) *Competition and Ownership in Land Passenger Transport*, pp. 515–533. Selected refereed papers from the 8th International Conference, Thredbo 8, Rio de Janiero, September 2003, Amsterdam. Elsevier.

Hall, P. (1977) *The World Cities* (second edition), London: Weidenfeld and Nicolson.

Hensher, D. A. (2003) 'Introduction', in D. A. Hensher (ed.) *Competition and Ownership in Land Passenger Transport*, pp. 1–5. Selected refereed papers from the 8th International Conference, Thredbo 8, Rio de Janiero, September 2003, Amsterdam: Elsevier.

Hidalgo, D., Custodio, P. and Graftieaux, P. (2007) Presentation of results from 'A Critical Look at Major Bus Improvements in Latin America and Asia: Case Studies of Hitches, Hic-ups and Areas for Improvement; Synthesis of Lessons Learned', Report produced with the Assistance of TRISP, a partnership between the UK Department for International Development and the World Bank. April 2007. Available at http:// siteresources.worldbank.org/INTTRANSPORT/Resources/336291–1153409213417/ CaseStudiesBBLhicups.pdf. See http://go.worldbank.org/W8FO3NQ680.

Hidson, M. and Müller, M. (2003) *Better Public Transport for Europe through Competitive Tendering – A Good Practice Guide*, ICLEI – Local Governments for Sustainability.

Hook, W. (2005) *Institutional and Regulatory Options for Rapid Bus Transit in Developing Countries: Lessons from International Experience*, Institute for Transportation and Development Policy, New York: ITDP.

Houghton, E. and Hensher, D. A. (2005) 'Negotiated and Competitively Tendered Performance-Based Contracts', in K. J. Button and D. A. Hensher (eds) *Handbook of Transport Strategy, Policy and Institutions*, Amsterdam: Elsevier, Chapter 31, pp. 527–546.

Kim, Gyeng-chul (2007) 'Sustainable Transport: Seoul's Challenges', presentation to Sustainable Urban Transport in Asia and the Pacific Region, *CITYNET Kuala Lumpur Regional Training Centre*, KLRTC. XI, 19 June 2007.

Kwon, W. Y. (1981) 'Seoul: A Dynamic Metropolis', in M. Honjo (ed.) *Urbanization and Regional Development*, Hong Kong and Singapore: Maruzen Asia on behalf of UNCRD, Nagoya, pp. 297–329.

Liu, Z. (1994) *Improving Seoul's Bus Network: Problems and Options, Final Report*, Harvard Institute for International Development and Seoul Development Institute.

Mackie, P. J., Preston, J. M. and Nash, C. A. (1995) 'Bus Deregulation: Ten Years On', *Transport Reviews* 15(3): 229–251.

Meakin, R. (2002) *Bus Regulation and Planning, Module 3c in Sustainable Transport: A Sourcebook for Policy-makers in Developing Cities*, Eschborn: Deutsche Gesellschaft für Technische Zusammenarbeit, GTZ.

Mees, P. (2000) *A Very Public Solution: Transport in the Dispersed City*, Melbourne: Melbourne University Press.

Mehta, R. (2002) 'Promoting Public Transport Through Restructuring and Creating Unique Public–Private Partnerships', in G. Tiwari (ed.) *Urban Transport for Growing Cities: High Capacity Bus Systems*, Delhi, India: Macmillan, pp. 177–188.

Örn, H. (2005) 'Urban Public Transport in an International Perspective', in G. Jönson and E. Tengström (eds) *Urban Transport Development: A Complex Issue*, Berlin: Springer, Chapter 5, pp. 45–64.

Poole, A. D., Pacheco, R. S. and De Melo, M. A. B. C. (1994) *Moving People: Transport Policy in the Cities of Brazil*, Ottawa: International Development Research Centre.

Pucher, J., Park, H., Kim, M. H. and Song, J. (2005) 'Public Transport Reforms in Seoul: Innovations Motivated by Funding Crisis', *Journal of Public Transportation* 8(5): 41–62.

Ravindran, V. (2007) 'Urban Transportation Strategies in the Klang Valley – Major Implications', presentation by the Head of Strategic Planning and Business Development Division, Syarikat Prasarana Negara Berhad, SPNB, to Sustainable Urban Transport in Asia and the Pacific Region, CITYNET Kuala Lumpur: Regional Training Centre, KLRTC. XI, 18 June 2007.

Rimmer, P. (1986) *Rikisha to Rapid Transit: Urban Public Transport Systems and Policy in Southeast Asia*, Sydney: Pergamon Press.

Roth, G. J. and Wynne, G. G. (1982) *Free Enterprise Urban Transportation*, Washington, DC: Council for International Liaison.

Sabariah, Jemali (2001) 'Commercial Vehicle Licensing: A Way Forward', paper presented at the National Seminar on Sustainable Transport Issues and Challenges, 7–11 September, RECSAM, in Penang, Malaysia.

Transportation Research Board (TRB) (2001) 'Contracting for Bus and Demand-Responsive Transit Services: A Survey of U.S. Practice and Experience', *Special Report* 258, Washington, DC: The National Academies Press.

Van de Velde, D. M. (2003) 'The Evolution of Organisational Forms in European Public Transport During the Last 15 Years', in D. A. Hensher (ed.) *Competition and Ownership in Land Passenger Transport*, pp. 481–513. Selected refereed papers from the 8th International Conference, Thredbo 8, Rio de Janiero, September 2003, Amsterdam: Elsevier.

Vasconcellos, E. A. (2001) *Urban Transport, Environment and Equity: The Case for Developing Countries*, London and Sterling, VA: Earthscan.

Westra, R. (2007) 'Evolution of RapidKL Past to Future', presentation by the Chief Executive Officer of Rangaian Penangkutan Integrasi Deras Sdn Bhd, RapidKL, to Sustainable Urban Transport in Asia and the Pacific Region, CITYNET Kuala Lumpur Regional Training Centre, KLRTC. XI, 18 June 2007.

White, P. (1995) 'Deregulation of Local Bus Services in Great Britain: An Introductory Review', *Transport Reviews* 15(2): 185–209.

World Bank (2002) *Cities on the Move: a World Bank Urban Transport Strategy Review*, Washington, DC: World Bank.

11 Planning for power

Lessons from three generations of Brazilian electricity reforms

Sunil Tankha

1 Towards an empirical and experimental approach to assessing the problems and solutions of public services

On 1 February 2001, Brazilian President Fernando Henrique Cardoso declared national electricity rationing. The country's hydropower reservoirs were almost dry, he announced, requiring all consumers – residential, commercial, industrial and government – to cut their electricity consumption by 20 per cent. Customers who would not comply were threatened with fines and even temporary disconnection. In 2001 also, California's electricity system practically collapsed, resulting in prolonged blackouts. Two years earlier, Chilean electricity consumers had suffered similarly when their hydropower reservoirs had also run dry, resulting in enforced and random power cuts. In 2003, problems in transmission grids led to a series of major blackouts in the United States and several European countries. Throughout the world, policymakers who had confidently forced through a transition from tight planning controls to dynamic market environments were scrambling to deal with power failures and emergencies.

In both developed and developing countries, policymakers privatised and deregulated public services hoping to encourage investment and simultaneously reduce prices through efficiency gains. Evaluations of electric power market privatisation and liberalisation initially seemed to demonstrate that significant benefits could be realised by rooting out the inefficiencies hidden behind government ownership, monopolies and regulatory structures. Wholesale electricity prices fell and the operating efficiencies of power firms increased. These gains persuaded many to follow the advice of policy entrepreneurs who were advocating a broader deregulation of electricity markets. The gains were, however, short-lived and illusory. Deregulated wholesale electricity markets soon began to exhibit severe price volatility and, more preoccupying, discouraged investment. Despite slow demand growth, liberalisation corresponded with a decrease in the security of supply.

The power industry is not the only one in which the promises of privatisation and liberalisation have disappointed. These reforms have failed to encourage sufficient investment and have led to quality of service problems in diverse public services such as transport (Tyrrall 2004), water and sanitation (Hall and

Lobina 2005), healthcare (Leonard 2002; EHMA 2000; Kumaranayake 1998) and education (Teixeira and Amral 2001; Riddell 1993). In many cases, they have also led to large price increases. What can explain this divergence between the expected results from reforms and the actual results? How did infrastructure markets fail in industrialised as well as in developing countries? What lessons can be learned from this experience? Most importantly, what are the policy responses and innovations that developing countries are constructing to deal with their infrastructure needs?

After over two decades of experience with privatisation and deregulation, most scholars accept that where privatisation and deregulation failed it was because of inadequate regulatory capacities and frameworks and bad market designs. For example, market imperfections are pervasive in infrastructure sectors and inadequate regulation can spark a struggle for the rents created by informational asymmetries, which regulatory institutions may find difficult to control. Another difficulty is that privatisation and deregulation involve trade-offs among competing policy objectives. Mediating and appropriately balancing among these competing objectives also requires institutional capabilities and skills. It is correct but, of course, not enough to conclude only that privatisation and deregulation require better institutional capacities and parallel efforts to increase competition and improve regulation. The difficulties related to creating appropriate and adequate regulatory frameworks are not insubstantial. Moreover, forcing institutional reforms and capacity building to fit into the requirements of a particular pre-defined reform programme is clearly unadvisable because the pre-requisites for such institutional capacity building are often not present in developing countries. Yet, certain dominant models of liberalisation are perva-sive for reasons of legitimacy and signalling, and despite their unsuitability for developing countries, attempts are made to tailor regulatory institutions to their requirements.

How can these problems be overcome? Theoretical enquiry and modelling provide a good beginning but are of limited utility in predicting appropriate structures and trade-offs because their predictions are probabilistic as well as case-specific. As models alone will be unlikely to provide complete answers under such conditions of uncertainty (Laffont and Tirole 1993), they must be complemented by a body of empirical cases where intuitive inductive reasoning is employed to contrast actual causal-chains against ideal ones and thereby identify the points at and means by which the virtuous causal-chain predicted by privatisation and deregulation proposals are circumvented. Such empirical cases are basically in-depth analyses of policy experiments, and learning from them has been recognised as critical to successfully implementing development pol-icies and projects under conditions of complexity and uncertainty (Rondinelli 1993). Policymaking, therefore, is to be based on a tripod of analyses including historical experience, theory and case studies (Laffont 2005).

This chapter presents one such policy experiment as both an analytic and illustrative tool: the case of the Brazilian electric power reforms. Between the mid-1950s and the mid-1980s, Brazil had built one of the world's largest and most sophisticated hydroelectric industries based on centralised planning and public investment. This model obsolesced in the 1980s because of a combination of external economic threats and internal economic mismanagement, after which the government embarked on an orthodox reform programme. This programme delivered some quick and positive results but eventually culminated in massive power rationing. After the disappointment with orthodox reforms, Brazilian power planners have sought to revitalise the industry through an interesting institutional mix of centralised planning and competition, which provides several insights on how to avoid the excesses of privatisation and liberalisation in infrastructure industries and to re-integrate state functions in their planning and operation.

The rest of the chapter is organised as follows. The following section analyses the causes and consequences of the rise and fall of public sector dominance in the Brazilian electric power industry, highlighting where, how and why its development differed from that predicted by the theories which underpin privatisation and deregulation. Section 3 explains why Brazilian power reforms were unable to provide sufficient investment at acceptable costs. Section 4 focuses on the policy imperatives of the Brazilian government following the failure of its power sector reform strategies and the steps it has taken to re-stabilise the sector, to re-integrate planning tenets to reduce probabilities of catastrophic failure and to increase the effectiveness of reform. Section 5 concludes.

2 From private to privatisation: the first generation of Brazilian power reforms

Privatisation policies have been underpinned by theoretical and rhetorical attacks on state ownership. The theoretical attacks are primarily based on property rights and public choice analyses and their recurring claims are that public enterprises are inefficient and incapable of the tasks set before them. The obvious limitations of these theories are not only that they do not satisfactorily address the existence of efficient public sector firms but also that they are too sanguine about the non-existence of related and similar problems in the private sector.

Planning, closely associated with public ownership, has also been criticised as inefficient and leading to incorrect allocation of resources and higher costs.[1] Neo-classical and neo-liberal economics has, however, pushed the markets versus planning dichotomy too far. Their fundamental argument is that central planning of *any* sort, not just that associated with Soviet-style integrated planning, is inherently inferior to markets because no planner can have either access to the diversity of information and of decision making that make markets efficient. Ignoring for the moment the inherent tautology of this argument, we find that there is one major weakness to this argument: market-based decision makers do not have perfect and cost-free access to information about demand and prices. Indeed, it was the costs associated with access to information (along with those associated with the enforcement of contracts) that led economists to explain the emergence of the firm and, indeed, these firms could easily be characterised as miniature planned economies.[2] The issue about efficiency and effectiveness of planning then moves away from one about notions of planning versus markets to one about the appropriate scale for a particular activity.

Abandoning a theory-driven approach in favour of an empirical one, this section employs detailed empirical observation of the Brazilian power industry to determine whether actual patterns match the theoretical predictions, and shows how the dynamics of ownership were more nuanced and significantly different from that which theories have predicted. It supports the claim that public ownership and planning, even given the unique constraints and resources with which they work, may deliver the results policymakers and the public want if they are endowed with the resources necessary to enable their missions. They may develop complex solutions to complex problems and manage resources effectively, thereby justifying the marshalling of public resources in their favour.[3] Moreover, this section shows that the need for privatisation in the Brazilian power industry did not arise simply because of public sector mismanagement and inefficiency but because of deeper systemic problems related to international economic interactions and domestic macroeconomic management.

State investment and planning in the expansion of the Brazilian electric power system

The modern networked electricity industry was brought to Brazil in 1900 by a group of Canadian investors. Over the next 50 years, this group – the Brazilian Traction, Light and Power Company (Light) – and the US-owned American & Foreign Power Company (Amforp) dominated Brazil's electricity industry. After the Second World War, however, disputes between the Brazilian government and the investors over acceptable prices, costs and returns intensified and culminated in stringent rate controls (McDowall 1988). Light and Amforp's investments dropped precipitously. In the wake of the private sector's retreat, President Juscelino Kubitschek's administration (1956–1961) committed itself to the expansion of the electric power sector and directed a quarter of all federal investments to it. This laid the foundation for a sustained power sector growth programme as a result of which the sector expanded at an annual rate of almost 10 per cent over the following decade.

Guiding the expansion was a comprehensive planning process initiated in 1962. Known as Canambra, after the three countries that participated in the planning process – Canada, the United States of America and Brazil – this planning exercise focused on the industrialised south-east region of Brazil.[4] Later exercises focused on the Amazon (1969) and the north-east (1970). The planning systems developed under Canambra were elaborate.[5] At one end, they studied the geography of the country, making inventories of potential hydroelectric projects and of their costs. At the other end, they studied the economy, determining economic trends and building scenarios of economic growth and the sectors in which economic growth would be concentrated. Based on these, Canambra developed projections of regional and national energy demand.

These plans had a determinative character. Once demand projections were made, the potential power projects were rank-ordered in terms of cost per unit of power produced and assigned to the various generation companies. The planning was done on a ten-year horizon and was continually modified at the margins in order to ensure that power infrastructure growth would accelerate or decelerate according to the latest revised projections of economic growth.

As the system became bigger, there was a gradual consolidation of firms and a centralisation of administrative functions. The industry finally settled into a stable institutional structure where federally owned companies took charge of generation and transmission and state government-owned companies were mainly responsible for distribution. At the apex was Eletrobrás, which the federal government established in 1962 to plan the expansion of the electricity system, finance power projects and coordinate the despatch of electricity from the various power plants. Eletrobrás was later transformed into the holding company for the federal generation and transmission companies (GENCOS). Meanwhile, the ownership of distribution companies (DISCOS) was transferred to the state governments, who were made responsible for developing the network and managing the retail operations within their jurisdictions.

From the planning perspective, this centralisation was useful. The Brazilian power industry was growing rapidly at a time when the country had few fossil energy reserves. What they had in abundance was water. Given its geography, large hydroelectric plants, built in a cascade fashion so that the water released from one would feed the reservoirs of another downstream, was the best option to produce reliable and affordable power. To maximise output from a given set of hydropower investments, power production needed a centrally coordinated and extensive interlinked transmission network. It fell upon the planning institutions to study, locate, inventory and optimally allocate investments towards the most efficient combination of hydroelectric plants and transmission lines. Canambra was the first of these planning institutions, which were eventually transferred to Eletrobrás after the former's mandate ended in 1969. Eletrobrás also developed state-of-the-art computational technology in managing complex hydroelectric systems which allowed them to produce 30 per cent more power with the same amount of installed capacity than would have been possible were the power production decisions decentralised. In the 1970s, consolidation was accentuated by the undertaking of massive projects such as Itaipu and Tucuri, which required a heavy concentration of financial resources. Power systems planning continued on a regional basis until 1980 when Eletrobrás created a Coordinating Group for Power Systems Planning (GCPS), thereby consolidating and centralising the planning of the generation and the transmission systems throughout the country.

Rather than cost overruns and delays, during this period Brazilian power firms achieved all planned targets. Moreover, the benefits of this programme were not concentrated in only the industrialised belt. Companies such as Chesf, which was charged with developing the hydroelectric potential of the São Francisco river basin, played a large part in catalysing development in the poorer semi-arid north-east of the country. The financial position of the industry was also strong. While electricity rates, especially at the retail level, had been stifled since the 1930s, in 1964 the government adopted a policy of "tariff realism" which set electricity rates at levels which were enough to cover operational costs as well as provide adequate return on capital. These rates also provided power companies with sufficient retained earnings so that they could finance a large part of the surge in investments, especially during the miracle years, a period between 1968 and 1973 when the Brazilian economy grew at rates of around 10 per cent per annum. Additional capital was leveraged through compulsory loans from large consumers and surcharges on electricity that were directed towards Eletrobrás investment programmes (Tendler 1968).

Brazilian success with state-led and planned power development can be explained principally by technical and institutional factors. In the power sector, the massive investments that are entailed require large degrees of coordination not only among the three sub-sectors (generation, transmission and distribution) but also in despatch from the least-cost combination of generating units. As power systems become more complex and geographically dispersed, tighter coordination yields larger benefits. Traditionally, these coordination and scale economies were obtained through vertical integration but Brazilian power planners, first under Canambra and then under Eletrobrás, developed an interesting combination of unbundling and coordination which enabled them to exploit these economies while promoting a degree of inter-firm competition and efficiency. In Brazil, planning remained centralised but hydropower construction and operation under public ownership was initially decentralised with several federally and state-owned GENCOS competing to build power projects in the same region. In the country's industrial centre of Rio de Janeiro, São Paulo and Minas Gerais, there were at one stage six different federal and state power-generating firms, in addition to the Light and Amforp companies. Competition arose in the generation sector because these companies, most of whose potential markets overlapped, had to sell to the federal government (under which concession-granting authority had been centralised by the 1934 Water Code) both a project and their ability to execute it. In an environment where the government's decision to finance one project usually meant other competing projects pushed by rival companies would fail to obtain financing, state-owned power companies generally fought fervently to push their own projects rather than follow a common cause (Tendler 1968). This rivalry amongst public power companies in many ways replicated the dynamics of private sector competition *for* the market and stimulated efficiency in the public sector. Although there was no competition *in* the market, and some companies did perform poorly after winning project concessions, the Brazilian public power sector generally escaped the debilitating effects of the typical curses on state-owned enterprise, such as the soft budget constraint and the lack of competition and market discipline, because the existence of multiple companies owned by the state as well as the federal governments meant that as they competed, the stronger companies distinguished themselves and the federal and state governments eventually subsumed the weaker companies into them. Once established, the competitive spirit remained entrenched in the public sector power generation companies.

These results diverged significantly from those predicted by theory. Poor performance in the public sector, as explained by property rights, agency and public choice theories assumes that agents derive little or no utility from job satisfaction but Tendler's study of the Brazilian power industry during its expansion drive in the 1960s indicates that performance was closely linked to a spirit of *pionerismo* which pervaded the industry, infused and nurtured by the nature of the task and the availability of resources to execute it (Tendler 1968).

The decline of state-led power development

Despite its achievements from the mid-1950s onwards, by the end of the 1980s Brazil's power industry was deeply in debt and in danger of serious power shortages. The main causes of this in Brazil, as in many other countries, were the oil price and interest rate shocks of the 1970s and 1980s. The steady and strong growth of the Brazilian electricity sector was one of the many victims of these external economic shocks and this unlatched windows to orthodox reform and privatisation. Paradoxically, the first oil price shock in 1973 benefited the industry because the government embarked upon a massive Keynesian investment-based economic recovery programme, gambling that it could pay Brazil's rapidly rising oil bills by growing even faster. This programme channelled billions into basic industries such as metals, fertilisers and petrochemicals, and infrastructures such as energy (including electric power), communications and transportation (Baer 2001). The second oil shock in 1978 and the interest rate shocks in the early 1980s left Brazil heavily indebted and unable to pay down or even roll over its debt. This led to a series of subsequent policies, each intended to deal with a particular macroeconomic problem, which distorted the economics of the power industry. First, the government equalised electricity rates throughout the country, compensating high-cost loss-making firms with financial resources transferred from firms with lower costs. This centralisation and equalisation of rates was done to combat high infrastructure prices in certain areas stemming from the expensive projects government had recently initiated as well as to make it easier to manage rate controls in the power sector. This strategy might have made sense were the Brazilian power industry monolithic but the ownership of power infrastructure in Brazil was diffuse and involved the federal, all the state and even some municipal governments. Predictably, the transfers of resources among firms reduced incentives for both credited and debited firms to be cost-efficient. Second and more seriously, the federal government abandoned the policy of "tariff realism" in 1977 and began to limit increases in electricity rates as a means to dampen inflation, fearing that high prices for infrastructure services would push price increases for goods and services in general. As a result, the return on assets of electric power companies in general fell to about 4 per cent as opposed to the 10 per cent which was legally guaranteed by the 1934 Water Code.[6] Finally, compounding the problem of inadequate rates, the federal government began to force SOEs – especially power and steel companies – to borrow abroad in order to obtain the foreign exchange that the government needed to finance Brazil's balance of payment deficits and to roll over its debt. Eroded by inflation, electricity rates lost a third of their real value between 1974 and 1984 (see Table 11.1) and power companies became increasingly dependent on foreign loans for investment (see Table 11.2). Financial resources began to be diverted from the power sector. Whereas in 1970 over 78 per cent of the financial resources in the industry had gone towards investment, by 1989 over 74 per cent of these resources went solely to debt service (Oliveira 1997). Perversely, it was no longer the infrastructure needs of the country that motivated public firms to take out foreign loans but the necessity to roll over the debt that pushed through large projects. Adding to the injury, the government often diverted funds from these loans so that public sector firms racked up debt yet developed no corresponding physical assets.

The result of these three financial shocks was that a dynamic state-owned industry was weakened with its investment and pricing policies increasingly being contaminated by macroeconomic compulsions. Till the late 1970s, the generation sector in Brazil was run efficiently and was technologically advanced. The distribution sector's performance was less consistent, with performance varying considerably across various states. The curtailment of investment programmes in the 1980s along with rate controls hurt efficiency in both sectors as overburdened and under-maintained networks began to fail with greater frequency.

While the theories of government failure, public choice in particular, indict private interests within public institutions for efficiency and performance problems, the Brazilian power industry's experience from the mid-1970s onwards indicates that a more credible explanation for performance problems was a tension between competing public interests, i.e. between the need to ensure

Table 11.1 Average real electricity rates 1964 = 100

	1964	1969	1974	1979	1984	1985	1986	1987	1988	1989	1990	1991
Real rates	100	150	145	106	98	93	97	102	101	71	73	72

Source: Eletrobrás.

Table 11.2 Source of power investments in %

	1967	1973	1979	1984
Internal	34.0	44.9	24.2	17.9
Forced loans	8.1	9.4	7.6	3.9
Government federal and state	31.9	20.3	6.1	6.0
Domestic loans	13.0	6.6	30.1	9.4
Foreign loans	13.0	18.8	32.0	62.8

Source: Eletrobrás.

economic growth and control inflation on the one hand and the financial and operational health of the public sector infrastructure companies on the other. As we will see in the following section, resolution between such competing public interests persists and does not become easier to work out under privatisation. Indeed, the incorporation of private sector investor interests, contrary to the arguments extolling efficiency gains from privatisation, often makes such resolution even more difficult.

3 Privatisation and deregulation: the second generation of Brazilian power reforms

The first step in reforming the Brazilian power industry had to reverse the financial distortions wrought by the power sector policies of the 1970s and 1980s. This was done in 1993 when the Brazilian Congress passed a series of laws eliminating the national uniform power rates and freeing power companies to charge prices that reflected operational costs and provided an adequate return on their capital. Other resolutions and decrees initiated market liberalisation by allowing utilities to negotiate rates directly with large, energy-intensive customers and by enabling free access to the federal transmission network, which facilitated, theoretically and legally, competition in the generation sector. The first step in reforming the industry was successful. Power rates were increased allowing the state-owned firms to recuperate their financial health. Most of these firms also began streamlining their workforce, forcing thousands of employees into early retirement programmes.

The second step in the reform process was privatisation, which hewed closely to the standard prescriptions of market deregulation pioneered in Chile and Great Britain. The generation and distribution segments were to be separated. DISCOS were privatised as 30-year concessions to be regulated by the price-cap method. GENCOS were to be auctioned as 35-year concessions and would be required to sell their power in competitive wholesale markets once these were established. Independent Power Projects (IPPs) were also allowed. This did not require much restructuring in Brazil since ownership of these two segments was already mostly separated with the federal government owning most of the generation assets and state governments owning most of the distribution networks. There were a few vertically integrated power companies owned by the state governments in Brazil's industrialised south-east and south, and only these would have to be restructured.

Both wholesale and retail markets were to be gradually liberalised. Before initiating GENCO privatisation in 1998, the government mediated the signing of initial power supply contracts among the DISCOS and GENCOS to facilitate a gradual transition to deregulated wholesale markets. These contracts were for eight years, with 25 per cent of the volume of energy contracted being released each year after the fourth, so that by the end of the eighth year the wholesale market would be completely liberalised. DISCOS were required to sign long-term power purchase agreements, with GENCOS, independent power producers

(IPPs) or self-generation units, for 85 per cent of their requirements and were allowed to completely pass through the cost of wholesale power to final tariffs, subject to a price ceiling, known locally as the *Valor Normativo* (VN). Their concessions contracts also allowed DISCOS to self-generate up to 35 per cent of their requirements and these were also subject to the VN. DISCOS' remuneration was placed under price-cap regulation as retail level liberalisation was initially restricted to large industrial consumers and full deregulation was expected to be concluded over a period of ten years.

Privatisation was initially very successful. Backed by regulatory contracts and pricing that were generous to investors, most of the DISCOS – representing about 80 per cent of the retail energy traded – were sold between 1995 and 1998, many at large premiums over their minimum reserve prices. DISCO profits jumped from US$115 million in 1993 to US$2 billion by 1996 (Mendonça and Dahl 1999). GENCO earnings also improved after several loss-making years. As DISCOS began to pay regularly for the power they received, GENCO profits reached US$200 million in 1996 even though the government still suppressed the rates the latter could charge (BNDES 2001). The rate increases and distribution privatisation allowed both GENCOS and DISCOS to recuperate their financial health, invest in improving and expanding the network, reduce power losses and improve services.

Beyond these initial gains, however, power privatisation failed to deliver on other public service priorities, the most important of which was investment in new generation capacity. This investment was never realised, primarily because privatisation policies and the economic stabilisation programmes within which they were embedded were not mutually reinforcing as policymakers had expected (Tankha 2009). In 1999, Brazil was forced into a large devaluation of its currency. The country had adopted a new currency, the Real, in 1994, pegging its value to the US dollar. This strategy, which had been successfully adopted in Argentina, arrested inflation but, maintaining the currency peg while at the same time allowing the domestic currency to be freely traded, required the government to pay high interest rates on its debt. The government's privatisation programme also helped maintain the peg as the influx of foreign investors increased demand for the Real. Under ideal scenarios, stability should have quickly translated into lower interest demands by foreign investors and a virtuous cycle of investment, productivity increases and economic growth. In reality, after an initial consumption and foreign investment based spurt in growth, the Brazilian economy stagnated. The high interest rates dampened domestic investment, (the initial consumption boom was satisfied mostly by underutilised capacity) and the strong currency made exports uncompetitive. Brazil's traditionally high trade and current account surplus quickly turned into a deficit. Economic stagnation prevented the government from reducing the external debt and this worried investors, who continued to demand high interest rates in exchange for holding even dollar-denominated debt (Baer 2001; Amann and Baer 2000). After the currency crises in Asia and Russia, the Brazilian government was forced to pay ever-higher interest rates to increasingly skittish investors and eventually forced to devalue the currency in 1999, which quickly lost over half its value.

By the time the Brazilian government finished privatising the distribution sector and was ready to being privatising GENCOS, the Real Plan had begun to collapse. The more the Real Plan weakened, the more privatisation stalled, becoming increasingly unattractive to both investors and consumers. Foreign investors who had taken over DISCOS wanted the electric power regulatory agency (ANEEL) to set much higher rates to compensate them for the losses they were incurring on the foreign exchange debt they had accumulated, but ANEEL, mindful that consumers were already complaining increasingly about price increases, was unwilling and unable to oblige (see Figure 11.1). Political opposition towards privatisation also hardened. Price increases for electric power were threatening to contribute to inflation. In the end, only the smallest of the Eletrobrás GENCOS, Eletrosul, was unbundled and its generation arm sold at its minimum price to the only investor that bid for it.

Problems with privatisation in an environment of currency instability were mostly responsible for derailing Brazilian power reforms but problems with deregulation were also a critical, albeit veiled, element in the subsequent crisis in the Brazilian power industry. The Brazilian government expected that given impending shortages in generation capacity private investors, motivated by potential profits, would step into the breach. To get power plants built, DISCOS

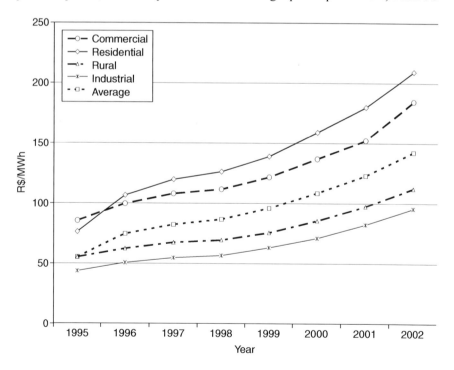

Figure 11.1 Retail electricity prices (source: ANEEL).

had to sign long-term power purchase agreements with investors so that the latter could get project finance. The prices DISCOS could offer were limited to the VN which ANEEL had established. For hydropower, the VN was around US$30, but thermal power plants, given the prevailing gas prices, were not viable at such prices. Investors, however, were not keen on building hydropower plants because they were considered too risky and required much larger amounts of capital. In risky situations investors prefer technologies with lower capital outlays (Teisberg 1993), so in Brazil investors were pushing for a solution aimed at enabling thermal power to be profitable. In response ANEEL did establish a separate, higher VN for thermal power but it was not high enough to reassure investors who were facing not only volatile gas prices but also foreign exchange risks, because the gas had to be imported and paid for in dollars while the retail rates were denominated in the local currency.

The regulatory agency and political establishment were reluctant to relax the limits on the VN because of a potential time-bomb that threatened to greatly increase wholesale power prices in deregulated markets. The initial contracts which DISCOS had signed with GENCOS had established a low price for wholesale power, which was made possible because a substantial part of the electricity being supplied came from hydropower plants whose capital costs had already been amortised, which allowed them to profitably supply power at a little over their operating costs of about US$5 per MWh. After the expiry of these contracts, this power, known locally as "old energy", stood to extract significant rents because the average wholesale prices would be dictated by the more expensive new investments. The potential rents were substantial, estimated at over US$1 billion (MME 2002). Before the collapse of the Real Plan, the initial contracts were a tool to smooth the transition to deregulated wholesale markets; after devaluation, they became a ticking time-bomb. With wholesale power prices likely to double after the expiry of the initial contracts and inflationary pressures resurging, the Treasury began to pressure ANEEL to control electricity rate increases. In this environment, uncertainty about how governments would deal with old energy dissuaded investors as political opposition coalesced around the issue.

With this paralysis, the power situation turned critical and in 2001 Brazil was forced to ration electricity for ten months. Initially, the rationing appeared as a surprise and the government claimed that the below-average rainfall over the previous years was to blame. However, it was known for several years that Brazil's hydropower reservoirs were running dangerously low – a BNDES newsletter had warned so as early as 1996 – and rationing was a result of both inadequate investment and the dismantling and marginalisation of electric power planning structures. As part of the power reforms, Eletrobrás' planning body, GCPS, was disbanded and its functions transferred to the Ministry of Mines and Energy (MME), but the institutional set-up to absorb this complex function was rudimentary. It was expected, rather, that as the sector would be liberalised, the market would make all the relevant decisions and planning would become vestigial. While the market's problems remained unresolved, there was no institution which had the ability to either monitor or resolve investment lacunae and Brazil steadily marched towards power rationing. The National Systems Operator's (ONS) charts could warn about the level of the reservoirs, ANEEL could monitor investments, but no agency had the power or the mandate to take decisive measures if investors did not respond to market or government incentives. The government even launched a Priority Thermoelectric Power Programme (PPT), channelling funds from the National Economic and Social Development Bank (BNDES) to private investors in order to persuade them to construct dozens of natural gas driven power plants with an installed capacity totalling over 17,000MW, but was unable to attract investors. Finally, the government ordered Petrobrás, Brazil's federally owned oil and gas company, to assume all risks and construct some of the thermoelectric power plants, but it was too late. In May 2001, ONS warned that immediate electricity rationing was essential to avoid a complete depletion of the reservoirs.

4 Embedding private enterprise, competition and markets inside plans: the third generation of Brazilian power reforms

The debacle with the power reforms programme provided an important campaigning point for the Workers Party (PT) to criticise the Cardoso administration's economic policies during the 2002 presidential elections. A working group closely associated with the party and consisting of power experts from the public sector power companies, and academics and researchers from local universities was established and began debating changes and proposing new models for the industry in conjunction with the campaign. After the PT's victory, it was this group's recommendations that formed the basis for the New Model for the Brazilian electricity sector rather than the suggestions of the official committee which the Cardoso administration had established to manage the rationing.[7]

The so-called New Model divides the retail electricity market into a regulated market, which makes up about 70 per cent of the total energy traded, and a liberalised market. Those whose consumption is greater than 3MW may purchase their power through DISCOS at regulated rates or they may opt for the deregulated market and source power directly from GENCOS, IPPs or other power sellers, or through self-generation. DISCOS are responsible for supplying the regulated market and must contract 100 per cent of their requirements and compulsorily do so through power auctions.

The so-called Model also divides the wholesale electricity supply into "old" and "new" energy markets. The "old" energy market is where the output of power plants licensed and/or operational before 2004, which covers the output of the amortised plants, is traded. Auctions for this energy are held every year for delivery commencing the following year and the associated PPAs have a duration of between five and ten years. Auctions for the "new" energy market are also held once annually and delivery of the power contracted in this market begins either five or three years after the contracts are signed. These PPAs associated with this market have a 20-year duration.

Based on the Single-Buyer Model, the New Model incorporates a hybrid of centralised planning and competition *for* the market, especially in the case of new energy. A non-profit public sector firm, the Electric Planning Company (EPE) has been established to execute studies of potential hydroelectric plants and obtain environmental clearances for them, in this manner recreating in the public sector a large part of the planning functions and structures formerly under Eletrobrás. The responsibility for generating the demand scenarios remains with the DISCOS who are required to prepare forecasts of their customers' demand five years in advance.[8] Based on these forecasts, they submit demands to EPE in terms of a stated load requirement from which EPE determines how much additional power capacity must be constructed. Competition is introduced into this process by EPE having investors bid for the right to supply this power. Each investor, which can be a public or private utility or an IPP, informs the EPE of the minimum annual revenues they require for undertaking the project. Investors may make these offers either for hydroelectric projects already prepared by EPE (which come with an environmental clearance) or they may propose their own projects (thermal, renewable, small hydro, etc.). EPE calculates the project's rates by dividing this annual revenue requirement by the assured energy produced by the project, as calculated by the MME. EPE then ranks these projects and selects them in terms of increasing rates until total supply equals the required load. The contracts that the power producers receive, a 30-year PPA, specifies both the amount of power to be supplied (on an annual basis) and the fixed rate (per MWh) at which it will be remunerated. EPE then bundles this energy and sells it to the DISCOS. EPE does not purchase the energy itself. Instead, DISCOS sign the PPAs directly with suppliers. Although the EPE mediates these contracts, the public agency does not enter into payment obligations.

The New Model prioritises security of supply. Determination of capacity requirements are made independent of movements in market prices, which should work well since electricity consumption is price inelastic. Once new capacity is contracted for, it is assured of a steady revenue stream for 30 years. Separating the markets for old and new energy ensures that low-cost plants do not price out new investments or that new investment contaminates the prices of the output of low-cost plants. In doing so, the New Model shifts market risks from high-cost plants to low-cost plants. Generally, if supply exceeds demand, it is the higher cost plants that are priced out of the market. Under the New Model, since new energy receives a guaranteed and fixed payment for 30 years, it is the old energy which will trade in shorter term markets and its prices and volumes will have to adjust in case consumption falls below demand projections. Although this shifts risks from one class of energy producer to another (i.e. from new to old), the planners believe that the system should work satisfactorily since old energy mostly has to recoup only its operational costs and, therefore, has more flexibility in setting prices.

After ensuring security of supply, keeping prices low is the major objective of the New Model. Its developers determined that going back to the principle of remunerating investors based on cost-of-service rather than through market-clearing prices would better deliver this objective. On one end, maintaining heterogeneity in wholesale power prices by paying each plant its actual average costs rather than a unique market-clearing price significantly reduces total costs as it prevents low-cost generators from earning significant rents. On the other end, having investors compete for the market ensures, a priori, a degree of discipline and efficiency. Guaranteeing a steady revenue stream, the model also takes market risk away from generation investors, reducing their cost of capital and making it easier for them to obtain project finance.

The model also tries to eliminate the problem of price and investment volatility brought about by market-clearing models for wholesale power by having investors bid on a fixed price through the life of the contract. Given that these contracts are signed in exchange for investors building pre-defined power plants of specified capacities rather than merely financial instruments, which may or may not be backed by physically available units of power, further removes elements of speculation from the process.

The New Model is designed to work with a mixed public–private ownership system. In Brazil, the public sector dominates power generation, producing 85 per cent of Brazil's electricity, while the private sector dominates distribution where they are responsible for 80 per cent of the market. Transmission is relatively equally divided, with 17 of the 26 firms belonging to the private sector, although the public sector transmission firms tend to be larger than the private sector ones. Allowing both public sector and private utilities to compete freely for the market provides an opportunity to accurately compare total price efficiency in the two sectors. If public sector utilities are significantly less efficient than private sector ones, they will not be able to match private sector price offers without incurring losses. If the private sector bids too high, the public sector will be able to undercut them.

The model allows not just public–private competition as described above, but also public–private partnerships as consortia including both state-owned and private power companies may bid to supply new power or to acquire power utilities. For example, in 2007, a consortium led by Cemig (a vertically integrated utility owned by the state of Minas Gerais) and CPFL (a domestic private power company) bought out a privatised DISCO, Light, from its French owners, EDF.

Finally, the New Model significantly reduces regulatory oversight and the problems caused by informational asymmetries. It places the responsibility for the determination of demand projections as well as the consequences of the errors therein not on a bureaucratic single-buyer but on the DISCOS. It makes EPE negotiate new power purchases through auctions to supply the market, thereby locking in these prices for 30 years. With this, there is less need to monitor prices in the wholesale markets. Similarly, monitoring the DISCOS' pass-through of wholesale power purchases is made easier because it is set as the average price in the wholesale markets (called the Reference Value or VR). The presence of a substantially large deregulated market in which large and sophisticated power consumers negotiate prices provides yet another means to compare and monitor prices in the regulated markets as prices in the two markets should move more or less in tandem.

Table 11.3 compares and contrasts the New Model with its predecessors. In designing this model, power planners in Brazil have made a measured return from market to plan. Replacing a strategy of comprehensive deregulation where control and oversight are automated through the market, the New Model uses markets not in an integrated and interlinked manner, but in discretely delineated areas to achieve targets established by a coordinated planning exercise. It is the plan that links the various elements of the power sector together as opposed to the market, which was supposed to do so under the earlier policy. Its origins can be traced to Brazil's early successful experiments with state-led electric power development. The New Model is, however, not a complete return to the state as substantial space has been left to the private and now more independent public sector firms to participate in the operational side of the sector.

The main weakness of the New Model is that it re-introduces some risks of government failure. There exists the danger that public sector firms might purposely underbid private investors in the competition to be selected to build a power plant, although in the long run this would be a self-defeating strategy as it would compromise their financial health and eventually prevent them from competing in future auctions for new power generation facilities. The model would also not prevent the government from forcing public sector GENCOS from bidding too low in such auctions in order to lower the price of electricity, but, as experience with all other power sector models has shown, in the event of a major crisis, government commitment to commercial rules is little related to ownership or liberalisation.

5 Conclusions

Although the neo-classical models upon which privatisation and liberalisation programmes were based in the 1980s and 1990 were pithy and sensible, they were inadequate in capturing and making sense of the complexities of public service delivery in industrialised, and even more so in developing countries. As the experience of the Brazilian power industry demonstrates, public agencies can perform well when they are given missions that excite and inspire their staff, and resources adequate to the task. Performance in these sectors, rather than being determined exclusively by ownership or even market structure, is a more complex phenomenon that needs to be studied in terms of institutional structures, human motivation, available economic resources, perspectives and prospective for the sector, and its strategic relevance. Problems with state ownership arise when competition amongst incompatible public sector goals intensifies but privatisation and deregulation cannot easily resolve these conflicts and may even exacerbate them. Implementation of the typical models of privatisation and liberalisation proposed for developing countries during the last decades have shown that planning systems have been prematurely dismantled in the expectation that markets would automatically provide the right amount of investment and quality of service. The solutions now being developed do not recommend going back to previous unsatisfactory models of public sector infrastructure management, but

Table 11.3 Comparison old, liberalised and new models

	Old model 1955–1995	Liberalised model 1995–2003	New model post-2003
Ownership	Federal (generation and transmission) and state governments (distribution)	Incomplete privatisation: distribution mostly privatised; generation partly privatised	Mixed: distribution mostly private; transmission mixed; generation mostly public
Planning	Centralised and determinative under Eletrobrás GCPS	Indicative weak; decentralised market	Partly decentralised and determinative under EPE
Despatch	Centralised under Eletrobrás GCOI	ONS	ONS
Wholesale price setting	Regulated, cost-of-service	Market; market clearing	Mixed; cost-of-service, auctions
Organisation responsible	MME (nominally); Eletrobrás	Wholesale Market Board	EPE
Contracting	100%	85%	100%
Distribution regulation and pass through of wholesale power	Cost-of-service; pass through at actual costs.	Price-cap; pass through subject to price ceiling called VN, a technically determined value that approximates long-term expansion costs	Price-cap; pass through subject to price ceiling called VR, the average price of the New Energy contracted through EPE
Industry structure	Federal GENCOS vertically integrated on G&T, distribution separate and generally owned by state governments	Vertically integrated tending towards unbundling	Unbundled
Regulatory capacity required	Low	High	Medium
Positive aspects	Long term planning, stability of contracts, low prices	Competitive market, private investment	Long-term planning, long-term PPAs, lower speculation, volatility and average prices
Negative aspects	Political interference, public sector performance risk	High prices, uncertainty of investment	Public sector performance risk

rather seek to reinsert the state and public sector institutions in addressing the coordination and distributional issues in which infrastructure markets have failed while allowing competition to create efficiency gains where feasible. Experience, as much as theory, dictates the principles upon which these solutions should be based.

Notes

1 See, for example, J. Kornai (1982) *Growth, Shortage and Efficiency*, Oxford: Blackwell.
2 For more material on this approach, I direct the reader to the works of R. Coase and O. E. Williamson.
3 By effective I mean whether the firms consistently achieved the targets that were established for them without inordinate delay and cost-overrun. I use the term effective instead of efficient here to avoid a fruitless debate on whether public sector power firms operated efficiently and could private firms have been even more efficient.
4 The participation of Canada and the USA was in the form of three engineering firms from these countries that the World Bank and Brazilian public authorities had jointly selected to execute a study of the hydroelectric potential and of the power market in Brazil.
5 A good Portuguese language history of electric power planning in Brazil is available in Eletrobrás (2002).
6 A. Gomes, C. Abarca, E. Faria and H. Fernandez (undated) "O Setor Eletrico", BNDES memo.
7 The Ministry of Mines and Energy's Emergency Management Committee had recommended further refinement of the deregulated market model, principally in allowing electricity prices to reflect scarcity values. The official commission recommendations are located in MME (2002), volumes 1–4. The reports of the group associated with the PT can be found in Sauer (2003) and Pinguelli (2002).
8 Penalties are imposed on the DISCOS if their forecasts are not accurate. If they underestimate demand, they will be forced to buy power on the spot market and are financially penalised. If they overestimate demand by more than 5 per cent, they will be allowed to sell their excess power in the spot market. They can keep any gains from these trades but have to absorb any losses. These penalties reflect substantially the consequences to which DISCOS would be subject under a deregulated market system.

Bibliography

Amann, E. and Baer, W. (2000) "The Illusion of Stability: The Brazilian Economy under Cardoso", *World Development* 28(10).

Baer, W. (2001) *The Brazilian Economy: Growth and Development* (fifth edition), Westport, CT: Praeger.

BNDES (2001) *Cadernos de Infra-estrutura: Setor Elétrico – Perfil das Concessionárias, Vol. 2*, Rio de Janeiro: The Brazilian Development Bank.

EHMA (2000) *The Impact of Market Forces on Health Systems: A Review of Evidence in the 15 European Member States*, Dublin: European Health Management Association.

Eletrobrás (2002) O Planejamento da Expansão do Setor de Energia Elétrica: A Atuação da Eletrobrás e do Grupo Goordenador do Planejamento dos Sistemas Elétricos (GCPS), Rio de Janeiro.

Hall, D. and Lobina, E. (2005) *The Relative Efficiency of Public and Private Sector Water*, London: Public Services International Research Unit, PSIRU.

Kumaranayake, L. (1998) "The Role of Regulation: Influencing Private Sector Activity within Health Sector Reform", *Journal of International Development* 9(4): 641–649.

Laffont, J. (2005) *Regulation and Development*, Cambridge: Cambridge University Press.

Laffont, J-J. and Tirole, J. (1993) *A Theory of Incentives in Procurement and Regulation*, Cambridge, MA: MIT Press.

Leonard, K. (2002) "When Both States and Markets Fail: Asymmetric Information and the Role of NGOs in African Health Care", *International Review of Law and Economics* 22: 61–80.

McDowall, D. (1988) *The Light: Brazilian Traction, Light and Power Company Limited 1899–1945*, Toronto: University of Toronto Press.

Mendonça, A. and Dahl, C. (1999) "The Brazilian Electrical System Reform", *Energy Policy* 27(2): 73–83.

Ministério de Minas e Energia (2002) *Comitê de Revitilização do Modelo do Setor Elétrico, Relatório de Progresso No. 1–2*, Brasilia.

Oliveira, A. (1997) Perspectivas da Reestruturação Financeira e Institucional do Setor Elétrico Brasileiro, Relatório de Pesquisa Patrocinado pelo PNUD/IPEA/FUNDAP.

Parker, D. and Kirkpatrick, C. (2005) "Privatisation in Developing Countries: A Review of the Evidence and the Policy Lessons", *Journal of Development Studies* 41(4): 513–541.

Pinguelli, L. (2002) *Diretrizes e Linhas de Ação Para o Setor Elétrico Brasileiro Rio de Janeiro*.

Riddell, A. (1993) "The Evidence on Public/Private Educational Trade Offs in Developing Countries", *International Journal of Educational Development* 13(4): 373–386.

Rondinelli, D. (1993) *Development Projects as Policy Experiments: An Adaptive Approach to Development Administration*, London: Routledge.

Sauer, I. (2003) *Reconstrução do Setor Elétrico Brasileiro*, Editora UFMS and Paz e Terra: São Paulo.

Tankha, S. (2009) "Lost in Translation: Explaining the Brazilian Power Reforms Failure", *Journal of Latin American Studies* 41(1): 51–90.

Teisberg, E. (1993) "Capital Investment Strategies under Uncertain Regulation", *RAND Journal of Economics* 24(4): 591–604.

Teixeira, P. and Amaral, A. (2001) "Private Higher Education and Diversity: An Exploratory Survey", *Higher Education Quarterly* 55(4): 359–395.

Tendler, J. (1968) *Electric Power in Brazil: Entrepreneurship in the Public Sector*, Cambridge, MA: Harvard University.

Tyrall, D. (2004) "The UK Railway Privatisation: Failing to Succeed", *Economic Affairs* 24(3): 32–38.

12 The fiscal and efficiency hypothesis of water utilities' privatization

A review of the evidence

Eduardo Araral Jr

Introduction

During much of the 1990s, water utilities worldwide experienced a wave of privatization. The rationale for this, much like the rationale for the wave of privatization of state-owned enterprises and other government services, is largely based on two hypotheses: the fiscal hypothesis and the efficiency hypothesis (Braadbaart 2001). The fiscal hypothesis suggests that privatization will relieve governments of the burden of investment financing particularly in the context of fiscal pressures faced by many developing countries in the 1980s. The efficiency hypothesis on the other hand suggests that water utilities' performance will improve under private ownership because it is "obviously" more efficient than the public sector.

These two hypotheses – widely supported by donors, think tanks and economists – is summarized by Franceys (1997) as follows:

> [P]rivate sector participation is seen to increase efficiency and introduce new ideas of finance but above all to require a new emphasis on proactive, performance oriented commercial management that aims to match the demand of its customers with their willingness to pay realistic charges and tariff.
>
> Franceys (1997)

The purpose of this chapter is to examine the validity of these hypotheses based on a meta-analysis of the international experience on water utilities' privatization. The extant literature on this subject remains fragmented as most studies either examine the efficiency argument in its various dimensions or some aspects of the fiscal argument. This chapter attempts to provide a broad synthesis of these two strands in the literature, explain the outcomes and draw out the key conclusions and policy implications.

The fiscal hypothesis

The essence of the fiscal argument, summarized by Palmer *et al.* (2003) is that "governments and government controlled parastatals rarely deliver services cost effectively nor can they usually raise the finance needed to expand service provision." In this view, the involvement of international water companies can facilitate cost-effective delivery of services and can also facilitate mobilizing long-term finance since participation on a risk-sharing basis of international water companies enhances confidence of creditors that investment programs will be implemented efficiently. The implication of this argument, therefore, is that aid should be used to leverage private sector investments in water (Franceys 1997).

The evidence

One of the most comprehensive and in-depth empirical reviews of the evidence on the fiscal hypothesis is provided by Hall and Lobina (2006). In their study, they have systematically debunked the myth that privatization will relieve governments of the burden of investment financing.

First, they find that most private contracts, notably lease and management contracts, involve no investment by the private company in extensions to unconnected households. In sub-Saharan Africa, for example, 17 lease and management contracts did not result in any investment by the private company to poor unconnected households. Concession contracts do involve investment by private companies to extend the network; however, the commitments agreed when these contracts were made are invariably revised, abandoned or missed. For instance, about 37 percent of all private investments in the water and sanitation sector worldwide became distressed (or were cancelled or renegotiated), including those of the largest concessions which accounted for 80 percent of these commitments (World Bank 2006).

The problem is more severe in Latin America and the Caribbean. Guash *et al.* (2003), for example, in a study of more than 1,000 concessions in infrastructure granted during 1985–2000 in that region, found that 74.4 percent of water and sanitation concession contracts were renegotiated very soon after their award, occurring on average 1.6 years thereafter. In Cape Verde, Gabon, Mali and South Africa, the story is pretty much the same.

Second, in most privatization contracts, actual investment on the ground particularly in connecting poor households often required public finance and/or guarantees from government or government-owned development banks. Table 12.1 provides an example of major build operate and transfer water projects which required public finance and/or government guarantees to deliver actual investments. In half of these projects the concessions were eventually terminated while a third were distressed and disputed.

Third, private water companies do not necessarily bring in new sources and volumes of investment finance. Hall and Lobina find that they rely heavily on the same sources that are available to the public sector. For instance, most private companies relied on sources that are also available to governments – donors, commercial and development banks, bonds and operating surplus. Private equity was rarely used by private investors.

Table 12.1 Major build operate transfer water projects with government guarantees

Country	Project	Companies	Problems for water distributor	Public guarantees	Status
China	Chengdu	Veolia	X	X	Distressed/disputed
China	Da Chang (Shanghai)	Thames Water, Bovis	X	X	Terminated
China	Shenyang	Suez	X	X	Terminated
China	Xian	Berlinwasser (Veikua/Thames)		X	Terminated
India	Bangalore	Biwater	X	X	Cancelled
India	Sonia Vihar (Delhi)	Suez	X	X	Distressed/disputed
Vietnam	Thu Duc (HCM City)	Suez, Pilecon	X	X	Terminated
Malaysia	Selangor	Puncak Niaga	X	X	
Thailand	Pathum Thani	Thames/Bois, Karnchang	X	X	
Turkey	Yuvacik (Izmit)	Thames	X	X	Distressed/disputed
Zimbabwe	10 dams plan	Biwater	X		Cancelled

Source: Hall and Lobina (2006).

Fourth, the contribution of multinational companies in water investments in poor countries is negligible and unlikely to increase. Most investors prefer to invest in middle-income countries (50 percent) compared to low-income countries (18 percent) where the need for water investment is greatest (Estache and Goicoehea 2005). Figures 12.1 and 12.2 illustrate this geographical disparity. Overall, as a proportion of investments in infrastructure worldwide, the share of private investment in water utilities is not significant. For instance, from 1990 to 2001, only 5 percent of the total private investment in all infrastructure projects in developing countries went to water investments.

As a result, since 1997, only roughly about 600,000 households (or 3 million people) in sub-Saharan Africa, South Asia and East Asia (excluding China) have been provided with a sustainable water supply arising from investments by private operators. This translates to roughly 900 people a day since 1997 which is way below the ideal of 270,000 people a day, the rate needed in order to meet the MDG target of reducing by half the proportion of people without sustainable access to drinking water and sanitation (Table 12.2).

In addition to the underinvestment by the private sector in water infrastructure, donors also held back their financing. For instance, from 1997 to 2002,

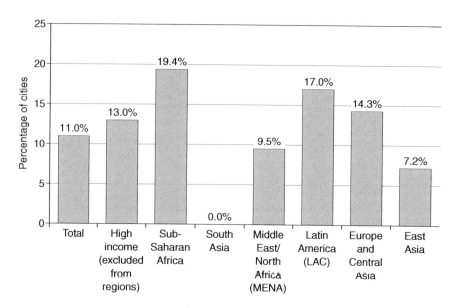

Figure 12.1 Percentage of cities with a population of over one million with water services operated by private companies by region (source: Hall and Lobina (2006)).

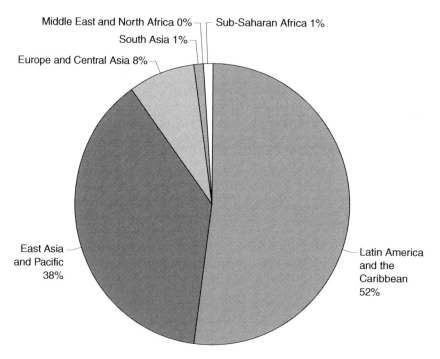

Figure 12.2 Geographic distribution of investments in water and sanitation infrastructure (source: World Bank (2004)).

Table 12.2 Estimated total new water connections financed by private operators in sub-Saharan Africa and Asia (ex-China)

	Region	Total number of new connections to households financed by private operator 1990–2005
Gabon	Africa	33,000
Nelspruit, South Africa	Africa	5,000
Jakarta, Indonesia	Asia	280,000
Manila, Philippines	Asia	267,000
Rest of sub-Saharan Africa and East Asia (excl. China)		15,000
South Asia	Asia	0
Total	sub-Saharan Africa and Asia (excl. China)	600,000

Source: Hall and Lobina (2006).

donor financing declined by 47 percent to \$7 billion. Briceno-Garmendia *et al.* (2004) attribute this to the over-optimistic expectations of private sector participation in the financing of infrastructure needs.

The efficiency hypothesis

Another argument widely used in support of water utilities' privatization is the efficiency hypothesis which suggests that performance will improve under private ownership because it is "obviously" more efficient than the public sector. The intellectual roots of the efficiency argument against public provision are drawn largely from public choice theories of government behavior. In this view, the poor performance of public water utilities in developing countries can be attributed to four fundamental incentive problems associated with public provision.

First, governments in developing countries often succumb to populist pressures to keep prices below cost even though these subsidies do not benefit the poor (Harris 2003). Second, public enterprises are faced with conflicts of interest because the owner is also the same as the regulator, and as a result performance contracts cannot be credibly enforced (Shirley and Nellis 1991). Third, public enterprises are faced with perverse organizational incentives arising from the non-credible threat of bankruptcy, weak competition, agency problems, rigidities and performance measurement problems (Stiglitz 2000; Weimer and Vining 1998). Fourth, state-owned enterprises are insulated from capital markets as they face soft budget constraints and therefore are not subject to market discipline.

Indeed, there is widespread evidence of efficiency problems plaguing public water utilities. A survey by the Asian Development Bank (2007) of 20 urban public water utilities throughout India provides an illustrative example of the problems faced by public water utilities: water is only available 4.3 hours a day on average; unaccounted for water (UFW) – water that has been produced but is eventually lost before it reaches the customers due to leaks, theft, unbilled consumption and inaccurate metering (a widely used measure of efficiency) – is 32 percent on average which also could be understated because metering covers only about 25 percent of households on average.

The story is the same for other urban public water utilities in other parts of Asia. For example, McIntosh and Yniguez (1997), in a study of 50 water utilities in 19 countries in Asia found that UFW stood at 60 percent. In Latin America, a survey of six publicly owned and operated water utilities in major cities showed that UFW goes up to as much as 51 percent (Shirley and Menard 2002) while in Lagos, Nigeria, it runs up to as high as 90 percent.

Thus, the confluence of poor performance of public utilities, fiscal pressures faced by developing countries, pressure from donors, arguments about the superior efficiency of privatized water supply and the public choice arguments of perverse incentives in the public sector have prompted many developing countries to involve the private sector in the provision and financing of goods previously provided by the public sector. On the basis of these assumptions, many of the previous debates about policy in infrastructure and services assume that achieving private sector operation is an objective in itself, and is always a desirable result (Hall and Lobina 2006). In fact, from 1990 to 2001, developing countries had seen over $755 billion of investment inflows in 2,500 infrastructure projects (Harris 2003).

The evidence

What has been the evidence on the efficiency hypothesis? Recently, there has been a stream of empirical evidence consistently and repeatedly showing that there is no systematic significant difference between public and private operators in terms of efficiency or other performance measures (Willner and Parker 2002; Clarke *et al.* 2003; Motta and Moreira 2004; Kirkpatrick *et al.* 2004; Estache and Rossi 2002; Estache *et al.* 2005; Hall and Lobina 2006; Perard 2007).

For instance, Willner and Parker (2002) observed that there is no consistent conclusion to be drawn in a survey of a large number of studies on the question of private versus public efficiency in developed, developing and transition countries. They find that in some cases, there is evidence of greater private sector efficiency, some showing greater public sector efficiency or no difference. They conclude that based on the empirical evidence, a change of ownership from public to private is not necessarily a cure for an under-performing organization.

Perard (2007), in a comprehensive review of 48 case studies and 22 econometric tests on the subject comparing the efficiency of public and private water utilities, also finds mixed results. For instance, 58 percent of the case studies indicate a positive influence of private sector participation while 27 percent indicate no difference. Of the 22 econometric tests reviewed, Perard finds that 68 percent of these studies indicate no difference between public and private provision.

Likewise, Estache *et al.* in 2005, summarizing the econometric evidence on water efficiency, also concludes that there is no statistically significant difference between the efficiency performance of public and private operators in the water sector. They find that for utilities it seems that, in general, ownership often does not matter as much as sometimes argued. They conclude that most cross-country papers on utilities find no statistically significant difference in efficiency scores between public and private providers. This finding is particularly significant since Estache has co-authored a number of earlier studies which have been used by the World Bank to argue for the superior efficiency of the private sector (Hall and Lobina 2006).

Experience from other parts of the world pretty much tells the same story. A study by the Clarke *et al.* (2003) in Latin America (Argentina, Bolivia and Brazil) compared cities which had private sector participation, and in cities which had no private sector involvement using household level data. They concluded that "while connections appear to have generally increased following privatization, the increases appear to be about the same as in cities that retained public ownership of their water systems." Similarly, in Brazil, a study by Motta and Moreira (2004) involving 4,000 sanitation operations shows that there is no significant difference between public and private operators in terms of the total variation in productivity. They note that regional operators have lower productivity levels than municipalities. In Chile, Bitrán and Valenzuela (2003) found that private sector operators had increased investment and labor productivity compared with public companies. However, they had also increased their rates by more, and had performed worse in dealing with unaccounted for water.

In Africa, Kirkpatrick *et al.* (2004) examined 110 African water utilities, 14 of them private, and found no significant difference between public and private operators in terms of cost. In contrast, Estache and Rossi (2002) in a smaller study of two private water operators in Africa, did find that the private operators were more efficient. However, they also found that institutional quality was a more important factor than private ownership in explaining differences in efficiency.

Likewise, the performance of privatized utilities in Asia is also mixed. For instance, the Asian Development Bank (2007), in a survey of 18 cities in Asia, including Jakarta and Manila – the world's largest privatization exercise, finds that they were performing significantly worse than most public sector operators on four indicators of coverage, investment, and leakage. In addition, Hall and Lobina (2006) find that the percentage of households connected to a water supply in Manila and Jakarta is lower than all other cities except one; the percentage with access to sewerage in Manila and Jakarta is lower than in any of the other cities except in Vientiane, Laos; capital expenditure (US dollars per connection) in Manila and Jakarta is much lower than in cities such as Delhi and Dhaka, even though these latter are in countries with lower per capita income; in terms of the levels of non-revenue water (leakage and unpaid consumption) Manila is worst, and Jakarta fourth worst. On six indicators (unit production costs, percentage of expenses covered by revenue, cost to consumers of constant level of usage per month, 24 hour supply, tariff level, connection fee) their performance is middling, not outstanding. However, Lobina and Hall find that the private cities perform relatively well on two indicators: revenue collection efficiency, and minimizing the number of staff per 1,000 connections.

Donors have taken cognizance of the steady stream of empirical evidence which has consistently and repeatedly shown the absence of systematic and significant difference between public and private operators in terms of efficiency or other performance measures. For instance, the IMF, in a policy paper on public–private partnership admits that "much of the case for public–private partnerships (PPP) rests on the relative efficiency of the private sector. While there is an extensive literature on this subject, the theory is ambiguous and the empirical evidence is mixed" (IMF 2004).

This conclusion is crucial since the question of private sector efficiency is central for justifying any form of PPP. The reason for this is that public sector borrowing is invariably cheaper than private sector borrowing, and therefore the key issue is whether PPPs result in efficiency gains that more than offset the higher borrowing costs. As the preceding review of the literature has shown, the assumption regarding the efficiency of privatized water supply is not supported by empirical evidence.

Explaining the failure of privatization

What could explain the apparent failure of water utilities' privatization? While much is known about the outcomes of water utilities' privatization, little is known about why this is the case. One explanation is provided by Shirley (2006) who attributes the failure of water utilities' privatization to the disregard by conventional economists of the local political and institutional realities surrounding urban water supply. In the conventional view, urban water supply is treated as a private good and priced to cover costs, including investments and externalities. In this view, water utilities should be operated as an enterprise operating under state regulation to assure access and quality, and poor consumers should be subsidized through means tested subsidies.

Using the case of the Buenos Aires water concession, Shirley suggests that the reason why few countries with weak institutions have followed the conventional advice has to do with four characteristics of urban water that is poorly understood by policy reform advocates: water is essential to life, local in supply, mysterious in information and dull in innovation. These characteristics, in turn, have important implications for urban sector water reform, which Shirley summarizes as follows:

First, water being essential to life is subject to strong beliefs. This leads to the strong belief that water should not be treated as a private good; it should be provided at very low cost or free and should be subject to government controls. Water being essential to life also implies that water politics is more intense and different from the politics of other utilities' reform such as power and telecommunication. Water reform – particularly the inevitable tariff reform that accompanies privatization – often succumbs to populist politics precisely because water is essential to life. The stickiness and intense controversy arising from water tariff reform could perhaps partly explain the difficulty of governments to credibly honor their commitments to private concessionaires to undertake water tariff reforms.

Second, water being dull implies low dynamic gains. However, as Shirley suggests, investors could still be motivated to sink capital in water and sanitation if states can credibly commit to assure a low but reasonable return over a long period. However the intense politics of water tariff reform raises issues of credible commitment problems on the part of governments.

Third, water being mysterious implies that the investors' information problems will be reflected in the design of the contract, and its vulnerability to renegotiation. For instance, the quality of water infrastructure – which is buried underground – is often difficult to ascertain ex-ante during contract negotiation. This information only becomes revealed during physical rehabilitation and concessionaires realize that they have underestimated the magnitude of costs involved. These pervasive information asymmetry problems could perhaps partly explain the fact that most water concessions were typically renegotiated shortly after contract agreement.

Conclusion and implications

The purpose of the chapter is to examine the validity of the fiscal and efficiency hypotheses that have been used to justify the wave of privatization of water utilities in the 1990s. Two major conclusions can be drawn from the preceding review of the literature.

First, contrary to expectations, privatization has not relieved governments of the burden of investment financing and that private finance is unlikely to play an important role in achieving water and sanitation targets of the Millennium Development Goals (Hall and Lobina 2006). The fact is that only 5 percent of the total private investment in all infrastructure projects in developing countries went to water investments. Most investors prefer to invest in middle-income countries compared to low-income countries where the need for water investment is greater (Estache and Goicoehea 2005). In addition, in most privatization contracts, public finance and/or guarantees from government or development banks are of central importance in delivering actual investment on the ground, particularly in connecting poor households. Furthermore, private water companies do not bring in new sources and volumes of investment finance – they rely heavily on the same sources that are available to the public sector.

Second, the efficiency claims of privatization are ambiguous as indicated by numerous case studies and econometric tests (Willner and Parker 2002; Clarke *et al.* 2003; Motta and Moreira 2004; Kirkpatrick *et al.* 2004; Estache *et al.* 2005; Hall and Lobina 2006; Perard 2007). These findings now appear to be the consensus view as even the main proponents of privatization such as the IMF and the WB have also admitted as much (Willner and Parker 2003).

Realizing this, donors have begun to reform their water financing programs. For instance, UK is batting for the front loading of donor investments in the water sector through long-term bonds backed by aid budgets of donor countries. USAID is exploring the route of improving the credit rating of public utilities and developing local bond markets as sources of finance. The ADB has doubled its financing commitment to the water sector to around US$2 billion a year for the period 2006–2010 as well as offering a host of knowledge products and other initiatives such as raising the political profile of water issues.

These findings have important implications on the role of private and public sectors in water supply. Indeed, the inherent characteristics of water – i.e. essential to life, local in supply, dull in innovation and mysterious in information – would imply a rethinking of the role of governments and private sector in water supply.

This does not imply a return to the old business model of water supply that has only led to poor performance of public water utilities. Local politicians who make decisions on water supply need to change their mindsets as well – i.e. to treat water as an essential economic good and adopt sustainable cost recovery measures. For this, they need to be convinced that *good water economics is also good water politics* – an important lesson in the case of the PPWSA in Cambodia. This message is important as more and more local governments assume responsibilities for water supply as a result of widespread decentralization efforts in the 1990s.

Convincing them that *good water economics is also good water politics* requires, among other things, that local governments provide a variety of financing mechanisms in order for them to make credible commitments to their electorate – i.e. be able to promise improved water services in exchange for adopting sustainable cost recovery mechanisms. One approach would be for national governments to provide water financing windows in the form of matching grants or competitive block grants for water investments. As the case of the Philippines shows, this financing window is an effective mechanism to generate local demand and facilitate progressive utilities' reform in smaller cities. Scale is important to ensure widespread adoption of water supply reforms. The Nehru Urban Renewal Program in India is one such example to provide federal assistance to state governments to deal with urban water supply issues.

Outside of government programs, domestic private companies also have important roles to play, despite the problems with the first generation experience of water utilities' privatization. For instance, domestic companies are also increasingly becoming important as they take over distressed concessions left by multinational companies. As the case of the two water concessions in Manila has shown, domestic water companies behave differently to multinational companies in terms of their approach in dealing with complex local problems.

This development of the increasing role of domestic companies has four policy implications. First is the need to rethink the role of fiscal policy instruments – for instance tax holidays and performance-based sovereign guarantees – to encourage domestic companies to invest in water utilities. Second, as more and more domestic companies succeed in running local utilities, the next logical step would be to experiment with water franchising models to expand outreach and coverage in areas outside of major cities. This is important as most un-served households are found in smaller cities. This model is currently being tested in the case of Cambodia using the PPWSA as the franchise for other provincial utilities. Third, along with the development of domestic water franchising models, there is also a need to develop water regulatory capacities at national and local government levels. Finally, as the experience of the first generation of water utilities' privatization has shown, many concessions became distressed, disputed or were eventually cancelled. This experience points to the importance of better understanding of the institutional economics of urban water supply particularly in the design of contracts and regulatory instruments.

Better approaches to providing water to urban poor communities would also have to be considered. Community-based approaches to urban water supply, particularly in slum areas, is an effective model of service delivery. In this model, organized urban poor communities assume responsibilities and accountability for water retail operations. Reputational mechanisms, group pressure and credible threat of disconnection have been shown to be effective mechanisms in dealing with urban poor communities as the experience of urban poor communities in Manila and Phnom Pen have shown. NGOs have a comparative advantage in organizing urban poor communities and have also been effective in raising the profile of water issues among local politicians and should be supported in this regard.

Finally, improving the governance of existing public water utilities should be a key focus of water supply reform as 90 percent of all water delivered through networks in developing countries is provided by these utilities. Small investments in information technology solutions, performance-based management, utilities' benchmarking and staff capacity building through twinning arrangements can go a long in way in terms of improving operational efficiencies. Beyond these, the creation of learning networks among public water utilities, nationally and regionally, can serve as important platforms for training, role modeling, benchmarking and the creation of markets for the reputation in water utilities' performance.

Bibliography

Araral, E. Jr (2008) "Public Provision for Urban Water: Getting the Fundamentals Right," *Governance: International Journal of Public Administration and Policy* 21(4): 527–549.

Asian Development Bank (2007) "Water in Asian Cities – Utilities Performance and Civil Society Views." Available at www.adb.org/Documents/Books/Water_for_All_Series/Water_Asian_Cities/regional_profiles.pdf.

Bitrán, G. and Valenzuela, E. (2003) "Water Services in Chile: Comparing Private and Public Performance Public Policy for the Private Sector," No. 255 March. Available at http://rru.worldbank.org/PapersLinks/Open.aspx?id=1998.

Braadbaart, O. (2001) "Privatizing Water: The Jakarta Concession and the Limits of Contract," paper presented at the Jubilee Workshop on "Water as a Life Giving and Deadly Force," Leiden, The Netherlands, June 14–16, 2001.

Briceno-Garmendia, C., Estache, A. and Shafik, N. (2004) "Infrastructure Services in Developing Countries: Access, Quality, Costs and Policy Reform," *World Bank Policy Working Paper 3468*, Washington, DC: World Bank.

Clarke, G., Kosec, K. and Wallsten, S. J. (2003) "Has Private Participation in Water and Sewerage Improved Coverage?: Empirical Evidence from Latin America," Working Paper 04–02, AEI-Brookings Joint Centre for Regulatory Studies, January 2004. Available at www.aei-brookings.com/admin/authorpdfs/page.php?id=325.

Estache, Antonio and Goicoehea, Ana (2005) "How Widespread Were Private Investment and Regulatory Reform in Infrastructure Utilities during the 1990s?" *Policy Research Working Paper 3595*, Washington, DC: World Bank.

Estache, A. and Rossi, M. (2002) "How Different is the Efficiency of Public and Private Water Companies in Asia?" *The World Bank Economic Review* 16(1): 139–148.

Estache, A., Perelman, S. and Trujillo, L. (2005) "Infrastructure Performance and Reform in Developing and Transition Economies: Evidence from a Survey of Productivity Measures," *World Bank Policy Research Working Paper 3514*, Washington, DC: World Bank. Available at http://wdsbeta.worldbank.org/external/default/WDSContent Server/IW3P/IB/2005/03/06/000090341_20050306101429/Rendered/PDF/wps3514. pdf.

Franceys, R. (1997) "Private Sector Participation in the Water and Sanitation Sector," report prepared for the Department for International Development (DFID), Occasional Paper # 3.

Garn, M., Isham, J. and Kahkonen, S. (2002) "Should We Bet on Private or Public Water Utilities in Cambodia? Evidence on Incentives and Performance from Seven Provincial Towns," Middlebury College Working Paper Series 0219. Available at http://ideas. repec.org/p/mdl/mdlpap/0219.html.

Guasch, J. Luis, Laffont, Jean-Jacques and Straub, Stephane (2003) "Renegotiation of Concession Contracts in Latin America," *World Bank Policy Research Working Paper*, Washington, DC: World Bank.

Hall, D. and Lobina, E. (2006) *Pipe Dreams: The Failure of the Private Sector to Invest in Water Services in Developing Countries*, Ferney-Voltaire: Public Services International; London: World Development Movement.

Harris, Clive (2003) "Private Participation in Infrastructure in Developing Countries," *World Bank Working Paper No. 5*, Washington, DC: World Bank.

International Monetary Fund (2004) Public–Private Partnerships March 12, 2004. Available at www.imf.org/external/np/fad/2004/pifp/eng/031204.htm.

Kirpatrick, C., Parker, D. and Zhang, Y-F. (2004) "State versus Private Sector Provision of Water Services in Africa: An Empirical Analysis," University of Manchester, Centre on Regulation and Competition, Working Paper Series, Paper # 70. Available at www. competition-regulation.org.uk/conferences/southafricasep04/kirkpatrick&parker& zhang.pdf.

McIntosh, Arthur and Yniguez, Cesar (eds) (1997) *Second Water Utilities Data Book: Asian and Pacific Region*, Manila: Asian Development Bank.

Motta, R. S. and Moreira, A. R. (2004) *Efficiency and Regulation in the Sanitation Sector in Brazil*, IPEA Discussion Paper No. 1059. Available at http://papers.ssrn.com/sol3/ Delivery.cfm/SSRN_ID651884_code347008.pdf?abstractid=651884&mirid=3.

Palmer, K., Cockburn, M. and Hulls, D. (2003) "Funding Johannesburg – Beyond the

Rhetoric: Delivering Water and Sanitation Targets," A CEPA Discussion Paper, Cambridge.

Perard, E. (2007) "Water Supply: Public or Private? An Approach Based on Cost of Funds, Transaction Costs, Efficiency and Political Costs," paper presented at the Conference on the Role of the State in Service Delivery, October 28–29, Lee Kuan Yew School of Public Policy, Singapore.

Shirley, M. (2006) "Urban Water Reform: What We Know, What We Need to Know," paper presented at the 10th Meeting of the International Society for New Institutional Economics, Boulder, CO.

Shirley, Mary and Menard, Claude (2002) "Cities Awash: A Synthesis of Country Cases," in Mary Shirley (ed.) *Thirsting for Efficiency: The Politics and Economics of Urban Water System Reform*, New York: Elsevier Science, p. 33.

Shirley, Mary and Nellis, John (1991) *Public Enterprise Reform: The Lessons of Experience*, Washington, DC: World Bank.

Stiglitz, J. (2000) *Economics of the Public Sector*, New York: W. W. Norton & Co.

Weimer, David and Vining, A. (1998) *Policy Analysis. Concepts and Practice*, Englewood Cliffs, NJ: Prentice Hall.

Willner, J. and Parker, D. (2002) "Relative Performance of Public and Private Enterprise under Conditions of Active and Passive Ownership," Centre on Regulation and Competition, Paper No. 22, October. Available at www.competition-regulation.org.uk/wpdl149/wp22.pdf.

—— (2003) "The World Bank as Privatization Agnostic," *Wall Street Journal*, 21 (July).

World Bank (2006) "Private Participation in Infrastructure Database." Available at http://ppi.worldbank.org/features/june2007/2006WaterDataLaunch.pdf.

13 Conclusion

Contradictions, contingencies and the terrain ahead

Scott A. Fritzen and Wu Xun

The pendulum – so goes the implicit or explicit argument in many of these contributions – is swinging again. States are once again reasserting their pre-eminent roles in service delivery and in the broad steering of their societies, clawing back authorities that under various guises of the New Public Management and privatization had been deleted, delegated, or otherwise diffused to market or social actors. Chapters in this collection have correlated these shifts in practice, across a range of sectors and settings, to shifts in ideology with regard to the role of government. Contributors have mapped some of the strategies being attempted to accomplish these shifts, and the mixed degree of implementation and success they have seen in various countries.

Yet this concluding chapter casts a critical light onto several of the assertions made in the above paragraph. Four broad perspectives are explored in so doing. First, we reflect on the metaphorical nature of the accounts underlying the reassertion of the state. Specifically, we explore the meanings embedded in the adoption of a "pendulum" versus "golden mean" metaphor for understanding these shifts. Second, we examine the tensions and ambiguities evident in the chapters, in essence casting doubt on whether we *are* witnessing a unifying phenomenon of the reassertion of the state. Third, we make some conjectures as to the "terrain ahead", in terms of the impact of the financial crisis and the broader forces constraining the reassertion to which it is giving great impetus. Finally, we attempt to draw some broader lessons or principles that seem embedded in the collection (despite the ambiguities noted).

Pendulum or golden mean?

Social and political explanation is inherently metaphorical; indeed, some philosophers have argued that metaphor-making gives rise to the structure of our consciousness itself (Hofstadter 2007). Less grandly, we would argue that it certainly underpins our understanding of the socio-political phenomenon of interest here: the shifting balance in the role of the state. Contributors in this volume can be seen (to use yet another metaphor) as torn between the adoption of two metaphors in studying the role of the state versus the market.

One is that of the "golden mean". It is worth remembering that the dawn of theorizing about government was normative and prescriptive with respect to its overarching roles. Early attempts to identify an ideal balance between state and society were rooted in religion or philosophy. These were later supplemented during the rise of the *Geisteswissenschaften* (Wagner 2007) in the nineteenth century by the examination of markets (most prominently with the rise of neo-classical economics) and a plethora of conceptual frameworks. Regardless of their varied conceptual constructions of politics (and economies), "philosophers" as different as Plato, Niccolo Machiavelli, Adam Smith and Milton Friedman shared an underlying assumption that there is an analytically or morally grounded "correct answer" to the question, a "golden mean" that brings the spheres into an appropriate balance (or a justified imbalance, as the case may be).

Closer to home, some contributors to this collection have put forward arguments that are at least partially grounded in a normative view of how states and markets should complement each other. For instance, Warner argues in Chapter 3 that the so-called reassertion of the state is "not a return to the direct public monopoly delivery model of old" – not a swing of the pendulum, in other words – but rather "heralds the emergence of a new balanced position which combined use of markets, deliberation and planning to reach decisions which may be both efficient and more socially optimal" (Warner, this volume, p. 00). As implied by the term "optimal", this line of thinking implies the potential to asymptotically approach the "golden mean" through a "rebalancing" of roles.

The normative or "golden mean" view has its advantages. It potentially offers a clearer foundation from which to describe disjunctions between the status quo and some idealized state of affairs, and hence a useful orientation for policy prescriptions. Yet it begs the question of whether and how a "golden mean" is ever reached, let alone maintained. How would we know when we see it? To take but one example, the question of what would happen if, amidst a general ideological predisposition towards the use of markets, expediency required massive and unprecedented coordinated government takeover of the commanding heights by otherwise "true believer" governments has been answered. It is, of course, "yes", in a story that continues to play out at present, and which rattles any narrative resting on the relative stability of state–market balances. In its stronger forms, the "golden mean" metaphor also implies somewhat heroic assumptions about the transferability of institutions and politics across porous cultural and geographical borders (Rose 2005).

An alternative metaphor – one in some sense embedded in the title of the collection – is less normative and more descriptive; it is that of pendulum shifts. In this view, movement in one direction, in one period, almost inevitably leads to the build-up of countervailing pressures that call for redress in the next period. B. Guy Peters (this volume, Chapter 2) follows this general line when he argues that "the decentralizing and delegation of the 'governance' models have necessarily been followed by the return of the State to a more authoritative position, using strategies of 'metagovernance' to reimpose some controls".

Indeed, one does not have to have a long memory to perceive several pendulum-like shifts in debates and, perhaps to a lesser extent, practices regarding the balance of state, society and market forces. This is a concept with a long past but a short history; there have arguably always been shifts, but the "past" that is in people's minds – the reference point from which one "re"-asserts the role of one or another construct – is of course ever shifting. To go back but a few cycles, we have seen the eras of:

- Strong war-time, development and welfare states at their apogee, in both the developing and developed world, across both capitalist and socialist blocks (roughly 1937–1979) (Peters 2001);
- The much discussed era of privatization and "New Public Management" (1980–1995) (Dunleavy and Hood 1994; Barzelay 2001);
- Increasing concerns to "bring the state back in" (Evans *et al.* 1985), for a number of reasons, many contradictory (1990–present);
- The re-emergence of the state "on steroids" and in crisis management mode, as a result of the ongoing global financial crisis (2008–present; see below).

All of which might lead one to wonder if the present collection is not, by virtue of the global crisis, charging through a very open door. Yet if the pendulum theory is accurate, the strength and rapidity of the current lurch suggests a consequent (precipitous?) retreat of state once the current situation stabilizes (on which some reflections are offered later in the chapter).

The primary advantage of the pendulum view is that it is dynamic, reflecting an appreciation of the way in which debates on the role of the state and market always take place in a social, political, and ultimately historical context that shapes its contours, pathways and possibilities. On the other hand, the pendulum analogy may suffer from containing too many embedded assumptions. It seems to assume that changes in the balance tend to be felt across sectors and contexts in a similar way across time. And it seems to prefigure a certain kind of narrative about the driving forces behind the common shifts *across boundaries*. Cross-national ideology, imitation and economic integration hence emerge as preferred drivers of the narrative, since whatever forces are posited must be assumed to work across boundaries. And the explanatory pathway of that narrative follows, perhaps a bit too predictably, a certain sequence to the narrative; the tendencies exhaust themselves, then force a correction of the excess, which in turn creates the inevitable countervailing pressures. It is a metaphor that carries the danger of a certain "just so" quality to its conclusions.

The case for contradiction and contingency

A close reading of the chapters in this collection suggests a more nuanced set of findings and underlying assumptions about the role of the state and the nature of its "reassertion" than might be assumed by the title. Several pieces present narratives that are characterized by three elements that in essence challenge a pendulum view of state–market–society balance, even in descriptive terms, and which, ironically, even challenge the view that they represent a common orientation towards a "reassertion". Taken together, the readings suggest the *ambiguous nature* of reforms that are generated by *multiple drivers* (some global, some local) in a *context-specific* and path-dependent manner. Let us unpack these three elements with some examples.

Ambiguity, even contradiction in the trends

Far from a single trend towards reassertion, several contributions depict reforms that are inherently ambiguous or that entail a number of contradictory elements. This could stem from any number of causes. One is the fact that there may be multiple levels on which the supposed "reassertion" may be taking place – theoretical, ideological, practical – and these may conflict in their application and effects. Anthony Cheung's description of civil service reform in Chapter 6 offers a fine example of the ironies and contradictions that make "reform" so difficult to capture. On the one hand, Hong Kong's colonial period "embraced a pro-civil service agenda" but was markedly market-oriented. On the other, its first post-colonial decade was characterized by "public sector downsizing and privatization" and the increased use of "contracting out, service vouchers, and public–private partnerships". Yet the ideological impetus and overall practical effect of these self-same reforms have been a significant movement towards the East Asian "developmental state" model: to wit, a reassertion of "the 'public' and the role of the state in economic and social management".

Or take the uses of the word "socialization" as a label of the Vietnamese Communist Party's policy towards the health sector as another example of this phenomenon. Jonathan London describes how it has been deployed simultaneously to justify increases in user payments and to promote a significant state project of redistributive expenditure in the sector (Chapter 8, this volume) – policy directions not easy to reconcile.

In short, the fact that all of these statements may be simultaneously accurate underscores the multiple levels on which political and administrative discourses of reform operate, and suggests that neither a "golden mean" nor a "pendulum" metaphor is likely to evince much explanatory power. Reforms are part of political strategies that are profoundly representational and symbolic, and in which different meanings can be attached to the same phenomenon by different observers (Stone 2001).

Ambiguities and interpretive contradictions may also stem from the large gap between the intended and unintended effects of reforms. Eduardo Araral's review of the "failure of water utilities' privatization" (this volume, Chapter 12) is instructive as an example of what in the systems literature goes by the name of "fixes that backfire" (Senge 1990). Water utility privatization, which was expected to improve management efficiency while reducing government's burden of investment financing, has had exactly the opposite effects in a large number of cases. The same might be said of decentralization reforms in China as well, as described by Painter and Mok in Chapter 9. What arose in part from a changing political strategy underlying the legitimation of Communist Party rule – the need to promote rapid economic growth – in fact created spaces for the fragmentation of authority relationships and inequalities in access to social services that are strong enough to galvanize vigorous challenges to local and, potentially, central-level politics.

Multiple causation

In explaining trends towards a reassertion, it is important to note the obvious: the chapters in the collection posit highly diverse drivers of the changes they set out to explain, calling into question the unity of the phenomenon itself.

Perhaps the most prominent driver mentioned by a range of contributors is ideology. The broad parameters of the debates over which sector should control the "commanding heights" of the economy were outlined in the introduction. Such macro-level currents, implicated in broad brush fashion in a range of chapters, were also shown to influence practices on a much more local stage. Consider the several examples given of New Public Management (NPM) reforms in this volume, for instance. Almost all of them were suggested to be highly problematic in their actual impacts (for in the narratives deployed by our contributors, this fact becomes the starting point for the call to "rebalance" state–market roles).

Yet the common impact of ideological currents is unlikely to offer a compelling explanation across contexts. That is not least because any attempt to delineate the ideology at work is likely to surface the kind of contradictions and ambiguities noted above. Take the NPM again as an example. One can narrow this reform ideology conceptually down to a preference for competition and a market orientation, as two of the chapters explicitly do (Walker *et al.*, Chapter 5; and Warner, Chapter 3). Yet NPM even in its heyday of the early 1990s was a very broad umbrella term used to advance reforms as different as organizational deconcentration and the application of yardstick competition to sub-units within an organization. Warner's suggestion that "[c]itizen engagement is more than the consumer orientation and competition advocated by New Public Management" is true as far as it goes, but neglects to mention that some prominent advocates of NPM called for measures far beyond "consumer orientation and competition" – including broad citizen engagement in policymaking (see for instance Osborne and Plastrik 2000, Chapters 6–8). Shared ideology is thus an important, but incomplete, explanation of recent shifts.

Other analysts posit different forces, again explicitly or implicitly, driving the reassertion of the state. Countries may succumb to external pressure or coercion, as some of the most vulnerable developing countries did in responding to donor demands for "structural adjustment" reforms against the backdrop of the "Washington consensus" (Srinivasen 2000). Imitation and policy learning across contexts may of course play their ostensibly more benign role (Rose 2005), not least in an era of economic interdependence. Changing perceptions of a socially or politically constructed "problem" may also call for reform and rebalancing; take the inequalities generated by the transition to a market economy (as in the Chinese and Vietnamese examples noted in this volume), or the "need" to compensate for an increasingly competitive global economic environment by reasserting the role of the state in promoting development (as in Cheung's case of Hong Kong). In these and in other cases we see, in keeping with the pendulum view, that the attempt to manage the side-effects of a particular development strategy or set of state–market roles has the potential to give rise to calls for redress, reform and rebalancing.

Contingent and path-dependent

Most of the examples in the collection show the dynamics of the renegotiation of state and market roles to be thoroughly grounded in *local* conditions and *recent* socio-political dynamics, both at the macro and micro level. This does not contradict a pendulum view – indeed, a pendulum is nothing if not path-dependent. But this contingent nature of the reforms does interact with the multiple causation and ambiguity noted above to make it difficult to paint a *common* picture of the movement towards reasserting the state. It also emphasizes that what will "work" to achieve any given set of objectives will be highly context-dependent.

The simple fact that reforms to "rebalance" the roles of state and market play out in different sectors within the same country or even local government context emphasizes the point that it is context-specific conclusions that must be drawn in these narratives. Pierre and Painter (this volume, Chapter 4), for example, point out that "the public sector has a multitude of objectives" as well as types of instrument at its disposal. This leads to these authors making predictions that belie the universality across sectors and instruments of bargains struck along the continuum of public and private roles: "[a]s a general rule ... the weaker the element of service production and the stronger the element of public authority, the more difficult the implementation of NPM becomes." Even from the normative perspective of their chapter, one might conclude that it is impossible to specify an appropriate *aggregate* balance of roles across the range of functions that need to be fulfilled in complex, modern states. Effective arguments will thus inevitably tend towards the sector-, policy instrument-, and site-specific.

While the individual contributions tend to support the above pattern of "contradiction and contingency", arguably the most powerful supra-national force in decades to be driving a realignment is one that we are in the midst of presently, namely global the financial crisis. The next section examines how this is likely to, in fact, significantly shape the contours of the debate going forward.

Reasserting the state amidst global financial crisis: opportunities and pitfalls

The chapters for this collection were first presented in a conference in Singapore in September 2007. By May 2009, the Dow Jones Industrial Average had lost more than a half of its market capitalization in a global economic crisis. Ignited by the collapse in the US subprime mortgage market, the effects of the crisis have rippled throughout the world economy, with the eventual magnitude of severity potentially rivalling that of the Great Depression in the 1930s. Large financial institutions have collapsed, and the volume of international trade has plummeted dramatically.

While arguments for reassertion of the state had gained momentum long before the current crisis (Evans *et al.* 1985; Sbragia 2000; Barrow 2005), there is no doubt that the crisis has provided additional fuel. It has exposed the vulnerability of the free market system; it was the *retreat* of the state from the regulation of financial markets that has been widely considered to be a major cause of the crisis. France's President Nicolas Sarkozy has claimed that the crisis signals "the return of the state and the end of the ideology of public powerlessness".

More importantly, the crisis is tacitly recasting the debate on the roles of the market and the state in three important ways. First of all, the fact that the crisis originated from the failure of financial markets in the US, the presumed exemplar of modern capitalism, provides at least highly suggestive evidence of fundamental flaws in market mechanisms. Despite the disastrous effects of similar crises in developing countries (Mexico, Argentina, Indonesia, Thailand, Russia etc.) in the last two decades, a rather unlikely notion of the "infallibility" of the free market system had achieved remarkable staying power in many quarters; defenders of market liberalization could always try to point to implementation issues, corruption and crony capitalism as the underlying causes for localized failure.

Second, while the globalization has often been posited as a leading factor contributing to the retreat of the state (Strange 1996), the crisis suggests that the absence of appropriate government oversight in one country can bring down the global economy in a globalized world. Any reconfiguration of the market and the state relationship must therefore take into consideration the global nature of its impacts.

Third, the speed at which economic wealth has evaporated during the crisis points to the importance of an appropriate time horizon in dealing with risks embedded in various institutional arrangements governing market–state inter-relationships. Even a long period of prosperity achieved through market liberalization may not be "long enough", given the risk of catastrophic failures embedded in a market-dominant approach.

Meanwhile, the crisis has inevitably given great impetus to an emerging consensus in favour of a more assertive role by the state in governing the economy. Massive government intervention to bail out banks and other financial institutions has pushed governments in many countries to take on roles as the managers and owners of these firms – roles that until recently were believed to be entirely inappropriate. Large-scale stimulus packages to combat the slowdown in private demand are in turn enabling governments to substantially increase spending on public services, reversing trends in some sectors.

These developments may be welcomed by many after decades of the dominance of market liberalism in policy thinking. Yet preoccupation with the crisis may also have the effect of hobbling careful deliberation on appropriate localized strategies for adjusting the role of states and markets. The fact that the crisis has hit many economies at the same time does not imply that responses to the crisis ought to be homogeneous across countries, or across sectors within countries. While public demand for extensive government interventions has never been stronger (driven by concerns over unemployment and economic instability), the movement towards the reassertion of the state now in full swing harbours several potential pitfalls.

First of all, the crisis may fuel unrealistic expectations about what the state is able to achieve; the threat of "state failure" has not receded along with the premature reports of its demise. The retreat of the state in the past two decades may in fact have set the state up for a failure to meet rising expectations in several important respects (Evans 1997). This "capacity gap" may take different forms, with varying effects in different contexts. One area of deficit is in the state's "penetrative capacity", its ability to gather sufficient information on changing economic and social conditions to decide on appropriate intervention strategies. It is well known that in most developing countries, the systematic collection of such information has often been relegated to low priority, aggregating the risk of states acting upon erratic or non-existent information. Another capacity deficit may lie in the expertise needed to perform new functions (and old ones that were always challenging) – such as rule making and enforcement in emerging economic areas. Sbragia (2000) argues that the state's "two faces" – that of the "provider of benefits" (as in most service–delivery agencies) and "builder of markets" (i.e. regulatory agencies) – can strain capacities of even highly institutionalized bureaucracies. And we should not forget the perpetual shortfalls of institutional capacity that result from weaknesses in programme planning, financial management, strategic planning and other key public management functions.

The second potential pitfall in reasserting the state lies in the potential reduction in the pressure for governments to improve performance. Whatever its limitations, NPM reforms such as contracting out and the creation of internal markets have in many cases increased the pressures on public sector organizations to perform better. In short, the swings of the pendulum could result in some of the positive inheritances of the previous agenda being uncritically rolled back, losing the opportunity to sustain policy learning.

A third possibility is that the current crisis may generate a roll-back in certain types of globalization. Barrow (2005) differentiates two conceptualizations of the state – as nation-state and as institution. The distinction may be critical in the backdrop of the current crisis, in which economic protectionism may be on the rise, as evinced by measures such as the "Buy America" provision included within the Obama administration's first stimulus package. The return specifically of the nation-state element of the state "on steroids" may ultimately erode more than the (at least in one view) hard-fought gains derived from multilateral trade liberalization over the past three decades.

Finally, the reassertion of the state obviously goes hand in hand with an increase in the discretionary powers of some very powerful government officials, raising the spectre of pervasive rent-seeking arrangements and corruption. Goel and Nelson (1998) showed that the bigger the government, the higher the levels of corruption in a country; the implication if their analysis is accepted is all too obvious. When the state is brought "back in" in a major way as a response to the immediate threats imposed by the crisis, concerns over governance quality and the control of rent-seeking and corruption may be sidelined.

While the reassertion of the state may be long overdue in many countries, our analysis suggests that it may take different forms across countries and across sectors within countries. Poorly construed strategies in moving state to the centre stage in economic management may replicate failures of the past. The next section summarizes some broader lessons embedded in the collection.

Strategic responses to the global economic crisis

It is a rare moment of time in history when virtually all countries are confronted with similar challenges: severe economic contraction, high unemployment rates, and sharply decreased domestic and external demand. The stakes are high, and governments will need to respond quickly, with both short-term measures and long-term strategies. Notwithstanding their diversity, the chapters in the present collection suggest some broad lessons for decision makers to consider.

First, the option of returning to old-fashioned state dominance should be rejected outright. Warner's conclusion (Chapter 3) that the reverse privatization process should not be equated to a return to the direct public monopoly delivery model of the old is echoed by Peters (Chapter 2). He argued that the capacity of the state to govern through command and control has been weakened substantially due to internal and external changes in governance patterns.

Second, governments should focus attention onto the identification of creative solutions by "retaining some of the gains achieved" (Peters, this volume, Chapter 2) in the era of the state retreat. Warner's chapter advocates for "the emergence of a new balanced position which combines the use of markets, democracy and planning to reach decision", mirroring in this point Barter's analysis of the transportation sector and Painter and Mok's analysis on education leading to similar proposals. Cheung's analysis (Chapter 6) suggests that even New Public Management can be strategically used as a means to strengthen the competence to state, instead of weakening or downsizing it as some of its detractors have asserted.

Third, while the reassertion of the state may be accepted as a general trend, the real story lies in the variations of its local manifestations. Ramesh's comparative analysis of the health sector in China, Singapore and Thailand (Chapter 7) provides a case in point. China's efforts in reasserting the role of the state as financiers of health care may aggravate the problems of rising expenditure, while in Thailand, public ownership of hospitals, tax-funding for the majority of the population and payment of providers on a capitation basis have been combined with some success to achieve affordable and equitable health care.

Finally, a clear implication of the volume is that much is to be gained by both governments and contributors to the debates by going beyond polarizing assertions of the relative virtues of the market and the state, and instead focusing attention onto the contextual variables that mediate their roles and impact. Tankha's suggestion in Chapter 11 is representative of this ethos; he notes that appropriate solutions (for the Brazilian energy sector, in this case) need to be rooted in a careful study of "the institutional structures, human motivation, available economic resources, perspectives and prospective for the sector, and its strategic relevance" (p. 00). When assessing the role of states and markets, the emerging consensus, prosaic as it may seem, is that "it all depends", as Ramesh and Araral asserted in the introduction. We share the hope of Walker *et al.*, expressed in Chapter 5, that "the next generation of public sector reformers will … pursue a more evidence-based reform agenda" (p. 00).

Bibliography

Barrow, C. W. (2005) "The Return of the State: Globalization, State Theory, and the New Imperialism*", *New Political Science* 27(2): 123–145.

Barzelay, M. (2001) *The New Public Management: Improving Research and Policy Dialogue*, Berkeley, CA: University of California Press.

Dunleavy, P. and Hood, C. (1994) "From Old Public Administration to New Public Management", *Public Management & Money* 14(3): 9–16.

Evans, P. (1997) "The Eclipse of the State? Reflections on Stateness in an Era of Globalization", *World Politics* 50(1): 62–87.

Evans, P. B., Rueschemeyer, D. and Skocpol, T. (1985) *Bringing the State Back In*, London: Cambridge University Press.

Goel, R. K. and Nelson, M. A. (1998) "Corruption and Government Size: A Disaggregated Analysis", *Public Choice* 97(1): 107–120.

Hofstadter, D. I. (2007) *I Am a Strange Loop*, New York: Basic Books.

McClelland, J. S. (1996) *A History of Western Political Thought*, New York: Routledge.

Osborne, D. and Plastrik, P. (2000) *The Reinventor's Fieldbook: Tools for Transforming your Government*, San Francisco, CA: Jossey-Bass.

Peters, B. G. (2001) *The Politics of Bureaucracy* (fifth edition), New York: Routledge.

Rose, R. (2005) *Learning from Comparative Public Policy: A Practical Guide*, New York: Routledge.

Sbragia, A. M. (2000) "Governance, the State, and the Market: What Is Going On?", *An International Journal of Policy and Administration* 13(2): 243–250.

Senge, P. (1990) *The Fifth Discipline: the Art and Practice of the Learning Organization*, New York: Doubleday.

Srinivasen, T. N. (2000) "The Washington Consensus a Decade Later: Ideology and the Art and Science of Policy Advice", *World Bank Research Observer* 15(2): 265–270.

Stone, D. (2001) *Policy Paradox: The Art of Political Decision Making* (third edition), New York: W.W. Norton & Co.

Strange, S. (1996) *The Retreat of the State*, New York: Cambridge University Press.

Wagner, P. (2007) "Public Policy, Social Science and the State: An Historical Perspective", in F. Fischer, G. J. Miller and M. S. Sidney (eds) *Handbook of Public Policy Analysis: Theory, Politics and Methods*, Boca Raton: CRC Press.

Index

Printed in Poland
by Amazon Fulfillment
Poland Sp. z o.o., Wrocław

76009396R00137